The 50 Greatest Players in New York Yankees History

Robert W. Cohen

TAYLOR TRADE PUBLISHING
Lanham • New York • Boulder • Toronto • Plymouth, UK

Published by Taylor Trade Publishing
An imprint of The Rowman & Littlefield Publishing Group, Inc.
4501 Forbes Boulevard, Suite 200, Lanham, Maryland 20706
www.rowman.com

10 Thornbury Road, Plymouth PL6 7PP, United Kingdom

Distributed by National Book Network

British Library Cataloguing in Publication Information Available

Library of Congress Cataloging-in-Publication Data

Cohen, Robert W.
  The 50 greatest players in New York Yankees history / Robert W. Cohen.
    p. cm.
  Includes bibliographical references and index.
  1. Baseball players—United States—Biography. 2. New York Yankees
(Baseball team)—Biography. I. Title. II. Title: Fifty greatest players in
New York Yankees history.
  GV865.A1C574 2012
  796.357'64097471—dc23   2011050650

ISBN 978-0-8108-8393-2 (hardcover : alk. paper)
ISBN 978-1-58979-815-1 (pbk. : alk. paper)
ISBN 978-0-8108-8394-9 (electronic)

Printed in the United States of America

*For Lily, whose warmth, generosity,
and love inspire me every day*

Introduction:
The Yankee Pedigree

The New York Yankees, Major League Baseball's most renowned and successful franchise, actually have their roots in the city of Baltimore, which the National League abandoned when it contracted from 12 to 8 teams in 1900. The American League experienced its inaugural season the very next year, with league president Ban Johnson and his financier friends forming the junior circuit to provide competition to the more established National League. Johnson and the new association's eight team owners promised better working conditions and higher pay to those players who chose to join the fledgling league, prompting many of the senior circuit's top stars to leave their former ball clubs. Led by player/manager John McGraw, the Baltimore Orioles served as one of the newly formed league's eight teams for two years, before Johnson insisted at a 1903 peace summit to unite the two leagues under similar rules that an American League franchise be established in New York. Johnson eventually succeeded in getting all but 1 of the 16 major-league owners to support his proposal, with the lone dissenter being John T. Brush of the New York Giants. Johnson arranged for Frank Farrell and Bill Devery to purchase the struggling Baltimore Orioles and subsequently move them to Manhattan. Meanwhile, Brush and McGraw displayed their mutual displeasure by joining forces just a few miles away, with Bush hiring McGraw to be his team's new manager.

Farrell and Devery wasted little time in securing a piece of land situated on Broadway, between 165th and 168th streets. They then constructed a ballpark that they named Hilltop Park, since it sat on one of the highest points in Manhattan. The stadium's location also prompted the nickname Highlanders to be affixed to the team.

Before the Highlanders played their first game, the team's owners secured the services of several former National League stars. Hall of Fame outfielder Willie Keeler, who batted .424 for Baltimore in 1897, took his talents from Brooklyn to Manhattan. Star pitchers Jack Chesbro and Jesse Tannehill both left Pittsburgh to don a New York uniform. Hall of Fame hurler Clark Griffith also traveled east, leaving the city of Chicago to serve as the team's player/manager.

The Highlanders experienced only a moderate amount of success in the 10 years they called Hilltop Park home, posting a winning record just four times. They had their best season in 1904, when they finished the campaign with a record of 92–59, just 1 1/2 games behind the American League champion Boston Americans. The Highlanders remained in the pennant race the entire year largely because of Jack Chesbro, who compiled one of the most amazing seasons in the history of the junior circuit. The right-hander established a 20th-century record by compiling a mark of 41–12 that made him one of only two pitchers since 1900 to win as many as 40 games in a season (Chicago's Ed Walsh was the other, posting 40 victories for the White Sox in 1908). Chesbro also finished the year with a 1.82 ERA, 239 strikeouts, 48 complete games, and 455 innings pitched. Not only did Chesbro's extraordinary performance enable the Highlanders to nearly capture their first league championship, but it also gained him widespread recognition as the team's first star player.

Other outstanding performers donned the team's colors in subsequent seasons, even as the franchise moved to the Polo Grounds in 1913 and officially became known as the New York Yankees. First basemen Hal Chase and Wally Pipp, pitcher Bob Shawkey, and Hall of Fame third baseman Frank "Home Run" Baker all starred for the Yankees during their formative years, bringing a level of respectability to a ball club that experienced little in the way of team success. However, the acquisition of Babe Ruth from the Boston Red Sox prior to the start of the 1920 campaign gave the Yankees their first true superstar. Ruth also legitimized the Yankees as a team, making them an annual pennant contender in the junior circuit. With the Babe leading the way, the Yankees finished atop the American League standings in six of the next nine seasons, also capturing their first three world championships during that time, including back-to-back titles in 1927 and 1928.

Joining Ruth on those consecutive world championship ball clubs was Lou Gehrig, who combined with the Bambino to give the Yankees the most formidable one-two punch in the history of the game. The heart and soul of the 1927 "Murderer's Row" squad, still considered by many baseball historians to be the greatest team ever assembled, Ruth and Gehrig anchored a club that featured future Hall of Famers Tony Lazzeri, Earle Combs, Herb Pennock, and Waite Hoyt.

After helping the Yankees win another world championship in 1932, Ruth eventually left New York at the conclusion of the 1934 campaign. Gehrig remained, though, being joined in 1936 by the team's next great player, Joe DiMaggio. Ably assisted by standout performers such as Bill Dickey, Joe Gordon, Red Rolfe, Tommy Henrich, Charlie Keller, Red Ruffing, Lefty Gomez, and Yogi Berra, the "Yankee Clipper" led the Yankees to 10 pennants and 9 world championships in his 13 years with the club, before passing the torch to Berra and Mickey Mantle.

The Yankees continued to excel under Mantle's leadership, winning 12 pennants and 7 World Series in his first 14 years with the team, before losing their elite status when age and injuries began to catch up with the star center fielder his final few seasons. Berra also thrived during that period, winning three Most Valuable Player Awards and annually earning All-Star honors. Meanwhile, Whitey Ford starred on the mound for New York during the Mantle years, with Bill Skowron, Bobby Richardson, Tony Kubek, Elston Howard, and Roger Maris making significant contributions.

Mantle's decline and subsequent retirement coincided with New York's fall from grace, leading to a dark period in team history frequently referred to as "the lean years." Steeped in mediocrity from 1965 to 1975, the Yankees experienced the longest drought in franchise history since the first two decades of the 20th century. Yet, they still managed to field a representative team in most of those seasons, with standouts such as Bobby Murcer, Thurman Munson, Roy White, and Mel Stottlemyre earning All-Star honors at various times.

Munson and White persevered through the lean years to share in the success that the Yankees experienced during the latter portion of the 1970s, when they won three consecutive pennants and two world championships. Reggie Jackson, Lou Piniella, Chris Chambliss, Graig Nettles, Ron Guidry, and Willie Randolph were among the many talented players who also contributed greatly to those championship ball clubs.

After advancing to the postseason in 1980 and 1981, the Yankees experienced another playoff drought from 1982 to 1994. Nevertheless, New York presented an extremely imposing lineup to opposing pitchers during the mid-1980s—one that featured Don Mattingly, Dave Winfield, and Rickey Henderson.

The arrival of future stars Bernie Williams, Derek Jeter, Jorge Posada, Andy Pettitte, Mariano Rivera, and Paul O'Neill during the mid-1990s ushered in the next great era of Yankee baseball. The Yankees captured 4 more world championships between 1996 and 2000, bringing their total to an astounding 26 World Series titles. They won their record 27th world championship in 2009, employing essentially the same philosophy used by most of their immediate predecessors— a heavy reliance on power, good pitching, and timely hitting, and an even greater dependence on star power.

FACTORS USED TO DETERMINE RANKINGS

With such a plethora of talented players from which to choose, it became quite difficult to select the 50 greatest players in New York Yankees history. Narrowing down the field to a mere 50 men proved to be challenging in itself. However, the matter of ranking the elite players that remained turned out to be an equally daunting task. Certainly, it was not particularly hard to settle on the top five or six players. The names of Joe DiMaggio, Mickey Mantle, Babe Ruth, Lou Gehrig, Yogi Berra, and Derek Jeter would likely appear at the top of virtually everyone's list, although the order might vary from person to person. Several other standout performers are universally considered to be among the best players ever to don the Yankee pinstripes. Don Mattingly, Mariano Rivera, Whitey Ford, Bernie Williams, and Thurman Munson head the list of other Yankee icons. But I needed to decide how to rank these men, who to exclude from my list, and what criteria to use in determining my rankings.

The first thing I decided to examine was the level of dominance a player attained during his time with the team. How often did he lead the American League in some major offensive or pitching statistical category? How did he fare in the annual MVP and/or Cy Young voting? How many times did he make the All-Star Team?

I also needed to weigh the level of statistical compilation that a player achieved while wearing the pinstripes. Where does a batter rank among the all-time Yankees in the major offensive categories? How high on the all-time list of Yankee hurlers does a pitcher rank in wins, ERA, complete games, innings pitched, shutouts, and saves? Of course, I also needed to consider the era in which the player performed when evaluating his overall numbers. For example, a modern-day starting pitcher such as Andy Pettitte was not likely to throw nearly as many complete games or shutouts as someone like Red Ruffing, who anchored New York's starting rotation during the 1930s. And the manner in which closers were used during the 1970s and 1980s made it far more difficult for men such as Sparky Lyle and Rich Gossage to amass the number of saves that Mariano Rivera has compiled during his career.

Other important factors that I needed to consider were the overall contributions that a player made to the success of the team, the degree to which he improved the fortunes of the ball club during his time in pinstripes, the manner in which he affected the team on and off the field, and the degree to which he added to the Yankee legacy of greatness. While the number of championships that the Yankees won during a particular player's years with the ball club certainly entered into the equation, I chose not to deny a top performer his rightful place on the list if his years in New York happened to coincide with a dark period in franchise history. As a result, the names of players such as Mel Stottlemyre and Bobby Murcer will appear in these rankings.

Another thing that I should mention is that when formulating my rankings, I considered a player's performance for only the time that he wore the pinstripes. That being the case, the name of a great player such as Rickey Henderson, who spent parts of only five seasons in New York, may appear lower on this list than one might expect. That being said, we are ready to take a look at the 50 greatest players in Yankees history, starting with number 1 and working our way down to number 50.

1

Babe Ruth

Lou Gehrig, Joe DiMaggio, and Mickey Mantle provided stiff competition to Babe Ruth for the number 1 spot, and each of them likely would have earned a first-place ranking on most other teams. But they all must settle for an honorable mention here due to the level of greatness that Ruth achieved during his 15 years in New York. The most colorful and charismatic player in baseball history, Ruth revolutionized the sport with his home run–hitting prowess, enabling it to survive the Black Sox scandal of 1919 and allowing the national pastime to reach new heights of popularity during the Roaring Twenties. Generally considered to be the greatest player in the history of the game, Ruth served as the sport's greatest ambassador and number one drawing card, dominating his era as no other player ever has. His arrival in New York in 1920 completely reversed the fortunes of both the Yankees and the Red Sox, turning his new team into perennial pennant contenders while relegating Boston to the second division for almost two decades. The Yankees have since captured 27 world championships, while the Red Sox have won only 2 more World Series, going 86 years before winning another Fall Classic.

George Herman Ruth spent six seasons with the Boston Red Sox before joining the Yankees in 1920, establishing himself during his time in Boston as arguably the American League's finest left-handed pitcher. After compiling a record of 18–8 and an ERA of 2.44 for the eventual world champions in 1915, Ruth evolved into the ace of Boston's staff the following year, winning 23 games, completing 23 of his 41 starts, throwing 323 innings, and leading the league with a 1.75 ERA and 9 shutouts. The Red Sox won the American League pennant, and Ruth helped them defeat Brooklyn in the World Series, allowing only 1 run and 6 hits during a 14-inning, 2–1 complete-game victory in his only start. Ruth had another sensational season in 1917, winning 24 games, compiling a 2.01 ERA, and leading the league with 35 complete games. However, the Babe continued to display increased proficiency at the plate over the course of his first few seasons, prompting the Red Sox to convert him into a full-time outfielder by 1919. After leading the Red Sox to their third world championship in four years in 1918 by continuing his streak of 29 2/3 consecutive scoreless innings on the mound in the Fall Classic, Ruth batted .322 and topped the American League with 29 home runs, 114 runs batted in, 103 runs scored, a .456 on-base percentage, and a .657 slugging percentage in his first full season in the outfield.

Fast becoming baseball's most popular and recognizable figure, Ruth demanded to be paid as such. However, Red Sox owner Harry Frazee, a theatrical producer who found himself deep in debt, refused to meet his disgruntled outfielder's demands. More concerned with financing a Broadway show called *No, No, Nanette*, Frazee sold Ruth to the Yankees for $100,000 in December of 1919, and the rest, as they say, is history.

Ruth compiled astounding numbers his first year in New York, batting .376 and leading the American League with 54 home runs, 137 runs batted in, 158 runs scored, a .530 on-base percentage, and an .847 slugging percentage. The Babe's level of dominance was so great that his 54 home runs were almost three times as many as the 19 homers AL runner-up George Sisler hit for the St. Louis Browns. In fact, the rest of the American League combined to hit only 315 long balls. Ruth's .847 slugging percentage also placed him 215 points ahead of Sisler, who finished second in that category with a mark of .632. The Yankees improved their win total from 80 to 95 in 1920, and they finished just 3 games behind the pennant-winning Cleveland Indians.

Fans of the game began coming out to ballparks in droves to watch Ruth hit a baseball farther than they previously imagined possible. Babe did not disappoint them in the least in 1921, batting .378, leading the league with a .512 on-base percentage and a slugging percentage of .846, and establishing new major-league records with 59 home runs, 171 runs batted in, and 177 runs scored. Babe's slugging figures once again surpassed those of every other player by an incredibly wide margin. His 59 homers were 35 more than the 24 that Ken Williams hit for the Browns, and his .846 slugging percentage was more than 200 points higher than the mark of .639 that Rogers Hornsby posted for the Cardinals in the National League. The Yankees captured their first pennant in 1921, compiling a record of 98–55 and finishing 4

1/2 games ahead of second-place Cleveland. However, they lost the World Series to the Giants, with whom they shared New York's Polo Grounds.

After a suspension-marred 1922 campaign, Ruth returned to the Yankees a humbled man in 1923, the year in which the team first began playing its home games in Yankee Stadium. Appearing in all of New York's 152 games, Ruth batted a career-high .393 and led the American League with 41 home runs, 131 runs batted in, 151 runs scored, a .545 on-base percentage, a .764 slugging percentage, and an American League record 170 walks. The Yankees won 98 games to easily win the AL pennant, and Babe earned league MVP honors. The team then captured its first world championship, defeating the Giants in six games in the World Series. Ruth aided the Yankee effort by batting .368 and hitting 3 home runs in the Fall Classic.

Ruth had another great year in 1924, winning his only batting title with a mark of .378, but he suffered through a horrific 1925 campaign in which he appeared in only 98 games due to a serious illness. With Babe absent from their lineup much of the year, the Yankees fell to seventh place in the American League, 28 1/2 games behind the pennant-winning Washington Senators.

Admonished by none other than the president of the United States during the subsequent off-season for "letting down the nation's youth," Ruth rededicated himself to his sport and returned to the New York lineup with a vengeance in 1926. He batted .372 and led the league with 47 home runs, 146 runs batted in, and 139 runs scored. The Yankees won 91 games to capture the American League pennant, but they came up short in the World Series, losing to the St. Louis Cardinals in seven games.

Angered by their loss to St. Louis in the Fall Classic, the Yankees approached the 1927 campaign as if they had something to prove. Led by the tandem of Ruth and Gehrig, the famed 1927 "Murderer's Row" Yankee squad dominated the baseball world, compiling an astounding 110–44 record during the regular season, with the Bambino breaking his own single-season home run record by hitting 60 long balls. Ruth also knocked in 164 runs, batted .356, and led the league with 158 runs scored, a .487 on-base percentage, and a .772 slugging percentage. The Babe punctuated his great season by batting .400, driving in 7 runs, and hitting 2 home runs against Pittsburgh during New York's four-game sweep of the Pirates in the World Series.

Ruth continued his prolific slugging in 1928, hitting a league-leading 54 home runs, to top the 50-homer mark for the fourth and final time in his career. He also led the league with 142 runs batted in,

163 runs scored, and a .709 slugging percentage. The Yankees repeated as American League champions and then gained a measure of revenge against St. Louis in the World Series by vanquishing the Cardinals in four straight games. Ruth batted .635 during the series, drove in 4 runs, and homered 3 times.

Substandard pitching and a superb Philadelphia Athletics team kept the Yankees out of the World Series the next three years. Nevertheless, Ruth continued his assault on American League pitching, topping the circuit in home runs and slugging percentage all three years, hitting a total of 141 homers, knocking in a total of 470 runs, and posting batting averages of .345, .359, and .373.

Although Ruth began to show signs of aging for the first time in 1932, the 37-year-old slugger still had an outstanding year, hitting 41 homers, driving in 137 runs, scoring 120 others, batting .341, and leading the league with a .489 on-base percentage. The Yankees returned to the top of the American League standings, finishing 13 games ahead of the second-place Athletics, before sweeping the Chicago Cubs in four straight games in the World Series. Ruth added to his legend in game 3 of the series when he hit his famous "called shot" against Chicago pitcher Charlie Root during New York's 7–5 victory. Babe batted .333 in his final World Series appearance, with 2 home runs and 6 runs batted in.

Ruth had his last productive season in 1933, before seeing his offensive numbers fall off dramatically the following year. The Yankees released the Babe at the conclusion of the 1934 campaign, and Ruth ended his career with the lowly Boston Braves in 1935, appearing in only 28 games and batting just .181 in his 72 official plate appearances. Babe experienced one final moment of glory with the Braves on May 25 of that year when he hit three home runs against the Pirates at Forbes Field, the last of which was the first ball ever hit completely out of that ballpark. The blast ended up being the last of Ruth's 714 round-trippers. He announced his retirement from baseball one week later and spent the remainder of his life waiting in vain for some major-league team to offer him a managerial job. Ruth died 13 years later from throat cancer, disappointed that he never got an opportunity to manage in the sport he helped to revitalize. Although most of Ruth's records have since been broken, his list of accomplishments is truly amazing. Upon his retirement, Ruth was the major league's all-time leader in home runs (714) and runs batted in (2,213). He scored 2,174 runs, batted .342, amassed 2,873 hits, and compiled a .474 on-base percentage. Ruth's .690 career slugging percentage is the highest in baseball history. Ruth holds Yankee career records for highest batting average (.349), on-base percentage (.484), and slugging percentage (.711), and he hit more home runs (659), scored more runs (1,959), compiled more total bases (5,131), and walked more times (1,852) than anyone else in team history. Ruth also ranks second in runs batted in (1,971) and third in hits (2,518). In addition, the Babe holds Yankee single-season marks for most runs scored (177), walks (170), and total bases (457), and he compiled the highest batting average (.393), on-base percentage (.545), and slugging percentage (.847) in club history.

Longtime manager Leo Durocher served as a backup infielder on the Yankees in 1928 and 1929. Durocher later said, "There's no question about it, Babe Ruth was the greatest instinctive baseball player who ever lived. He was a great hitter, and he would have been a great pitcher."

Sportswriter Tommy Holmes said on the day of Ruth's funeral, "Some 20 years ago I stopped talking about the Babe for the simple reason that I realized that those who had never seen him didn't believe me."

Hall of Fame pitcher Lefty Gomez joined Ruth on the Yankees during the latter stages of Babe's career. Gomez later said of his former teammate, "He was a circus, a play and a movie, all rolled into one. Kids adored him. Men idolized him. Women loved him. There was something about him that made him great."

YANKEE CAREER HIGHLIGHTS

Best Season

There are so many great seasons from which to choose, with Ruth's performances in 1920, 1923, 1924, 1927, 1930, and 1931 all ranking among his finest. However, many baseball historians still consider Ruth's 1921 campaign to be the greatest single-season performance ever turned in by a major-league player. Ruth batted .378, collected 204 hits, amassed 16 triples and 44 doubles, and led the majors with 59 home runs, 171 runs batted in, 177 runs scored, 457 total bases, 145 walks, a .512 on-base percentage, and a slugging percentage of .846. Ruth's 177 runs scored and 457 total bases remain major-league records.

Memorable Moments/Greatest Performances

One of only three players to hit as many as three home runs in a single World Series game (Reggie Jackson and Albert Pujols are the others),

Ruth accomplished the feat twice. Although the Yankees lost the 1926 World Series to St. Louis in seven games, Ruth made baseball history by homering three times during New York's 10–5 game 4 victory. He concluded the Fall Classic with 4 home runs, 5 runs batted in, 11 walks, and a .300 batting average.

Ruth duplicated his earlier feat two years later, again hitting 3 home runs against the Cardinals, this time during New York's Series-clinching game 4 victory. He concluded the Fall Classic with a .625 batting average and 9 runs scored.

Nevertheless, the most memorable moment of Ruth's career likely occurred in game 3 of the 1932 World Series against the Chicago Cubs. Jeered throughout the contest by Chicago players and fans alike, Ruth stepped into the batter's box with the score tied 4–4 in the fifth inning. After taking two consecutive called strikes from Chicago pitcher Charlie Root, the Babe raised two fingers in the air. While some accounts suggest that Ruth's gesture merely signified he still had one strike remaining in the count, others firmly contend that he "called his shot," hitting the very next pitch into the center field bleachers. Either way, the blast brought the Wrigley Field crowd to its feet, effectively thrusting a dagger into the collective hearts of the Cubs players and leading the Yankees to a 7–5 victory and a four-game sweep of the overmatched Cubs.

NOTABLE ACHIEVEMENTS

- Hit more than 50 home runs four times.
- Topped 40 homers on seven other occasions.
- Surpassed 150 RBIs five times.
- Scored more than 150 runs six times.
- Batted over .370 on six occasions.
- Collected more than 200 hits three times.
- Topped 400 total bases twice.
- Compiled on-base percentage in excess of .500 five times.
- Posted on-base percentage over .450 five other times.
- Compiled slugging percentage in excess of .800 twice.
- Posted slugging percentage over .700 seven other times.
- Led AL in home runs 10 times; RBIs, 5 times; runs scored, 7 times; walks, 11 times; on-base percentage, 9 times; slugging percentage, 11 times; total bases, 5 times; and batting average, once.

- Major League Baseball's single-season record holder in runs scored (177) and total bases (457).
- Holds Yankee single-season records for highest batting average (.393), on-base percentage (.545), and slugging percentage (.847).
- Holds Yankee career records for most home runs (659), runs scored (1,959), total bases (5,131), and walks (1,852) and highest batting average (.349), on-base percentage (.484), and slugging percentage (.711).
- First major-league player to surpass 30, 40, 50, and 60 home runs in a season.
- First major-league player to reach 200, 300, 400, 500, 600, and 700 home run plateaus.
- One of only three players in major-league history to hit 3 home runs in one World Series game (1926 and 1928).
- 1923 AL MVP.
- Six-time *Sporting News* All-Star selection.
- Two-time AL All-Star.*
- Hit 15 World Series home runs, placing him second on the all-time list.
- Played for 7 pennant-winning clubs in New York.
- Played for 4 world championship teams in New York.

*Major League Baseball played its first All-Star Game in 1933.

2

Lou Gehrig

Although the utter dominance of Babe Ruth enabled him to edge out Lou Gehrig for the top spot in these rankings, Gehrig clearly deserved to be placed in the number 2 position. While the more colorful and charismatic Ruth consistently grabbed the headlines in the New York newspapers during their 10 full seasons together, Gehrig took a back-seat to no one in terms of total offensive production. Arguably the greatest RBI man in the history of the game, the "Iron Horse" drove home more runs over the course of his career than any other Yankee player; he also holds 5 of the top 10 single-season RBI marks in team history, including the all-time AL mark of 184, which he established in 1931.

Henry Louis Gehrig appeared briefly in a Yankee uniform for the first time shortly after he graduated from New York's Columbia University near the end of the 1923 campaign. He made another brief appearance for the team the following year before joining New York for good in 1925. Replacing Wally Pipp as the team's starting first baseman, Gehrig played in New York's final 126 contests, hitting 20 home runs, driving in 68 runs, crossing the plate 73 times himself, and batting .295. Little did anyone know at the time that Gehrig would go on to play in another 2,004 consecutive games en route to establishing a major-league record that endured for 56 years.

Gehrig appeared in every game for New York for the first of 13 consecutive seasons the following year, establishing himself as one of the American League's top first basemen by hitting 16 home runs, driving in 112 runs, scoring 135 others, and batting .313. Inserted behind Babe Ruth into the number 4 spot in New York's batting order, Gehrig enabled the Yankees to place the league's most formidable one-two punch in the middle of their lineup, helping them capture the AL pennant. Although the Yankees lost the World Series to the St. Louis Cardinals in seven games, the 23-year-old first baseman displayed the sort of clutch hitting that eventually became his trademark, batting .348 and knocking in 4 runs against St. Louis pitching.

Gehrig developed into a full-fledged star in 1927, rivaling his teammate Ruth as the game's greatest player. As New York's renowned "Murderer's Row" squad romped to 110 victories and the American League pennant, Ruth and Gehrig waged an assault on the Babe's single-season record of 59 home runs, which the "Bambino" established six years earlier. A phenomenal month of September enabled Ruth to pull away from his teammate in the home run race, but the individual battle waged between the two men provided much of the impetus for New York's great season. Although Ruth grabbed most of the headlines by setting a new home run mark, it was Gehrig who captured league MVP honors for his exceptional performance. The Yankee first baseman finished second in the league in home runs (47), runs scored (149), batting average (.373), hits (218), triples (18), walks (109), and slugging percentage (.765); he placed third in on-base percentage (.474); and he topped the circuit with 175 runs batted in, 52 doubles, and 447 total bases. Gehrig punctuated his great season by batting .308 and knocking in 4 runs during New York's four-game sweep of Pittsburgh in the World Series.

The Yankees repeated as American League champions in 1928, and Gehrig had another outstanding year, leading the league with 142 runs batted in, 47 doubles, and a .467 on-base percentage while placing second in the circuit with 27 homers, 139 runs scored, a .648 slugging percentage, and 210 hits. He also finished third in the league with a .374 batting average. Gehrig followed up his exceptional campaign by annihilating St. Louis pitching during New York's four-game sweep of the Cardinals in the World Series. In addition to hitting 4 home runs and batting .545 in the Fall Classic, Gehrig knocked in 9 runs—just 1 fewer than the Cardinals scored the entire series.

Although New York failed to repeat as American League champions in any of the next three seasons, Gehrig continued to perform at an extremely high level. After posting solid numbers in 1929, the slugging first baseman hit 41 homers, batted a career-high .379, scored 143 runs, collected 220 hits, and topped the circuit with 174 runs batted in and 419 total bases in 1930. He followed that up by leading the league in five offensive categories in 1931, including home runs (46), runs scored (163), and an all-time AL record 184 runs batted in.

Even though Gehrig continued to compile magnificent numbers year after year, he remained in Babe Ruth's shadow their entire time together. Quiet, reserved, and dignified, Gehrig stood in stark contrast to the loud, boisterous, and colorful Bambino, to whom the writers paid far more attention. Asked about playing in Ruth's shadow, Gehrig responded, "It's a pretty big shadow. It gives me lots of room to spread myself."

However, Gehrig began to surpass the aging Ruth as New York's greatest player in 1932, posting better numbers than the Babe in most offensive categories. Firmly entrenched as the team's number one star by 1934, Gehrig took center stage for the first time in his career, capturing the American League Triple Crown by topping the circuit with 49 home runs, 165 runs batted in, and a .363 batting average.

Ruth left the Yankees at the conclusion of the 1934 campaign, leaving Gehrig to carry much of the offensive burden in New York. After compiling outstanding numbers again in 1935, Gehrig once again found himself sharing the spotlight with another great player when Joe DiMaggio joined the Yankees in 1936. The extraordinary all-around talents of the brilliant rookie center fielder drew much of the media attention away from Gehrig. Nevertheless, it was the Iron Horse who ended up capturing league MVP honors for the second time in his career by leading his team to the first of four consecutive world championships. Gehrig topped the circuit with 49 home runs and 167 runs scored, and he placed among the league leaders with 152 runs batted in and a .354 batting average.

After another big year in 1937, Gehrig saw his offensive numbers drop precipitously the following season, causing Yankee fans to wonder if New York's 35-year-old captain was nearing the end of his career. It later surfaced that Gehrig's declining performance resulted directly from a relatively unknown disease that he incurred called *amyotrophic lateral sclerosis*—one that attacks the central nervous system. The fatal illness gradually sapped Gehrig of his strength, causing him to take himself out of the lineup for the first time in almost 14 years on May 2, 1939, after playing in 2,130 consecutive games.

Two months later, on July 4, 1939, an emotional Gehrig made the most famous speech in sports history. Fully aware that he did not have long to live, the Yankee captain told a teary-eyed packed house at Yankee Stadium, "Fans, for the past two weeks you have been reading about the bad break I got. Yet today I consider myself the luckiest man on the face of this earth." Gehrig died less than two years later, on June 2, 1941, at only 37 years of age.

Both Gehrig's speech and the tragic manner in which his career and life ended have contributed greatly to his legend. Nevertheless, the Yankee first baseman was one of the greatest players in baseball history. He ended his career with 493 home runs, 1,995 runs batted in, 1,888 runs scored, 2,721 hits, a .340 batting average, a .447 on-base percentage, and a .632 slugging percentage. He ranks second in team history in hits, runs scored, batting average, on-base percentage, slugging percentage, and total bases. In addition to holding the Yankee career record for most runs batted in, Gehrig ranks first in doubles (534) and triples (163). The Iron Horse also holds the major-league record for most career grand slams (23). The Yankees won 7 pennants and 6 World Series in his 14 full seasons with the team.

Yet, sportswriter John Kieran once said of Gehrig in the *New York Times*, "His greatest record doesn't show in the book. It was the absolute reliability of Henry Louis Gehrig. He could be counted upon. He was there every day at the ballpark bending his back and ready to break his neck to win for his side. He was there day after day and year after year. He never sulked or whined or went into a pout or a huff. He was the answer to a manager's dream."

Discussing his amazing streak, during which he appeared in 2,130 consecutive games, Gehrig said, "This 'Iron Man' stuff is bunk. It is true that I have considerable physical strength, but that isn't the answer. There have been many powerful players in baseball who weren't in there every day. It wasn't exceptional strength in my case, nor even exceptional endurance. It was the determination to be in there and to hustle every minute of the time I was there that has made that record a reality."

CAREER HIGHLIGHTS

Best Season

It would be extremely difficult to argue too strenuously with anyone who claimed that Gehrig's Triple Crown season of 1934 was the finest of his career. After all, the Iron Horse not only led the league with 49 home runs, 165 runs batted in, and a .363 batting average but also topped the circuit in total bases (409), on-base percentage (.465), and slugging percentage (.706). A strong argument could also be waged on behalf of Gehrig's 1930, 1931, and 1936 campaigns. Nevertheless, the feeling here is that Gehrig had his finest all-around season in 1927, when he captured AL MVP honors by finishing in the top 3 in the league in 11 different offensive categories. In addition to hitting 47 home runs, scoring 149 runs, collecting 218 hits, batting .373, amassing 18 triples, and compiling a .474 on-base percentage, Gehrig led the league with 175 runs batted in and established career highs with a league-leading 52 doubles and 447 total bases.

Memorable Moments/Greatest Performances

Gehrig had the greatest game of his career on June 3, 1932, when he became the only player in Yankee history to hit 4 home runs in one game.

An exceptional clutch hitter throughout his career, Gehrig also saved several of his greatest performances for the World Series. He batted .545 with 4 home runs and 9 runs batted in during New York's four-game sweep of St. Louis in the 1928 Fall Classic. Gehrig also terrorized Chicago Cubs pitchers in the 1932 Series, hitting 3 homers, driving in 8 runs, and batting .529 during the four-game sweep. Over the course of his career, Gehrig hit 10 home runs, knocked in 35 runs, and batted .361 in 34 World Series games.

Still, Gehrig's most memorable moment occurred on July 4, 1939, when he added to his legacy of greatness and raised himself to a new level of baseball immortality by telling Yankee fans that he considered himself to be the "luckiest man on the face of the earth."

NOTABLE ACHIEVEMENTS

- Hit more than 40 home runs five times.
- Surpassed 150 runs batted in seven times.
- Scored more than 150 runs twice.
- Batted over .370 three times.
- Collected more than 200 hits eight times.
- Surpassed 20 triples once.
- Topped 400 total bases five times.
- Compiled on-base percentage in excess of .450 on eight separate occasions.
- Posted slugging percentage in excess of .700 three times.
- Led AL in home runs three times; RBIs, five times; runs scored, four times; total bases, four times; on-base percentage, five times; slugging percentage, twice; walks, three times; doubles, twice; hits, once; and triples, once.

- AL MVP in 1927 and 1936.
- 1934 AL Triple Crown winner.
- Only Yankee player to hit 4 home runs in one game.
- Major League Baseball's all-time leader with 23 grand slams.
- Knocked in American League record 184 runs in 1931.
- Holds Yankee career records for most RBIs (1,995), doubles (534), triples (163), and extra base hits (1,190).
- Six-time *Sporting News* All-Star selection.
- Six-time AL All-Star (1933–1938).
- Seven-time AL champion.
- Six-time world champion.

3

Joe DiMaggio

A valid case could be made for slotting either Joe DiMaggio or Mickey Mantle into the number 3 spot in these rankings. Both men were terrific all-around players who excelled in every aspect of the game. Mantle had more raw power than DiMaggio, and he hit 175 more home runs over the course of his career. However, Mickey did so in almost 2,300 more plate appearances and almost 1,300 more official at bats than "Joltin' Joe," who lost three peak seasons to time spent in the military during World War II. Ironically, each man compiled an on-base plus slugging (OPS) of exactly .977 over the course of his career, with Mantle holding an edge in on-base percentage due to his superior ability to draw bases on balls and with DiMaggio posting a higher slugging percentage. The factors that enabled DiMaggio to edge out Mantle for the number 3 position ended up being his slight superiority as an all-around hitter, his greater run production, and his superior defensive skills. In addition to posting a career batting average that exceeded Mantle's by 27 points (.325 to .298), DiMaggio amassed many more triples (131 to 72) and doubles (389 to 344), struck out far fewer times (369 to 1,170), and knocked in more runs (1,537 to 1,509) in far fewer trips to the plate. DiMaggio also developed a reputation for being a superb defensive outfielder, while Mantle was generally considered to be merely good. As a result, DiMaggio claims the third spot here, while Mantle must settle for a fourth-place finish.

The most complete player of his era, Joe DiMaggio is considered by most baseball historians to be the first true "five-tool" player ever to grace a major-league ball field. In fact, prior to leaving the game for three years to serve in the military during the Second World War, DiMaggio may well have been the greatest all-around player in baseball history. His tremendous ability, along with the stylish grace and elegance he exhibited while patrolling centerfield in Yankee Stadium for 13 seasons, enabled the "Yankee Clipper" to reach icon-like status, turning him into a true American hero.

Born Giuseppe Paolo DiMaggio Jr., the eighth of nine children to Italian immigrants, Joseph Paul DiMaggio had already made a name for himself in his native California by the time he joined the Yankees in 1936. Honing his baseball skills under the watchful eye of former major-league outfielder Lefty O'Doul while playing for the San Francisco Seals from 1933 to 1935, DiMaggio became a West Coast legend by hitting in a Pacific Coast League record 61 consecutive games from May 27 to July 25, 1933. DiMaggio later said, "Baseball didn't really get into my blood until I knocked off that hitting streak. Getting a daily hit became more important to me than eating, drinking or sleeping."

DiMaggio joined the Yankees prior to the start of the 1936 season, after being purchased for $25,000 and 5 players. He made his major-league debut on May 3, 1936, batting third in the New York lineup, just ahead of Lou Gehrig. The Yankees had not won the American League pennant since 1932, but with Gehrig and DiMaggio leading the way, they captured the first of four consecutive world championships in the brilliant rookie's first year with the team. Displaying his vast array of skills, DiMaggio excelled in the field and at the bat. He intimidated opposing base runners with his powerful throwing arm, accumulating a league-leading 22 outfield assists while establishing himself as one of the game's top offensive performers by hitting 29 homers, driving in 125 runs, scoring 132 others, batting .323, and compiling 206 hits, 44 doubles, and a league-leading 15 triples. DiMaggio's exceptional all-around performance earned him the first of 13 selections to the All-Star Team and an eighth-place finish in the AL MVP voting.

DiMaggio improved on those numbers his second year in the league, having perhaps the finest season of his career. Despite playing in spacious Yankee Stadium, noted for its distant fences in left-center and center field, the right-handed hitting DiMaggio slugged a league-leading 46 home runs, knocked in 167 runs, topped the circuit with 151 runs scored, batted .346, stroked 215 hits and 15 triples, and led the league with 418 total bases and a .673 slugging percentage. He also compiled more than 20 assists in the outfield for the second of three consecutive times. For his efforts, DiMaggio was awarded a second-place finish in the league MVP voting.

DiMaggio continued to build on his reputation as the finest all-around player in the game over the course of the next three seasons, leading New York to the world championship in 1938 and 1939. In the first of those years, he hit 32 homers, drove in 140 runs, scored 129 others, and batted .324. After drawing the ire of the fans early in 1939 for missing the first few weeks of the season due to a contract dispute, DiMaggio demonstrated that he was well worth the money he extracted from the Yankee front office. The game's greatest player not only led the league with a career-high .381 batting average but also hit 30 home runs and drove in 126 runs in only 120 games and 462 official at bats. DiMaggio earned AL MVP honors for the first of three times for his extraordinary performance. He then won his second straight batting title the following year, hitting .352 while also clubbing 31 homers and knocking in 133 runs, to earn a third-place finish in the league MVP balloting.

It was in 1941, though, that the Yankee Clipper became a true American folk hero. DiMaggio edged out Ted Williams (who batted .406 for the Red Sox that year) for league MVP honors by hitting 30 home runs, scoring 122 runs, batting .357, and driving in a league-leading 125 runs en route to leading the Yankees to their fifth world championship in his first six years with the team. More important, DiMaggio carved out a permanent place for himself in the record books and mainstream American culture by hitting in a major-league record 56 consecutive games. As DiMaggio continued to hit in game after game from May 15 to July 16, he reached legendary status, prompting songs to be written about him and transposing himself into more than just a baseball player. He became the idol of millions and arguably the most famous man in America. Adding to his glorification was the DiMaggio "mystique," an aura that seemed to surround him as he glided gracefully after fly balls in the outfield, slugged home runs with a near-perfect swing, moved swiftly but effortlessly around the bases, and carried himself majestically, both on and off the field. Not only did fans of the game look up to DiMaggio, but other players admired and respected him as well.

Stan Musial, certainly one of the greatest players ever to don a major-league uniform, expressed his reverence for the Yankee Clipper when he stated, "There was never a day when I was as good as Joe DiMaggio at his best. Joe was the best, the very best I ever saw."

Ted Williams, to whom DiMaggio was often compared, said, "DiMaggio was the greatest all-around player I ever saw. I give it to him over Mays [Willie] simply because he was a better hitter than Mays. I saw him play, I saw what he could do, and I'm positive that he was a better hitter than Mays."

Williams continued to express his admiration for DiMaggio by saying, "I can't say enough about DiMaggio. Of all the great major leaguers I played with or against during my 19-year career, he was my idol. I idolized Joe DiMaggio!"

DiMaggio had something of an off year in his final season before joining the war effort. Although he drove in 114 runs and scored 123 others in 1942, he hit "only" 21 homers and batted "just" .305. Clearly not the same player after he returned to the major leagues in 1946, DiMaggio batted only .290, with just 25 home runs, 95 runs batted in, and 81 runs scored. Despite being named AL MVP for the third and final time in 1947, DiMaggio actually posted subpar numbers once again, hitting just 20 homers, driving in only 97 runs, and batting .315. However, Joltin' Joe showed that he still had something left the following year, batting .320, scoring 110 runs, and leading the American League with 39 home runs and 155 runs batted in, to earn a second-place finish in the league MVP voting.

The 1948 campaign turned out to be DiMaggio's last great season. Injuries cut into his playing time significantly in each of his last three years, although he remained an extremely productive player to the end. After missing half of the 1949 campaign with an injured instep, DiMaggio returned to the Yankee lineup to bat .346, hit 14 home runs and drive in 67 runs over the team's final 76 games. He followed that up by clubbing 32 homers, knocking in 122 runs, scoring 114 others, and batting .301 in 1950. DiMaggio batted just .263, with only 12 homers and 71 RBIs in 1951, prompting him to announce his retirement at the end of the season. In making the announcement, DiMaggio declared, "I made a solemn promise to myself that I wouldn't try to hang on once the end was in sight. It wasn't easy to pass up $100,000, but with me it was all or nothing. . . . I feel like I have reached the stage where I can no longer produce for my club, my manager, and my teammates. I had a poor year, but even if I had hit .350, this would have been my last year. I was full of aches and pains and it has become a chore for me to play. When baseball is no longer fun, it's no longer a game, and so, I've played my last game."

DiMaggio's great pride caused him to leave the game at age 36, when he probably could have played another two or three seasons. He refused to allow himself to perform at a level that failed to reach the expectations either he or his fans set for himself. DiMaggio often said that he felt a need to always play his very best because there might be one person in the stands who never saw him play before, and he wanted to make certain that he left a favorable impression on that one fan.

Later in life, the level of importance DiMaggio placed on his public image, his obsessive and somewhat narcissistic nature, and revelations regarding his preoccupation with money caused much of the luster to be rubbed off the DiMaggio mystique. Yet, he remained an icon-like figure until he died on March 8, 1999. And although later generations of fans came to widely accept the notion that Willie Mays and a few others may have been slightly better all-around players, there is little doubt that the man named "baseball's greatest living player" in a 1969 poll conducted to coincide with the centennial of professional baseball was one of the greatest players who ever lived. In addition to winning three Most Valuable Player Awards, DiMaggio finished in the top 10 in the voting seven other times. He is the only player in baseball history to be selected to the All-Star Team in every season in which he played. His 56-game hitting streak remains one of baseball's most hallowed records, and it is still considered to be one of the most unbreakable marks in all of professional sports. In addition to all his other remarkable batting feats, DiMaggio amazingly hit 361 home runs and struck out a total of only 369 times over the course of his career.

Some of the luster may have been rubbed off the DiMaggio mystique in recent years, but he remains one of the most heroic figures in baseball history. Ted Williams noted in his book *The Hit List*, "Joe DiMaggio's career cannot be summed up in numbers and awards. It might sound corny, but he had a profound and lasting impact on the country. How many athletes can make that claim? Despite what Simon and Garfunkel sang about him, every baseball fan knows that DiMaggio could never really leave us. For many fans he's become baseball's knight in shining pinstripe armor. Hell, for some he was almost the embodiment of the American dream."

CAREER HIGHLIGHTS

Best Season

DiMaggio's exceptional 1941 campaign is perhaps the one with which he is most closely associated. In addition to hitting 30 homers, scoring 122 runs, batting .357, and leading the AL with 125 runs batted in and 348 total bases en route to capturing league MVP honors, the Yankee Clipper etched his name into baseball lore by compiling the longest hitting streak in the history of the game. DiMaggio also performed brilliantly in 1939, when he batted a career-high .381 and drove in 126 runs in only 120 games. Nevertheless, the feeling here is that DiMaggio had his finest all-around season in 1937, when he batted

.346 and established career highs with 46 homers, 167 runs batted in, 151 runs scored, 215 hits, 418 total bases, and a .673 slugging percentage. DiMaggio topped the junior circuit in four offensive categories, and he placed in the top three in four others. His second-place finish to Detroit's Charlie Gehringer in the MVP balloting was a travesty—DiMaggio should have won the award easily.

Memorable Moments/Greatest Performances

DiMaggio is perhaps remembered best for hitting safely in an all-time record 56 consecutive games in 1941, and that was clearly his greatest feat. He also hit three home runs in a game on three occasions over the course of his career.

Still, DiMaggio may well have turned in his most memorable performance over a three-day period, from June 28 to June 30, 1949, when he provided the impetus for New York's successful second-half run to the American League pennant. After missing the first 69 games of the season due to an ailing heel, DiMaggio returned to the Yankee lineup on June 28, delivering a single and a home run against Boston at Fenway Park to lead his team to a 6–4 victory over the first-place Red Sox. DiMaggio subsequently hit three more homers in the next two games, leading the Yankees to a three-game sweep of the Red Sox that helped shift the momentum of the pennant race.

NOTABLE ACHIEVEMENTS

- Surpassed 30 homers on seven occasions, topping the 40-mark once.
- Knocked in more than 100 runs nine times, topping 150 RBIs twice.
- Scored more than 100 runs eight times, topping the 120-mark on five occasions.
- Batted over .350 three times.
- .381 batting average in 1939 is second-highest in franchise history.
- Collected more than 200 hits twice.
- Topped 400 total bases once (1937).
- Compiled slugging percentage in excess of .600 four times.
- Led AL in home runs, RBIs, batting average, and slugging percentage two times each; runs scored and triples, once each; and total bases, three times.

- AL MVP in 1939, 1941, and 1947.
- Holds major-league record for longest consecutive hitting streak (56 games in 1941).
- Eight-time *Sporting News* All-Star selection.
- Thirteen-time AL All-Star.
- Ten-time AL champion.
- Nine-time world champion.

4

Mickey Mantle

A series of debilitating injuries prevented Mickey Mantle from ever living up to the enormous potential he displayed when he first joined the Yankees in 1951. Yet, even at less than 100 percent, Mantle had a brilliant 18-year career with the Yankees that clearly established him as the greatest switch hitter in baseball history and one of the most exceptional players ever to play the game.

After being signed by scout Tom Greenwade at the tender age of 17 in 1949, Mantle spent two years in the Yankee farm system before being promoted to the big club at the start of the 1951 campaign. The shy 19-year-old immediately had huge expectations thrust on him by manager Casey Stengel and the New York media. Considered by most to be the heir apparent to the aging Joe DiMaggio in center field, Mantle was built up by Stengel as someone who would eventually become DiMaggio, Babe Ruth, and Lou Gehrig all rolled into one. Observing the switch-hitting outfielder's blinding speed and awesome power from both sides of the plate, the Yankee manager proclaimed, "He should lead the league in everything. With his combination of speed and power, he should win the triple batting crown every year. In fact, he should do anything he wants to do." Adding to the pressures placed on Mantle was the uneasiness that the insecure country boy felt over being in the big city for the first time in his life.

Unable to live up to his advanced billing early in his rookie season, Mantle found himself striking out frequently and often being booed by Yankee fans, who believed everything they had read and heard about the talented youngster. Before long, the struggling outfielder was sent down to the minor leagues, where he eventually righted himself. Returning to New York later in the year, Mantle finished his rookie season with decent numbers, hitting 13 home runs, knocking in 65 runs, and batting .267 in 341 at bats. However, he experienced the first in a series of crippling injuries in that year's World Series, which ended up limiting his playing time and robbing him of much of his great speed throughout the remainder of his career.

Playing right field in Yankee Stadium, Mantle moved toward right center to catch a fly ball hit by the Giants Willie Mays. With Mantle all set to make the play, centerfielder Joe DiMaggio called off his teammate at the last moment. Stopping abruptly to avoid a collision, Mantle caught his right foot in an outfield drainage ditch, seriously injuring his leg and causing him to be carried off the field on a stretcher. The injury prevented Mantle from ever again playing at 100 percent capacity.

Yet, even at less than 100 percent, Mantle had enough natural ability to become a truly great player. He was thick throughout his 5'11", 200-pound frame, extremely muscular, and also exceptionally fast, even after losing some of his great speed. Although Mantle always maintained that he was a better right-handed hitter, he had equal power from both sides of the plate, possessing the ability to drive the ball more than 500 feet as either a left-handed or right-handed batter.

Returning to the Yankees at the start of the 1952 campaign, Mantle took over the starting center field job from the recently retired DiMaggio. Although he continued to strike out regularly, fanning a total of 111 times, Mantle had a solid second season, hitting 23 home runs, driving in 87 runs, scoring 94 others, batting .311, and making the All-Star Team for the first of 11 straight times. He also performed quite well in each of the next three seasons, averaging 28 home runs, 98 runs batted in, and 118 runs scored from 1953 to 1955, and batting over .300 in two of those years. Mantle led the American League with 129 runs scored in 1954, and he topped the circuit with 37 home runs, a .433 on-base percentage, and a .611 slugging percentage in 1955. Yet, disappointed by Mantle's frequent strikeouts and the slugger's inability to reach the lofty level that had been predicted for him when he first arrived in the big leagues, Yankee fans continued to voice their displeasure toward the slugger by booing him whenever he failed to fully live up to their expectations.

Mantle finally became the darling of the fans in 1956, when he put together the kind of season that most people always believed he was capable of having. Mantle won the American League Triple Crown by leading the league with 52 home runs, 130 runs batted in, and a .353 batting average. He also topped the circuit with 132 runs scored and a .705 slugging percentage en route to being named the league's

Most Valuable Player for the first of three times and being awarded the Hickok Belt as the top professional athlete of the year. Mantle had another great season in 1957, hitting 34 home runs, knocking in 94 runs, batting .365, winning his second consecutive MVP Award, and leading the Yankees to their sixth pennant in his first seven years with the team. However, even though Mantle was among the league's best players in 1958 and 1959, his numbers fell off somewhat, causing Yankee fans to begin jeering him once again. The attitude of the fans toward Mantle began to permanently change the following season, though, after New York's disappointing third-place finish in 1959 prompted the team to acquire Roger Maris from the Kansas City Athletics for five players.

Mantle and Maris engaged in the first of two consecutive home run races in 1960, with Mickey edging out his new teammate for the league lead, 40 to 39. Mantle also knocked in 94 runs, batted .275, and topped the circuit with 119 runs scored. But Maris finished just ahead of Mantle in the league MVP voting, winning the award for the first of two straight times. And as the season progressed, fans of the team began to develop a strong connection to Mantle. Even though they realized that Maris's contributions were critical to the success of the team, the right fielder began to draw their ire as he challenged Mantle for the home run title. Since they considered Mickey to be a "true" Yankee, fans of the team rooted for the center fielder to win the home run crown, and they correspondingly rooted against Maris whenever he stepped to the plate. Mantle subsequently became their hero, something he remained the rest of his career, while they begrudgingly accepted Maris as a necessary evil.

The feelings of the fans toward Mantle and Maris intensified the following year, when the two men waged an epic battle in pursuit of Babe Ruth's single-season home run record en route to leading New York to its first world championship since 1958. As the Yankees systematically devastated their opponents on the way to capturing the 1961 AL pennant, fans of the team expressed their affection for Mantle more and more, since they felt that, as a "true" Yankee, he should be the one to break Ruth's record. Maris was cast as an interloper, while Mantle was cheered wildly every time he came to the plate. The fans also believed that Mantle was the better all-around player of the two men, even though Maris was the one who eclipsed Ruth's record, edging out Mantle for league MVP honors for the second consecutive year in the process. Nevertheless, the numbers posted by Mantle over the course of the campaign would seem to justify the feelings of the fans. He finished second in the league to Maris in home runs, with 54, placed among the league leaders with 128 runs batted in, a .317 batting average, and a .452 on-base percentage, and he topped the circuit with 132 runs scored and a .687 slugging percentage.

The New York press began to choose sides as well. Far more comfortable in the big city than he was earlier in his career, Mantle became a much easier interview than the shy and often uncooperative Maris. Fully understanding the types of answers that members of the media appreciated, Mantle took every opportunity to oblige them. Reporters began writing stories that praised Mantle for the courage he displayed as he continued to play through more and more pain as his career wore on. Their articles helped make Mickey a folk hero of sorts, enabling him to reach icon-like status, not only in New York, but throughout the entire country. In subsequent seasons, Mantle experienced the kind of popularity enjoyed by few players in the history of the game.

Mantle captured his third MVP trophy in 1962, leading the Yankees to their third straight pennant and second consecutive world championship. Although he missed almost 40 games and compiled only 377 official at bats, Mantle's 30 home runs, 89 runs batted in, 96 runs scored, .321 batting average, and league-leading .488 on-base percentage and .605 slugging percentage enabled him to edge out teammate Bobby Richardson for league MVP honors.

Mantle's 1963 season was cut short by one of the most serious injuries he sustained during his career. Playing in Baltimore, the center fielder ran into a wire fence in the outfield, breaking his left foot and tearing the cartilage in his left knee. Mantle appeared in only 65 games for the Yankees that year, hitting 15 home runs, driving in 35 runs, and batting .314, in just 172 official at bats.

Mantle returned to the team's everyday starting lineup the following year, leading the Yankees to their fifth consecutive pennant. Despite limping noticeably and playing in constant pain, Mantle finished among the league leaders with 35 home runs, 111 runs batted in, a .303 batting average, and a .591 slugging percentage. He also topped the circuit with a .426 on-base percentage. The center fielder finished second to Baltimore's Brooks Robinson in the league MVP voting. The Yankees lost the World Series to the Cardinals in seven games, but Mantle batted .333 during the Fall Classic, drove in eight runs, and hit the final three of his World Series record 18 home runs.

The 1964 campaign turned out to be Mantle's last big offensive year. He missed huge portions of the 1965 and 1966 seasons with injuries, and the Yankees shifted him to first base before the start of the 1967 campaign to alleviate the pressure on his aching legs. Playing in great pain until he finally retired at the end of 1968, Mantle never again put up huge offensive numbers. But he remained a productive player whenever his ailing body enabled him to take the field. Mantle ended his career with 536 home runs, 1,509 runs batted in, 1,677 runs scored, 2,415 hits, a .298 batting average, a .423 on-base percentage, and a .557 slugging percentage. His 536 homers were the third-most in baseball history at the time of his retirement. In addition to winning three Most Valuable Player Awards, Mantle finished in the top five in the balloting on six other occasions. He helped lead the Yankees to 12 pennants and 7 world championships in his 18 years with the team.

As popular as Mantle eventually became with the fans, he was equally beloved by his teammates. In his book *Few and Chosen*, former teammate and close friend Whitey Ford referred to Mickey as "a superstar who never acted like one. He was a humble man who was kind and friendly to all his teammates, even the rawest rookie. He was idolized by all the other players."

Ford also noted, "Often he played hurt, his knees aching so much he could hardly walk. But he never complained, and he would somehow manage to drag himself onto the field, ignore the pain, and do something spectacular."

Clete Boyer once expressed his admiration for his teammate by saying, "He is the only baseball player I know who is a bigger hero to his teammates than he is to the fans."

Roy White, who played with Mickey only during the latter stages of Mantle's career, talked about the inspiration he was to him:

> I was really impressed with the way he played the game, how hard he played the game, and the way he hustled, especially with the bad legs he had. I have a vivid memory of him in DC Stadium, after a double-header on a Sunday. It was something like 120 [degrees] down on the floor of the DC Stadium, in July. Looking at him afterwards wrapping the tape off his legs . . . just sitting there totally exhausted. He had played both games. Mickey would hit a one-hopper over to second base, and he would run all-out to first base. How could you give any less watching a guy like that play the game?

Opposing players also held Mantle in high esteem because they knew the effort that he had to go through late in his career just to be able to take the field to start a game. They also admired his sense of fair play, which prevented him from ever trying to embarrass the opposition. Early in his career, the Yankee front office suggested to

Mickey that he do something colorful, such as tip his cap to the fans, whenever he hit a home run. However, Mantle rejected the notion, preferring instead to circle the bases with his head down for fear of embarrassing the opposing team's pitcher. Explaining his actions, Mantle later said, "After I hit a home run I had a habit of running the bases with my head down. I figured the pitcher already felt bad enough without me showing him up rounding the bases."

It was Mantle's humility and courage that made him a hero to opposing players as well as to his own teammates.

Hall of Fame outfielder Carl Yastrzemski once said of Mantle, "If that guy were healthy, he'd hit 80 home runs."

Former Chicago White Sox second baseman Nellie Fox stated, "On two legs, Mickey Mantle would have been the greatest ballplayer who ever lived."

Injuries prevented Mantle from ever realizing his full potential. But Mickey's accomplishments were also diminished somewhat by the frivolous lifestyle he led, which was prompted by his fear of dying young. Mantle's father and grandfather both passed away at an early age, and Mantle believed the same fate awaited him. Stating, "I'm not gonna be cheated," Mantle lived life just as hard as he played baseball. He drank, stayed up until all hours of the night, and was frequently unfaithful to his longtime wife, Merlyn, whom he married in 1951. Had Mantle taken better care of himself, he likely would have been able to add significantly to the extremely impressive numbers he compiled during his career. And as Mickey later said, "If I'd known I was gonna live this long, I'd have taken a lot better care of myself."

Unfortunately, Mantle realized his transgressions too late in life. After being treated for alcoholism at the Betty Ford Clinic in 1994, Mickey discovered that the manner in which he abused his body through the years had left him with inoperable liver cancer. The idol of millions, Mantle displayed dignity and humility in his final days, telling all those fans who had looked up to him as a role model through the years, "This is a role model. Don't be like me."

Mickey Mantle died on August 13, 1995, at the age of 63. At his funeral, sportscaster Bob Costas eulogized his lifetime hero by describing him as "a fragile hero to whom we had an emotional attachment so strong and lasting that it defied logic." Costas added, "In the last year of his life, Mickey Mantle, always so hard on himself, finally came to accept and appreciate the distinction between a role model and a hero. The first, he often was not. The second, he always will be. And, in the end, people got it."

CAREER HIGHLIGHTS

Best Season

Mantle compiled extraordinary numbers in 1957 and 1961. In the first of those years, he led the AL with 121 runs scored and established career highs with a .365 batting average, a .512 on-base percentage, and a league-leading 146 bases on balls. Four years later, Mantle hit 54 homers, drove in 128 runs, batted .317, and topped the circuit with 132 runs scored, 126 walks, and a .687 slugging percentage. Nevertheless, there is little doubt that Mantle's Triple Crown season of 1956 was the finest of his career. In addition to leading the league with 52 home runs, 130 runs batted in, and a .353 batting average, Mickey topped the circuit with 132 runs scored, a .705 slugging percentage, and 376 total bases.

Memorable Moments/Greatest Performances

Over the course of his career, Mantle hit a number of tape measure home runs, any of which could qualify as being among his most memorable feats. He also hit three home runs in a game once, and he hit four consecutive homers over a two-game span on another occasion. Yet, two particular blasts tend to stand out as the most memorable of Mantle's career.

Mantle hit the first of those momentous round-trippers on October 10, 1964, in game 3 of the World Series against the St. Louis Cardinals. Leading off the bottom of the ninth inning with the score tied 1–1 and the series deadlocked at one game apiece, Mantle hit reliever Barney Schultz's first pitch into the right-field upper deck, to give the Yankees a 2–1 victory and a 2–1 lead in the series. The homer was Mantle's 16th in World Series play, enabling him to pass Babe Ruth as the Fall Classic's all-time home run king. Although the Yankees dropped the series to the Cardinals in seven games, Mantle homered two more times, raising his record total to 18.

Even more historic was the home run that Mantle hit against Baltimore's Stu Miller on May 14, 1967. The drive into Yankee Stadium's lower right-field stands made Mantle the sixth member of the 500–home run club.

NOTABLE ACHIEVEMENTS

- Hit more than 50 home runs twice.
- Knocked in more than 100 runs four times.

- Scored more than 100 runs nine times, topping the 120 mark on six occasions.
- Batted over .350 twice.
- Drew more than 100 bases on balls 10 times.
- Compiled on-base percentage in excess of .450 on three occasions.
- Compiled slugging percentage in excess of .600 six times.
- Led AL in home runs four times; runs scored, six times; walks, five times; slugging percentage, four times; on-base percentage and total bases, three times each; and RBIs, batting average, and triples, once each.
- AL MVP in 1956, 1957, and 1962.
- 1956 AL Triple Crown winner.
- 1956 *Sporting News* Major League Player of the Year.
- 1956 Hickok Belt winner.
- Holds major-league record for most World Series home runs (18).
- Member of 500-home run club.
- Six-time *Sporting News* All-Star selection.
- Sixteen-time AL All-Star.
- 1962 Gold Glove winner.
- Twelve-time AL champion.
- Seven-time world champion.

5

Yogi Berra

Derek Jeter and Mariano Rivera merited consideration for the number 5 spot, but in the end, the decision here was to go with Yogi Berra. Rivera is the greatest closer in the history of the game, and he has arguably performed his specific role as well as any other Yankee. But he is a pitcher who typically takes the mound for just one or two innings at a time, prompting me to place Jeter and Berra ahead of him. Jeter has also performed magnificently throughout his career, and he has posted numbers in most offensive categories that far surpass the figures compiled by Berra during his Hall of Fame career. Jeter has also helped lead the Yankees to 7 American League pennants and 5 world championships. However, Berra established an even greater legacy of winning in his 17 full seasons in New York, leading the Yankees to 14 pennants and 10 world championships. And while Jeter never finished any higher than second in the league MVP voting, placing in the top five a total of three times, Berra earned AL MVP honors on three occasions. Yogi also placed second in the balloting two other times. As much as anything, that last fact ended up pushing Berra just ahead of Jeter, into the fifth position in these rankings.

Short, stocky, and lacking grace in the field and at the bat, Lawrence Peter Berra hardly looked like a future Hall of Famer when he first joined the Yankees in 1946. But by the end of his 18-year career, Berra had established himself as one of the greatest catchers in baseball history and as one of the winningest players in the history of professional team sports. Berra was so successful that longtime Yankee manager Casey Stengel considered him to be his good-luck charm, relying heavily on his catcher during his 12-year managerial stint in New York. Stengel once said of Berra, "He'd fall in a sewer and come up with a gold watch." Stengel stated on another occasion, "They say he's funny. Well, he has a lovely wife and family, a beautiful home, money in the bank, and he plays golf with millionaires. What's funny about that?"

Berra actually almost never became a Yankee. Yogi originally tried out for the St. Louis Cardinals in 1942 with childhood friend Joe Garagiola, whom the Cardinals elected to sign instead of him. Thinking that he had been spurned by St. Louis, Berra signed a contract with the Yankees for the same $500 bonus that Garagiola received from the Cardinals. However, the thing that very few people knew at the time was that St. Louis team president Branch Rickey planned to leave the Cardinals shortly thereafter to take over the operation of the Brooklyn Dodgers. Once in charge in Brooklyn, the extremely astute Ricky intended to sign Berra for the Dodgers. His plans failed to come to fruition, though, when New York scooped up Berra in the interim.

Brooklyn's loss turned out to be the Yankees' gain. After playing briefly for the Norfolk Tars of the Class B Piedmont League in 1942, Berra enlisted in the US Navy, for whom he served as a gunner's mate in the D-Day invasion during World War II. Berra returned to professional baseball in 1946, spending most of the year with the Newark Bears before being called up by the Yankees for the final few games of the regular season. He joined the Yankees for good the following year, appearing in 83 games and batting .280, with 11 home runs and 54 RBIs in only 293 official at bats.

Yogi appeared awkward behind the plate during the early stages of his career, and he leaned heavily on Yankee coach Bill Dickey to teach him the tricks of the trade. Dickey, an exceptional defensive catcher during his Hall of Fame career with the team, discussed his young pupil's lack of refinement behind the plate: "Right now, Berra does about everything wrong, but Casey [Stengel] warned me about that. The main thing is he has speed and agility behind the plate and a strong enough arm. He just needs to be taught to throw properly. I know he can hit. I'd say Berra has the makings of a good catcher. I won't say great, but certainly a good one."

Yogi ended up exceeding all expectations. He developed into an outstanding defensive receiver, leading all American League catchers in games caught, chances accepted, and putouts eight times each; double plays, six times; assists, three times; and fielding percentage, once. Deceptively quick and mobile, Berra left the game with AL records for catcher putouts (8,723) and chances accepted (9,520). He was also an exceptional handler of pitchers and a superb signal caller. Casey Stengel once noted, "Why has our pitching been so great? Our catcher, that's why. He looks cumbersome, but he's quick as a cat."

It was as a hitter, though, that Berra truly excelled. After hitting 14 home runs, knocking in 98 runs, and batting .305 in 1948, Yogi began a string of 10 consecutive seasons in which he hit at least 20 home runs. He surpassed 100 RBIs in five of those years, also topping the .300 mark in batting on two occasions. Berra had his finest statistical season in 1950, when he hit 28 homers, drove in 124 runs, scored 116 others, and batted a career-high .322. He finished third in league MVP voting that year, before winning the award for the first of three times the following season. Berra earned league MVP honors in 1951 for leading the Yankees to their third consecutive world championship by hitting 27 home runs, knocking in 88 runs, and batting .294. He won the award again in 1954, even though New York finished second to Cleveland in the American League pennant race. Berra batted .307, hit 22 homers, and knocked in a career-high 125 runs. Berra captured his final MVP trophy the following year, leading the Yankees to their seventh pennant in his first nine full seasons with the team by hitting 27 home runs, driving in 108 runs, and batting .272. Berra had another outstanding season in 1956, when he hit 30 homers, knocked in 105 runs, scored 93 others, and batted .298. He finished second to teammate Mickey Mantle in the league MVP voting. Berra placed in the top five in the balloting a total of seven times during his career.

Mickey Mantle established himself as New York's best all-around player during the middle stages of Berra's career, and opposing pitchers dreaded the thought of pitching to the Yankee center fielder with men on base. But Berra developed a reputation for being one of the game's best clutch hitters, and some opponents feared him even more than Mantle. Rival manager Paul Richards once called Berra "the toughest man in the league in the last three innings."

Former teammate Hector Lopez said, "Yogi had the fastest bat I ever saw. He could hit a ball late that was already past him, and take it out of the park. The pitchers were afraid of him because he'd hit anything, so they didn't know what to throw. Yogi had them psyched out and he wasn't even trying to psyche them out."

A notorious bad-ball hitter, the lefty-swinging Berra tended to swing at anything near the plate. He golfed low pitches into the right field seats and lined high offerings into the outfield for base hits. Blessed with tremendous bat control, Yogi rarely struck out. Five times during his career, he had more home runs in a season than strikeouts. He struck out only 12 times in 597 at bats in 1950, and he whiffed a total of only 414 times over the course of 18 big-league seasons.

An outstanding performer in the World Series as well, Berra holds major-league records for World Series games (75), at-bats (259), hits

(71), doubles (10), singles (49), games caught (63), and catcher putouts (457). He hit 12 home runs and drove in 39 runs in the Fall Classic. The Yankees won 10 of the 14 World Series in which he appeared. Both figures are all-time records.

Berra remained a productive offensive player until 1962, when his skills finally began to erode. He spent his last two years with the Yankees as a part-time player, before retiring at the conclusion of the 1963 campaign. He ended his career with 358 home runs, 1,430 runs batted in, 1,175 runs scored, 2,150 hits, and a .285 batting average. The numbers he compiled over the course of his career place him among New York's all-time leaders in five offensive categories, with his home run and RBI totals earning him a top-five ranking. Berra earned 14 selections to the AL All-Star Team, and the *Sporting News* named him to its All-Star squad on five separate occasions.

Yet, in spite of the tremendous amount of success that Berra experienced during his career, many people tended to view him as a somewhat comical figure, known as much for his malaprops (often referred to as "Yogi-isms") as for his greatness as a ballplayer. Among the more notable quotes that have been attributed to Yogi are the following:

- "Always go to other people's funerals, otherwise they won't come to yours."
- "Baseball is 90 percent mental, and the other half is physical."
- "Even Napoleon had his Watergate."
- "He hits from both sides of the plate. He's amphibious."
- "I never said most of the things I said."
- "So I'm ugly. So what? I never saw anyone hit with his face."
- "Nobody goes there anymore. It's too crowded."
- "It ain't over till it's over."
- "It's like déjà vu, all over again."
- "When you come to a fork in the road, take it."

However, those people closest to Berra have always been keenly aware of his tremendous baseball acumen that enabled him to manage two teams to the World Series after his playing career ended.

The Yankees first hired Berra as their manager after he retired at the conclusion of the 1963 campaign. Although Yogi led the team to the American League pennant in his first year as skipper, he found himself unceremoniously relieved of his duties after New York lost the 1964 World Series to the St. Louis Cardinals in seven games. The crosstown rival New York Mets subsequently hired Berra to be manager

Casey Stengel's first base coach. He remained in that position until 1972, when he took over as field manager following the sudden death of Gil Hodges. Berra piloted the Mets to the National League pennant in 1973, leading them to a major upset over the heavily favored Cincinnati Reds in the League Championship Series. He then directed them to within one game of the world championship, with New York finally losing the World Series to the Oakland Athletics in seven games.

Berra remained Mets manager until he was fired by the team in August 1975. He rejoined the Yankees the following year, serving as a coach under former Yankee teammate and longtime friend Billy Martin. Yogi was a member of the New York coaching staff when the team won consecutive World Series in 1977 and 1978. He continued to function in the same capacity until Yankee owner George Steinbrenner named him the team's manager prior to the start of the 1984 campaign. Berra agreed to stay on as manager in 1985 after receiving assurances from Steinbrenner that he would not be fired in the middle of the season. However, the Yankee owner went back on his word, letting Berra go only 16 games into the season. Berra later said that the manner in which Steinbrenner delivered the news to him upset him far more than the firing itself. Instead of addressing Yogi personally, Steinbrenner dispatched GM Clyde King to inform Berra of his dismissal. A rift subsequently developed between Berra and Steinbrenner, with the former vowing never to return to Yankee Stadium as long as Steinbrenner owned the team. Yogi finally recanted some 15 years later, after the Yankee owner publicly apologized to him. Berra returned to the stadium he called home for 18 seasons on July 18, 1999, for "Yogi Berra Day." This national treasure has been a frequent visitor to Yankee Stadium ever since, bringing smiles to the faces of current Yankee players and fans.

CAREER HIGHLIGHTS

Best Season

Berra won three AL MVP Awards. Yet, he ironically posted his best offensive numbers in 1950, a season in which teammate Phil Rizzuto copped the honor and Berra finished third in the balloting. Yogi hit 28 home runs, knocked in 124 runs, and established career highs with 116 runs scored, 192 hits, 30 doubles, 318 total bases, a .322 batting average, and a .383 on-base percentage.

Memorable Moments/Greatest Performances

Always an outstanding World Series performer, Berra provided Yankee fans with several thrills in postseason play. In game 3 of the 1947 Fall Classic, he hit the first pinch-hit home run in series history. Berra batted .429 and drove in 4 runs against the Dodgers in the 1953 Fall Classic. He again tormented Dodger pitchers in the 1956 World Series, batting .360, hitting 3 homers, and knocking in 10 runs in leading the Yankees to a seven-game victory over the "Boys of Summer."

However, Berra perhaps experienced his greatest moment in game 5 of the 1956 series, when he caught Don Larsen's perfect game—the only one ever thrown in postseason play. Having called every pitch of Larsen's perfecto, Berra leaped into the pitcher's arms after the tall right-hander recorded the final out, providing the national pastime with one of its most indelible images.

NOTABLE ACHIEVEMENTS

- Surpassed 20 home runs 11 times, reaching the 30-mark on two occasions.
- Knocked in more than 100 runs seven times, leading the Yankees in RBIs seven straight seasons at one point.
- Batted over .300 twice.
- AL MVP in 1951, 1954, and 1955.
- Holds major-league records for most World Series games (75), at bats (259), hits (71), doubles (10), singles (49), games caught (63), and catcher putouts (457).
- Five-time *Sporting News* All-Star selection.
- Fifteen-time AL All-Star.
- Fourteen-time AL champion.
- Ten-time world champion.

6

Derek Jeter

One of the most popular and well-respected players in franchise history, Derek Jeter has worn the pinstripes with pride for the past 17 seasons. A product of the Yankee farm system, Jeter has earned numerous personal honors over the course of his career while also establishing a tremendous legacy of winning in New York since he first joined the team late in 1995. With Jeter serving as their starting shortstop, the Yankees have won 12 AL East titles, 7 American League pennants, and 5 world championships. Jeter's outstanding leadership ability, timely hitting, solid defense, and exceptional base running have all contributed significantly to the success that the team has experienced during his time in New York, earning him general recognition as one of the finest all-around players of his generation and as the greatest shortstop in the rich history of the Yankees.

Born in Pequannock, New Jersey, in 1974, Derek Sanderson Jeter moved with his family to Kalamazoo, Michigan, at the age of four. However, he continued to spend his summers in the Garden State, becoming a huge fan of the Yankees and gaining the inspiration to play professional baseball by watching Dave Winfield perform in right field for his favorite team. Selected by the Yankees right out of high school with the sixth overall pick of the 1992 amateur draft, Jeter received an opportunity to pursue his dream when he signed with the team just one day after celebrating his 18th birthday. The lanky shortstop spent the next three years working his way up the New York farm system, succeeding at every level at which he performed. After earning a brief call-up to the major-league club in 1995, Jeter assumed the team's starting shortstop job the following year. Displaying the quiet confidence for which he became so well noted, the 21-year-old shortstop homered on opening day and subsequently went on to win AL Rookie of the Year honors by hitting 10 home runs, driving in 78 runs, scoring 104 others, and batting .314. He continued to exhibit the poise of a veteran during the playoffs and World Series, helping the Yankees capture their first world championship in 18 years by batting .361 in New York's 15 postseason contests.

After a solid sophomore campaign, Jeter embarked on an exceptional run during which he helped lead the Yankees to three consecutive world championships. He batted .324 for New York's record-setting 1998 team while collecting 203 hits and topping the junior circuit with 127 runs scored en route to earning a third-place finish in the AL MVP voting. Jeter followed that up with arguably his finest all-around season, establishing career highs with 24 home runs, 102 runs batted in, 134 runs scored, a .349 batting average, and a league-leading 219 hits in 1999. Jeter subsequently batted .339, amassed 201 hits, and scored 119 runs for New York's 2000 world championship ball club. The shortstop also became the first player in baseball history to be named MVP of both the All-Star Game and the World Series in the same year. After leading the American League to victory in the annual All-Star tilt by becoming the first Yankee since Yogi Berra to hit a home run in the Midsummer Classic, Jeter helped the Yankees dispose of the crosstown rival New York Mets in five games in the World Series by batting .409 and hitting two homers.

Although the Yankees failed to win another world championship in any of the next eight seasons, Jeter continued to perform exceptionally well, earning AL All-Star honors virtually every year and proving to be one of the team's most reliable players during the postseason. He had one of his finest seasons in 2006, earning a close second-place finish in the AL MVP balloting by driving in 97 runs; stealing 34 bases; placing among the league leaders with a .343 batting average, 118 runs scored, 214 hits, and a .417 on-base percentage; and winning his third consecutive Gold Glove. Meanwhile, even though the Yankees failed to win the World Series from 2001 to 2008, Jeter's reputation as one of the finest clutch performers of his generation continued to grow. He posted batting averages of .500 against Anaheim in New York's four-game ALDS loss in 2002, .346 against Florida in the 2003 World Series, and .500 against Detroit in the Yankees' 2006 ALDS loss.

Discussing Jeter's ability to perform well under pressure, Reggie Jackson (also known as "Mr. October" for his ability to excel during the postseason) said, "In big games, the action slows down for him where it speeds up for others. I've told him, 'I'll trade my past for your future.'"

Former Yankee teammate Charlie Hayes noted, "The thing that sets Derek apart is that he's not afraid to fail."

Discussing his shortstop, former Yankee manager Joe Torre once stated, "This kid, right now, the tougher the situation, the more fire he gets in his eyes. You don't teach that."

Jeter even drew praise from Michael Jordan, who certainly knows something about winning. The greatest player in NBA history had this to say about the Yankees shortstop: "I love his work ethic. He has a great attitude. He has the qualities that separate superstars from everyday people, and a lot of it is attributable to his great family background."

As for Jeter's ability to play the field, Ozzie Smith said, "What kind of shortstop is Derek Jeter? Well, a very effective one, to be sure. I think he's a sleeker and leaner model of a Cal Ripken. He's out of the Cal Ripken mold in that he's tall and rangy, has a great arm, covers a lot of ground, and he's a great offensive player."

An instinctive and extremely intelligent player as well, Jeter has always demonstrated a knack for being in the right place at the right time, as evidenced by his famous "flip" to Jorge Posada at home plate in game 3 of the 2001 American League Division Series against the Oakland Athletics. This intrinsic quality has helped to separate Jeter from the many other outstanding players of his time, making him the winningest player of his generation and allowing him to succeed even after his physical skills began to diminish.

After posting solid numbers in each of the previous two seasons, a 35-year-old Jeter batted .334, collected 212 hits, and scored 107 runs in 2009 en route to earning a third-place finish in the league MVP voting. He subsequently helped the Yankees capture their 27th world championship by batting .400 against Minnesota in the ALDS, before compiling 11 hits and a .407 batting average against Philadelphia in the World Series.

Although Jeter's performance slipped somewhat in 2010 and 2011, he remains an effective player who continues to add to his baseball legacy. In recent years, he has surpassed Luis Aparicio as Major League Baseball's all-time hits leader among shortstops, and he has moved into first place on the Yankees' all-time hits list, passing the immortal Lou Gehrig in the process. In 2011, Jeter became the first Yankees player ever to accumulate 3,000 career hits.

Heading into the 2012 campaign, Jeter has 240 career home runs, 1,196 runs batted in, 1,769 runs scored, 3,088 hits, 492 doubles, 339 stolen bases, and a lifetime batting average of .313. In addition to compiling more hits than any other Yankee, he ranks first on the team's all-time list in stolen bases (339), games played (2,426), total plate appearances (11,155), and official at bats (9,868). Jeter also is second in club history in doubles, third in runs scored, fourth in total bases (4,430), tenth in home runs, and tied for fifth in batting average. Although Jeter has never won a batting title, he has finished second in the league in hitting twice, and he has finished third in the batting race another two times. He has earned 7 top 10 finishes in the AL MVP voting, placing second in the balloting once and coming in third on another two occasions. More important, the Yankees have advanced to the playoffs in 15 of the 16 seasons in which Jeter has served as their starting shortstop.

CAREER HIGHLIGHTS

Best Season

Jeter had a tremendous all-around year in 2006, knocking in 97 runs; stealing 34 bases; finishing among the AL leaders with 118 runs scored, 214 hits, and a .343 batting average; winning a Gold Glove; and earning a second-place finish in the league MVP voting. Nevertheless, I elected to go with his 1999 campaign instead. In his finest statistical season, Jeter established career highs with 24 home runs, 102 runs batted in, 134 runs scored, 219 hits, a .349 batting average, a .438 on-base percentage, and a .552 slugging percentage. The shortstop's exceptional performance earned him a sixth-place finish in the MVP balloting and helped the Yankees capture their second of three consecutive world championships. Jeter also had a fabulous postseason, batting .455 against Texas in the ALDS, hitting .350, with a home run and 3 RBIs against Boston in the ALCS, and batting .353 and scoring 4 runs during New York's four-game sweep of Atlanta in the World Series.

Memorable Moments/Greatest Performances

Jeter has experienced many memorable moments over the course of his career, the last of which occurred this past season. On July 9, 2011, he became the 28th member of the 3,000-hit club, doing so in grand fashion by homering off David Price of the Tampa Bay Rays in the third inning at Yankee Stadium. On September 11, 2009, Jeter surpassed Lou Gehrig as the Yankees' all-time hits leader when he singled to right field against the Baltimore Orioles' Chris Tillman for the 2,722nd hit of his career. Less than one month earlier, on August

16, 2009, Jeter recorded his 2,673rd and 2,674th hits, enabling him to tie and surpass Luis Aparicio for the most hits by a shortstop in major-league history.

However, aside from those personal milestones, most of the signature moments of Jeter's career have fittingly taken place during the postseason, giving credence to the moniker of "Captain Clutch" that he acquired over time.

The first such instance took place in Jeter's rookie season of 1996. With the Yankees trailing the Baltimore Orioles 4–3 in the bottom of the eighth inning of game 1 of the ALCS, Jeter lofted a fly ball to deep right field. With Orioles right fielder Tony Tarasco apparently readying himself to make a play on the ball by the fence, 12-year-old Jeffrey Maier reached over the wall and caught the ball, pulling it back into the stands. Although replays showed conclusively that the ball would not have reached the stands had Maier not reached over onto the field of play, the umpires awarded Jeter a home run. The Yankees subsequently went on to win the contest in 11 innings and the series in five games.

The 2001 postseason turned out to be an even more eventful one for Jeter. With the Yankees clinging to a 1–0 lead and facing elimination in game 3 of the ALDS against the Oakland Athletics, Jeter made a season-saving defensive play. With Jeremy Giambi on first base, Oakland outfielder Terrence Long doubled down the right-field line against Yankees pitcher Mike Mussina. As Giambi rounded third base and headed for home, Yankees right fielder Shane Spencer retrieved the ball and made an errant throw that sailed over the head of cutoff man Tino Martinez. However, Jeter saved the day by cutting across the infield, grabbing the ball as it dribbled down the first-base line, and flipping it backhanded to catcher Jorge Posada, who tagged Giambi on the leg just before he crossed home plate with the tying run. The Yankees went on to win the game 1–0, and they subsequently won the series as well.

Some two weeks later, Jeter provided more heroics in game 4 of the World Series. With game 4 of the Fall Classic being played at Yankee Stadium on October 31, the contest entered the bottom of the 10th inning tied at 3–3. At midnight, the scoreboard in center field read "Attention Fans, Welcome to NOVEMBER BASEBALL." Moments later, Jeter drove an offering from Arizona Diamondbacks relief pitcher Byung-Hyun Kim into the right field stands for a game-winning home run. Although the Yankees eventually lost the series to Arizona in 7 games, the blast earned Jeter his nickname "Mr. November."

NOTABLE ACHIEVEMENTS

- Batted over .300 on 11 occasions, topping the .330 mark four times.
- Scored more than 100 runs 13 times.
- Collected more than 200 hits seven times.
- Stole at least 30 bases four times.
- Knocked in more than 100 runs once (1999).
- Led AL in hits and runs scored once each.
- Led AL shortstops in fielding percentage twice and in assists and putouts once each.
- Member of 3,000-hit club.
- Yankees' all-time leader in hits (3,088) and stolen bases (339).
- Major League Baseball's all-time hits leader among shortstops.
- Major League Baseball's record holder for most hits (191) and runs scored (107) in postseason play.
- 1996 AL Rookie of the Year.
- 2000 All-Star Game MVP.
- 2000 World Series MVP.
- Two-time *Sporting News* All-Star selection.
- Twelve-time AL All-Star.
- Won 4 Silver Sluggers.
- Five-time Gold Glove winner.
- Seven-time AL champion.
- Five-time world champion.

7

Mariano Rivera

Generally considered to be the greatest closer in baseball history, Mariano Rivera has achieved a level of excellence over the course of his career that few others can even approach. Since being converted from a starter to a reliever in his first big-league season, the Panamanian-born right-hander has relied almost exclusively on one pitch to dominate opposing hitters for the past 16 years. Rivera has compiled more saves than any other relief pitcher in the history of the game (603 as of this writing), has posted the lowest career ERA of any pitcher during the "live ball" era (2.21), and holds numerous postseason records, including most career saves (42), lowest career ERA (0.70), and most consecutive scoreless innings pitched (34 1/3). Perhaps more than any other player, "Mo," as he is affectionately known to his teammates, has been responsible for the incredible success that the Yankees have experienced during his time in New York, particularly from 1996 to 2000, when they won four world championships in five years.

After initially signing with the Yankees as an amateur free agent at the age of 20 in 1990, Mariano Rivera spent five years working his way up the team's farm system before finally getting a chance to pitch at the major-league level in 1995. Rivera struggled somewhat in his first year in pinstripes, compiling a 5.51 ERA while splitting his time between the starting rotation and the bullpen. However, the hard-throwing 25-year-old right-hander opened eyes during the postseason when he struck out 8 batters and allowed only 3 hits in 5 1/3 scoreless innings against Seattle during New York's first-round playoff loss to the Mariners.

Given an opportunity to serve as setup man for closer John Wetteland the following year, Rivera thrived in his new role, compiling a record of 8–3 and a 2.09 ERA and setting a Yankees single-season record for strikeouts by a reliever by fanning 130 batters in 108 innings of work. Rivera's extraordinary performance earned him a third-place finish in the Cy Young voting. He subsequently allowed just 1 earned run in 14 1/3 innings pitched during the postseason in helping the Yankees win their first world championship in 18 years. Rivera's superb pitching convinced team management to insert him into the role of closer when Wetteland became a free agent at season's end.

Rivera soon made Yankee fans forget all about Wetteland, saving 43 games in his first year as closer while compiling a 1.88 ERA. He became even more effective over the course of that 1997 campaign after he added to his pitching repertoire a cut fastball that eventually became his signature pitch. However, Rivera faltered somewhat during the postseason, surrendering a game-tying home run to Cleveland's Sandy Alomar Jr. in game 4 of the ALDS that eventually led to New York's first-round playoff loss.

Undaunted by his playoff failure, Rivera rebounded the following year to begin an amazing run during which he clearly established himself as the best closer in the game. He saved a total of 117 games for the Yankees from 1998 to 2000, serving as arguably the most important member of their three consecutive world championship ball clubs. Particularly effective in 1999, Rivera compiled a 1.83 ERA, led the major leagues with 45 saves, and allowed just 43 hits in 69 innings of work while striking out 52 and walking only 18. After saving six games and pitching 13 1/3 scoreless innings during the previous year's postseason, Rivera earned World Series MVP honors in 1999 by recording 2 saves and a win during the Yankees' four-game sweep of the Atlanta Braves. He concluded the campaign having pitched 43 consecutive scoreless innings across the regular season and postseason.

The Yankees failed to win the World Series again until 2009, but Rivera continued to perform brilliantly throughout the period, leading the AL in saves another two times and compiling an ERA below 2.00 in five of the next eight seasons. He saved at least 30 games in all but one of those years, topping the 40 mark on four occasions. And even though the Yankees came up short in their bid to win another world championship, Rivera pitched extremely well each postseason, saving a total of 15 games between 2001 and 2007, and posting an ERA below 2.00 in all but one playoff series during that time.

When the Yankees finally returned to the top of the baseball world in 2009, Rivera predictably made huge contributions to their success.

After saving 44 games and compiling a 1.76 ERA during the regular season, he saved another five games during the postseason and allowed just 1 run in 16 total innings of work. Although he is 42 years old as of this writing, Rivera shows virtually no signs of slowing down. He saved 44 games and compiled a 1.91 ERA in 2011.

It is the combination of Rivera's remarkable consistency and amazing longevity that has prompted most baseball experts to anoint him as the greatest closer in the history of the game. Hall of Fame starter-turned-closer Dennis Eckersley called him "the best ever, no doubt." Former Yankee manager Joe Torre said of Rivera, "He's the best I've ever been around. Not only the ability to pitch and perform under pressure, but the calm he puts over the clubhouse." Meanwhile, in discussing Rivera's looming presence at the end of games, Alex Rodriguez said, "He's the only guy in baseball who can change the game from a seat in the clubhouse or the bullpen. He would start affecting teams as early as the fifth inning because they knew he was out there. I've never seen anyone who could affect a game like that."

Opposing players also admire Rivera for the level of professionalism he has demonstrated throughout his career. Fellow closer Joe Nathan said, "I look up to how he's handled himself on and off the field. . . . You never see him show up anyone and he respects the game. I've always looked up to him, and it's always a compliment to be just mentioned in the same sentence as him."

Longtime Texas Rangers infielder Michael Young echoed Nathan's sentiments: "I respect Mo more than anybody in the game. The guy goes out there, gets three outs and shakes [Jorge] Posada's hand. You appreciate someone who respects the game like he does, respects the people he plays with and against, and obviously his results speak for themselves."

CAREER HIGHLIGHTS

Best Season

Rivera has had a number of absolutely brilliant years that could easily be classified as the finest of his career. He compiled a record of 5–2 in 2003, posted an ERA of 1.66, saved 40 games, struck out 63 batters in 70 2/3 innings, and surrendered only 61 hits to the opposition. The following year, Rivera led the league with a career-high 53 saves, compiled a 1.94 ERA, and struck out 66 batters in 78 2/3 innings of work, while allowing opposing batters only 65 hits.

However, the two finalists for Rivera's greatest season ended up being his 2005 and 2008 campaigns. In the first of those years, he compiled a career-best 1.38 ERA, won seven games, converted 43 of 47 save opportunities, struck out 80 batters in 78 1/3 innings of work, allowed a total of only 72 base runners (50 hits, 18 walks, 4 hit batsmen), and limited opposing hitters to a batting average of only .177. Rivera's extraordinary performance earned him a second-place finish in the Cy Young voting and a ninth-place finish in the league MVP balloting.

In 2008, Mo finished 6–5, with an ERA of 1.40, 39 saves, and 77 strikeouts in 70 2/3 innings pitched. He also allowed only 49 men to reach base (41 hits, 6 walks, 2 hit batsmen), holding opposing hitters to a batting average of just .165. The primary obstacle to selecting 2008 as Rivera's best season ended up being the Yankees' failure to make the playoffs for the only time in his career. Nevertheless, the fact that Rivera walked only 6 men all year long, blew just 1 save opportunity, and compiled a career-best 97.5 save conversion rate made it impossible to overlook his fabulous 2008 campaign, which edged out 2005 in a photo finish.

Memorable Moments/Greatest Performances

Rivera's extraordinary postseason pitching has afforded him many memorable moments, including being on the mound to record the final out of the Yankees' 1998, 1999, 2000, and 2009 World Series victories. He also threw the final pitch at the "old" Yankee Stadium, retiring Baltimore's Brian Roberts on a groundout on September 21, 2008.

Although Rivera has always put his team before himself, he experienced two of his greatest individual moments during the latter stages of the 2011 campaign. After becoming just the second pitcher to record as many as 600 career saves on September 13, Rivera surpassed Trevor Hoffman as Major League Baseball's all-time saves leader six days later by closing out a 6–4 win against the Minnesota Twins at Yankee Stadium. Rivera's record 602nd save gave further affirmation as to his place as the greatest closer in baseball history.

While Rivera has pitched brilliantly throughout his postseason career, he delivered one of his most memorable postseason performances against the arch-rival Boston Red Sox in game 7 of the 2003 American League Championship Series. Entering the contest in the ninth inning with the score tied 5–5, Rivera pitched three scoreless innings, holding the Red Sox at bay until Aaron Boone won the pennant for the Yankees with a walk-off home run in the bottom of the 11th. Rivera earned Championship Series MVP honors by recording 2 saves and the game 7 victory. The Yankees subsequently lost the World Series to the Florida Marlins in six games, but Rivera continued his exceptional pitching during the Fall Classic, concluding the postseason with 5 saves and having allowed only 1 earned run in 16 total innings of work.

NOTABLE ACHIEVEMENTS

- Surpassed 50 saves twice.
- Topped 40 saves six other times.
- Compiled ERA below 2.00 on 11 occasions.
- Led AL in saves three times.
- Holds Yankee team records for most saves in a single season (53), most strikeouts by a reliever in a single season (130), and most consecutive save opportunities converted (36).
- Holds numerous major-league records, including most career saves (603), highest career save conversion rate (89.33%), and most seasons with at least 30 saves (14).
- Holds several postseason records, including most career saves (42), lowest career ERA (0.70), most consecutive scoreless innings pitched (34 1/3), most consecutive save opportunities converted (23), and most times in a career recording the final out of a World Series (4).
- Holds All-Star Game records for most selections as a reliever (12) and most saves (4).
- Career ERA of 2.21 is lowest of any pitcher whose career began after 1920.
- Five-time AL Rolaids Relief Man Award winner.
- 1999 World Series MVP Award winner.
- 2003 ALCS MVP Award winner.
- 2009 *Sporting News* Pro Athlete of the Year Award winner.
- Six-time Sporting News Reliever of the Year Award winner.
- Twelve-time AL All-Star.
- Seven-time AL champion.
- Five-time world champion

8

Bill Dickey

The first in a long line of outstanding Yankee catchers, Bill Dickey would likely be better remembered today had he not been replaced almost immediately by Yogi Berra after he retired at the conclusion of the 1946 season. Dickey also had the misfortune of spending his entire career being overshadowed by other Yankee greats, such as Babe Ruth, Lou Gehrig, and Joe DiMaggio. Nevertheless, Dickey, who was both an outstanding hitter and an exceptional defensive receiver, deserves to be mentioned high on the list of all-time Yankees since he rivaled Mickey Cochrane as Major League Baseball's premier catcher of the first half of the 20th century.

Born in Bastrop, Louisiana, on June 6, 1907, William Malcolm Dickey made his major-league debut with the Yankees during the latter stages of the 1928 campaign, appearing in 10 games and batting just .200 in his 15 plate appearances. The lanky 6'1", 195-pounder became the team's starting catcher the following year, beginning a record string of 13 consecutive seasons in which he appeared in at least 100 games behind the plate. Dickey batted .324 in his first full season, before compiling averages of .339 and .327 in 1930 and 1931, respectively.

Although Dickey posted impressive batting averages in each of his first three seasons, he exhibited little in the way of power, combining for a total of only 21 home runs. However, he began to establish himself as a more integral part of New York's offense in 1932, when he reached new career highs in home runs (15) and runs batted in (84) while surpassing the .300 mark in batting for the fourth of six consecutive times. Dickey earned the first of his six nominations to the

Sporting News All-Star Team and then celebrated by batting .438 and driving in 4 runs against the Cubs during New York's four-game sweep of the National League pennant winners in the World Series.

Dickey had another outstanding season in 1933, driving in 97 runs, batting .318, and appearing in Major League Baseball's inaugural All-Star Game. Injuries cut into Dickey's playing time and offensive production in each of the next two seasons, but he still managed to catch more than 100 games each year, total 26 home runs and 153 RBIs those two campaigns, and earn his second All-Star Game nomination in 1934. During 1934's Midsummer Classic, it was Dickey who ended Carl Hubbell's strikeout string, following whiffs by Babe Ruth, Lou Gehrig, Jimmie Foxx, Al Simmons, and Joe Cronin with a single to center field.

Healthy again in 1936, Dickey began a string of four consecutive seasons that were the most productive of his career. In helping the Yankees capture four straight world championships, he surpassed 20 home runs and 100 RBIs each year while batting well over .300 each season. Dickey hit 22 homers, knocked in 107 runs, scored 99 others, and batted a career-high .362 in 1936. His .362 batting average was the highest single-season mark ever posted by a catcher (tied by Mike Piazza of Los Angeles in 1997), until Joe Mauer hit .365 for Minnesota in 2009. Dickey placed fifth in the league MVP voting at season's end. He finished fifth in the balloting again the following year, when he batted .332, scored 87 runs, and established new career highs with 29 homers and 133 runs batted in. Dickey continued to excel in each of the next two seasons, hitting 27 home runs and knocking in 115 runs in 1938 and hitting 24 long balls, driving in 105 runs, and scoring 98 others in 1939. He placed second to Jimmie Foxx in the league MVP voting in 1938, before punctuating his great season by batting .400 against the Cubs during New York's four-game sweep of Chicago in the World Series.

Dickey never again posted huge offensive numbers, but he remained the finest defensive receiver in the game until he retired. Known for his strong throwing arm, ability to handle a pitching staff, and exceptional signal-calling talent, Dickey was in many ways the heart and soul of the Yankee dynasty of the late 1930s.

Bill Werber was a backup infielder on the Yankees for two seasons, before serving as starting third baseman for four teams over the course of the next 10 years. Werber later discussed the impression that Dickey made on him during his two years in New York: "Bill Dickey was the heart of the team defensively and commanded tremendous respect from the Yankee pitchers. Once the game started, he ran the show."

Dickey also earned the respect of his opponents around the league, albeit in a totally different fashion. Although he was known mostly for his quiet demeanor off the field, Dickey occasionally displayed the same fiery temperament on the diamond that helped lead the Yankees to 8 pennants and 7 world championships in his 16 years with the team. Dickey's temper became apparent for all to see on July 4, 1932, at Washington's Griffith Stadium when he fractured the jaw of Washington outfielder Carl Reynolds with one punch following a collision at home plate. The incident resulted in a $1,000 fine and a one-month suspension for Dickey.

Known also for his close friendship with Lou Gehrig, Dickey was seen by many as the Yankees' new leader on the field after their captain was stricken with the fatal illness that came to bear his name.

After seeing his role behind the plate gradually diminish from 1941 to 1943, Dickey spent two years in the navy during World War II. He returned to the Yankees in 1946, appearing in 54 games before taking over the managerial reins from Joe McCarthy at midseason. Dickey resigned at the end of the year, but he came back to New York to serve as a coach under Casey Stengel from 1949 to 1957. Dickey served primarily as first-base coach and as special catching instructor to Yogi Berra, who later credited his tutor with turning him into a solid defensive receiver.

Dickey was inducted into the Hall of Fame in 1954, and he later shared a joint ceremony with Berra at Yankee Stadium when the team retired their famous number 8 jersey. Dickey passed away in Little Rock, Arkansas, on November 12, 1993, at the age of 86.

Bill Dickey ended his career with 202 home runs, 1,209 runs batted in, 930 runs scored, and a .313 batting average. In addition to surpassing 20 homers and 100 runs batted in four times each, he scored more than 90 runs twice and batted over .300 a total of 11 times. Dickey appeared in 11 All-Star Games and finished in the top 10 in the league MVP voting on five occasions. Considered to be the finest defensive receiver of his time, Dickey posted a lifetime .988 fielding percentage and held the records for putouts and fielding average by a catcher at the time of his retirement.

Perhaps Dickey's greatest contributions to the Yankees, though, could not be measured by his statistics. He was a tremendous team leader who affected the game in any number of ways. An admiring sportswriter named Dan Daniel once wrote, "Dickey isn't just a catcher. He's a ball club. He isn't just a player. He's an influence."

CAREER HIGHLIGHTS

Best Season

It's really a close call between Dickey's 1936 and 1937 campaigns. He performed most proficiently in the first of those years, establishing career highs with 99 runs scored, a .362 batting average, and a .617 slugging percentage while hitting 22 homers and driving in 107 runs in only 112 games. However, with injuries forcing Dickey to relinquish his catching duties for 41 games, he failed to affect his team as much as he would have had he been fully healthy. As a result, I will opt instead for Dickey's 1937 season, when he appeared in 140 games, batted .332, compiled a .417 on-base percentage and a .570 slugging percentage, and established career bests with 29 homers and 133 runs batted in.

Memorable Moments/Greatest Performances

In addition to being the finest defensive receiver of his time, Dickey performed several outstanding batting feats. He hit grand slams on consecutive days in 1937, leaving the park with the bases loaded on both August 3 and 4. Dickey torched the crosstown Giants in game 2 of the 1936 World Series, hitting a 2-run homer and driving in 5 runs. He also had a big series against the Reds in 1939, hitting 2 home runs and knocking in 5 runs, including the game winner in the bottom of the ninth inning of the opening contest. However, Dickey had his greatest day on July 26, 1939, when he slammed 3 straight homers against the St. Louis Browns during a 14–1 Yankee win.

NOTABLE ACHIEVEMENTS

- Topped 20 homers and 100 RBIs four straight seasons, from 1936 to 1939.
- Batted over .300 in 10 of 11 seasons at one point.
- Compiled on-base percentage in excess of .400 on five occasions.
- Six-time *Sporting News* All-Star selection.
- Eleven-time AL All-Star.
- Eight-time AL champion.
- Seven-time world champion.

9

Whitey Ford

The greatest starting pitcher in the rich history of the Yankees, Whitey Ford was among the premier hurlers of his time. A fierce competitor and a master of the mental aspects of pitching, Ford won more games (236), threw more shutouts (45), struck out more batters (1,956), and pitched more innings (3,171) than any other Yankee hurler, while establishing World Series records for most wins (10), losses (8), games started (22), innings pitched (146), and strikeouts (94). The fact that the left-handed-throwing Ford had the good fortune to spend his entire career pitching for the dominant team of his era in a ballpark that boasted distant outfield fences in left and left-center field certainly aided his numbers considerably. Nevertheless, Ford's overall effectiveness as a hurler is indisputable. He compiled an ERA under 3.00 in 11 of his 16 seasons, never allowing the opposition more than 3.24 runs per nine innings in any single campaign. Ford's lifetime 2.75 earned run average is the lowest among starting pitchers whose careers began after the advent of the "live ball era" in 1920. His career record of 236–106 gives him a lifetime winning percentage of .690—the third-best all-time and the highest of any modern pitcher with at least 200 wins. He allowed an average of only 10.94 base runners per nine innings, and his 45 career shutouts included eight 1–0 victories. Ford accomplished all he did despite possessing only average physical size and athletic ability.

Born in New York City on October 21, 1928, Edward Charles Ford grew up in the Astoria section of Queens, just a few miles south of Yankee Stadium. After graduating from the Manhattan School of Aviation, Ford signed an amateur free agent contract with the Yankees in 1947. He began his professional baseball career shortly thereafter, being given the nickname "Whitey" while in the minor leagues due to his exceptionally blonde hair. Ford spent almost three years working his way up New York's farm system, finally making his major-league debut with the team at the age of 21, on July 1, 1950. Displaying the same craftiness and calm demeanor on the mound that eventually earned him the nickname "The Chairman of the Board," Ford went on to compile a 9–1 record over the season's final three months, helping the Yankees to their second of five straight American League pennants. He continued his success against the Philadelphia Phillies in the World Series, throwing 8 2/3 innings of shutout ball in the game 4 clincher.

Ford spent the 1951 and 1952 campaigns serving in the army during the Korean War, but he returned to the Yankees in 1953 to give them the deepest starting staff in the majors. Joining veteran hurlers Allie Reynolds, Vic Raschi, and Eddie Lopat, Ford gave New York a "Big Four" that rivaled that of the Cleveland Indians—the team that challenged the Yankees for preeminence in the American League throughout the first half of the decade. The depth of New York's starting staff enabled manager Casey Stengel to work Ford into the rotation gradually, without putting too much pressure on him. Ford learned a great deal from Reynolds, Raschi, and fellow left-hander Lopat, who taught the youngster many tricks of the trade.

After compiling marks of 18–6 and 16–8 his first two full seasons, Ford established himself as the ace of the Yankee staff in 1955. Finishing the year with a record of 18–7, he tied for the league lead in wins. Ford also topped the circuit with 18 complete games, and he placed second in the loop with an ERA of 2.63, en route to earning the first of four selections to the *Sporting News* All-Star Team. He finished out the campaign in grand fashion, throwing consecutive one-hitters during the month of September.

Ford followed up his outstanding 1955 season with another exceptional year in 1956, finishing the regular season with a record of 19–6, 18 complete games, and a league-leading 2.47 earned run average. He again topped the circuit in ERA two years later, when he compiled a career-best mark of 2.01.

Despite the tremendous amount of success that Ford experienced during the first half of his career, he likely would have posted even better numbers had manager Casey Stengel not limited his starts over the course of each season. Stengel preferred to start Ford every fifth or sixth day, manipulating his rotation so that his best pitcher faced the league's stronger teams.

Reflecting on the manner in which Stengel handled him his first several seasons, Ford noted, "Casey and Jim Turner [former Yankee pitching coach] . . . there were certain clubs they wanted me to pitch against. I know I would never miss Chicago, Cleveland, or Detroit. If I had to rest an extra day, they would do it in order for me to pitch against certain clubs."

However, when Ralph Houk replaced Stengel as manager in 1961, he installed a regular four-man rotation, allowing Ford to pitch on only three days' rest for the first time in his career. The left-hander ended up making 39 starts, finishing the campaign with a league-leading record of 25–4, topping the circuit with 283 innings pitched, striking out a career-high 209 batters, and winning the Cy Young Award. After winning 17 games the following year, Ford led the American League with a record of 24–7 and 269 innings pitched in 1963. He likely would have won the Cy Young Award again had the trophy been presented to the best pitcher in each league at the time. However, the award went instead to the National League's Sandy Koufax, who posted even better numbers for the pennant-winning Dodgers. Koufax also bested Ford twice in that year's World Series, with the latter losing the Dodgers' game 4 clincher despite allowing only two hits and one unearned run.

The 1963 campaign turned out to be Ford's last truly dominant season. Although he pitched extremely well the following year, compiling a record of 17–6 and a 2.13 ERA, he began experiencing circulatory problems in his pitching arm that hindered his performance the remainder of his career. Never a particularly hard thrower to begin with, Ford threw the ball with less velocity than ever, thereby forcing him to get by more on guile and courage than anything else. His inability to make more than one start in the 1964 World Series against the Cardinals eventually led to New York's downfall, since the team found it necessary to start rookie right-hander Mel Stottlemyre in the decisive seventh game on only two days' rest.

Despite lacking the same velocity on his pitches that he had earlier in his career, Ford experienced a considerable amount of success his last few seasons as a full-time starter because, even at his peak, he depended more on his intelligence and resourcefulness than on sheer physical ability to get out opposing batters. At 5'10" and 180 pounds, Ford lacked great size and physical strength. However, he handled himself on the mound like a surgeon, controlling games with his mastery of the mental aspects of pitching and with his pinpoint control. Batters had to deal with his wide variety of pitches, ranging from his outstanding changeup to his excellent curve and good fastball. He also had one of the league's best pickoff moves, and he fielded his position extremely well.

In discussing one of the techniques that he used to get out opposing hitters, Ford said, "You would be amazed how many important outs you can get by working the count down to where the hitter is sure you're going to throw to his weakness, and then throw to his power instead."

As for his purported use of the spitball, Ford said, "I never threw the spitter, well maybe once or twice when I really needed to get a guy out real bad."

Although Ford later admitted to occasionally cheating by doctoring balls in various ways, he proclaimed, "I didn't begin cheating until late in my career, when I needed something to help me survive. I didn't cheat when I won the 25 games in 1961. I don't want anybody to get any ideas and take my Cy Young Award away. And I didn't cheat in 1963 when I won 24 games. Well, maybe a little."

In spite of his physical woes, Ford returned to the team in 1965, putting together one more solid season by going 16–13. However, the pain in his pitching arm became so bad in 1966 that he found himself unable to take the mound on a regular basis. After undergoing shoulder surgery during the year, Ford attempted a comeback in 1967, but he soon realized his pitching days were over. He announced his retirement in late May, after lasting just one inning in his final start. Ford entered the Hall of Fame seven years later, with his close friend and former teammate Mickey Mantle.

Although Ford surpassed 20 victories just twice during his career, he won at least 16 games eight other times. He also posted an ERA below 2.50 on five occasions and threw more than 250 innings four times. In addition to capturing Cy Young honors in 1961, Ford finished in the top five in the AL MVP voting twice.

Former Yankee manager Ralph Houk had high praise for the left-hander, saying, "Whitey was the greatest pitcher that I ever managed, and, I think, one of the greatest pitchers that there's been around. He could make the hitter do almost anything he wanted him to do. He could throw his curveball, changeup, slider—anything he wanted, on any count."

Ford's teammates had the utmost confidence in his abilities. Johnny Blanchard, who occasionally caught Ford when neither Yogi Berra nor Elston Howard did, said, "When you had Whitey bases loaded and nobody out, you were in trouble. That's how tough he was."

Mickey Mantle said of his close friend, "I don't care what the situation was, how high the stakes were—the bases could be loaded and the pennant riding on every pitch, it never bothered Whitey. He pitched his game. Cool . . . crafty . . . nerves of steel."

Mantle added, "If the World Series was on the line and I could pick one pitcher to pitch the game, I'd choose Whitey Ford every time."

CAREER HIGHLIGHTS

Best Season

Ford had several exceptional years, any of which could easily be classified as the finest of his career. He finished 19–6 with a league-leading 2.47 ERA in 1956. Although Ford won only 14 games in 1958, he led the American League with 7 shutouts and a career-best 2.01 ERA. Ford went 24–7 in 1963, with a 2.74 ERA and a league-leading 269 innings pitched. He also performed brilliantly the following year, going 17–6, with a 2.13 ERA and a career-high 8 shutouts, despite being plagued by circulatory problems in his pitching arm.

Nevertheless, the 1961 campaign is generally considered to be Ford's signature season. Although the left-hander's 3.21 ERA ranked among the highest of his career, it must be remembered that earned run averages throughout all of baseball skyrocketed that year, with the prolific offensive numbers posted in both leagues causing the powers that be to increase the size of the strike zone one year later. In addition to leading all AL hurlers with a 25–4 record and 283 innings pitched, Ford struck out a career-high 209 batters en route to earning Cy Young honors and a fifth-place finish in the league MVP voting.

Memorable Moments/Greatest Performances

Ford pitched brilliantly during the first week of September 1955, hurling a one-hitter against Washington on the second of the month and following that up five days later with another one-hitter, this time against Kansas City. In between, he threw 1 1/3 hitless innings against the Senators to earn a save. Still, Ford's crowning achievement came during the 1961 World Series, when he broke Babe Ruth's World Series record of 29 2/3 consecutive scoreless innings, earning in the process series MVP honors. Ford's record skein eventually reached 33 2/3 innings.

NOTABLE ACHIEVEMENTS

- Two-time 20-game winner (1961 and 1963).
- Topped 16 victories eight other times.

- Compiled ERA below 3.00 in 11 of 16 seasons.
- Led AL pitchers in wins and winning percentage three times each; ERA, shutouts, and innings pitched, twice each; and complete games, once.
- All-time Yankee leader in wins (236), shutouts (45), strikeouts (1,956), and innings pitched (3,171).
- Holds World Series records for most wins (10), losses (8), games started (22), innings pitched (146), strikeouts (94), and consecutive scoreless innings pitched (33 2/3).
- Holds lowest career ERA (2.75) of any starting pitcher whose career began after 1920.
- Career winning percentage of .690 is third-best ever and highest of any modern pitcher with at least 200 wins.
- 1961 Cy Young Award winner.
- Four-time *Sporting News* All-Star selection.
- Eight-time AL All-Star.
- Eleven-time AL champion.
- Six-time world champion.

10

Don Mattingly

Had Don Mattingly's performance not been compromised by a bad back the second half of his career, he likely would have landed a few spots higher in these rankings. The six-time AL All-Star posted some truly prolific offensive numbers his first few years in New York, before back problems robbed him of much of his power his last several seasons. Mattingly's injury woes very much reflected the star-crossed nature of his career, which coincided with one of the least successful periods in franchise history. Mattingly arrived in the Bronx for the first time in 1982, just one year after the Yankees appeared in the World Series against the Los Angeles Dodgers, and he remained with them until 1995, one year before they won their next world championship. Although Mattingly's bad timing eventually caused him to be recognized as the greatest Yankee player never to win a championship, it did not prevent him from becoming one of the most beloved athletes in the history of New York sports.

Selected by the Yankees in the 19th round of Major League Baseball's 1979 amateur draft, Donald Arthur Mattingly spent four years working his way up the New York farm system, excelling at every level at which he competed. After posting batting averages of .349, .358, and .316 his first three seasons, the lefty-swinging Mattingly compiled a mark of .315 at Triple-A Columbus in 1982, earning his first call-up to the big-league club in early September. Appearing in only seven games, Mattingly batted just .167 over the season's final month, prompting the team to send him back to the minors for the start of the 1983 campaign.

Mattingly returned to New York two months into the 1983 season, earning a permanent roster spot by impressing team brass with his solid hitting and deft fielding. In addition to doing a solid defensive job wherever the Yankees put him, the 22-year-old first baseman/outfielder batted .283, hit 4 home runs, and drove in 32 runs in just over 300 total plate appearances.

After shifting back and forth between the outfield and first base early in 1984, Mattingly eventually established himself as New York's starting first baseman. Displaying soft hands and exceptional range, Mattingly ended up leading all AL first sackers in fielding percentage for the first of four times while finishing second in assists. In addition, he quickly developed into one of the junior circuit's most formidable batsmen, hitting 23 home runs, knocking in 110 runs, scoring 91 others, and leading the league with 44 doubles, 207 hits, and a .343 batting average. Mattingly's mark of .343 enabled him to barely edge out teammate Dave Winfield for the batting title. The first baseman captured league leadership honors by going 4 for 5 on the season's final day. Mattingly's exceptional all-around performance earned him the first of four straight selections to the *Sporting News* All-Star Team and a fifth-place finish in the league MVP voting.

While Mattingly's quick ascension into stardom may have surprised some members of the Yankee front office, virtually everyone within the organization expected him to hit at the major-league level. The biggest surprise ended up being the youngster's emergence as a power hitter. Primarily a gap-to-gap hitter when he first arrived in New York, Mattingly worked extensively with team batting instructor Lou Piniella and quickly learned to look for the inside pitch that he might drive into Yankee Stadium's short right-field porch. The first baseman's short, compact swing, tremendous bat speed, and intelligence at the plate also made him an outstanding two-strike hitter, enabling him to rarely strike out. He fanned only 33 times in more than 600 official at bats in his first full season.

Mattingly followed up his breakout season with a spectacular 1985 campaign in which he placed among the league leaders with 35 home runs, 107 runs scored, 211 hits, a .324 batting average, and a .567 slugging percentage while topping the circuit with 145 runs batted in, 48 doubles, and 370 total bases. Mattingly earned the first of five consecutive Gold Gloves for his outstanding defensive work at first base, was voted the American League's Most Valuable Player, and was selected as the Major League Player of the Year.

Fast becoming a Yankee icon, Mattingly had an equally brilliant 1986 campaign, after which a media poll named him the best player in the game. In arguably his finest all-around season, the first baseman finished near the top of the league rankings with 31 homers, 113 runs batted in, 117 runs scored, and a career-high .352 batting average. He also led the league with 53 doubles, 238 hits, 388 total bases, and a .573 slugging percentage while amazingly striking out only 35 times in 742 total plate appearances.

Mattingly's 53 doubles and 238 hits both established new Yankee records. He might have captured his second batting title as well had Boston's Wade Boggs not elected to sit out the season's final few games to protect his slim lead over Mattingly in the batting race. "Donnie Baseball's" extraordinary performance earned him a second-place finish to pennant-winning Boston's Roger Clemens in the league MVP balloting.

Widely recognized as one of the sport's truly great hitters, Mattingly drew praise from teammates and opponents alike. Yankee reliever Dave Righetti saw Mattingly when the latter first arrived in New York, and he spent the next several seasons admiring his teammate. Righetti recalled, "[Mattingly] had so much confidence. He could hit with strikes on him. . . . He wasn't worried about it."

Roger Clemens noted, "You could never get in a pattern with Donnie. He'd shoot you to left and pull you to right and, as a pitcher, that's difficult to deal with."

Third baseman Mike Pagliarulo said of his former teammate, "The only way he was gonna' get out was if you threw the ball in the dirt five feet in front of home plate where he couldn't reach it. Otherwise, he was gonna' put the bat on it and get a hit."

New York Mets star pitcher Dwight Gooden faced Mattingly only a few times in exhibition games. The hard-throwing right-hander once commented, "I'm glad I don't have to face that guy every day. He has that look that few hitters have. I don't know if it's his stance, his eyes or what, but you can tell he means business."

Meanwhile, Gene Michael, who observed Mattingly from various vantage points within the Yankee organization, discussed his fielding ability by saying, "Nobody could play defense better than him at first base. He was the best first baseman defensively you'd ever want to see."

Mattingly continued his assault on American League pitching in 1987, hitting 30 homers, knocking in 115 runs, scoring 93 others, and batting .327. The first baseman also accomplished two historic feats, tying a major-league record by hitting home runs in 8 consecutive games and establishing a new major-league mark by hitting 6 grand slams over the course of the season. The 10 home runs that Mattingly hit during his 8-game streak also established a new record, as did his concurrent streak of 10 games with at least 1 extra base hit. Meanwhile, Mattingly's 6 grand slams were ironically the only ones he hit during his career.

Despite his brilliant performance in 1987, Mattingly experienced adversity for the first time in his young career. After missing a total of only two games the previous two seasons, the first baseman spent two weeks on the disabled list in June after injuring his back during a fielding drill. Although Mattingly returned with a vengeance, embarking on his record-tying home run streak shortly thereafter, the disk problem that surfaced in his back served as a portent of things to come.

Despite making his fifth consecutive All-Star appearance and winning his fourth straight Gold Glove, Mattingly had a slightly subpar 1988 season, hitting only 18 home runs, driving in just 88 runs, scoring 94 others, and batting .311. He also committed a career-high 9 errors at first base, while being forced to sit out 17 games due to occasional back stiffness.

Mattingly battled through his back problems in 1989, finishing the year with 23 home runs, 113 runs batted in, and a .303 batting average. However, his chances of fulfilling his dream of advancing to the postseason appeared to be dwindling. Yankee owner George Steinbrenner's constant meddling in the affairs of the team and several ill-advised personnel decisions made by the front office gradually reduced the Yankees to a laughing stock by the end of the decade. After winning at least 85 games and finishing second twice in Mattingly's first five full seasons, New York finished fifth in the AL East in 1989, with a record of only 74–87.

The 1990 campaign turned out to be the low point of Mattingly's career. Having to adjust his batting stance to compensate for the ever-increasing pain in his lower back, the first baseman struggled terribly at the plate the first half of the season, before finally going on the disabled list in July. He returned to the club some two months later, finishing the year with career lows in home runs (5), runs batted in (42), runs scored (40), and batting average (.256). The Yankees also reached their nadir, finishing last in the AL East with a record of only 67–95.

After undergoing extensive physical therapy during the off-season, Mattingly returned to the Yankees in 1991 to appear in a total of 152 games. However, still suffering from constant back pain, he played only 127 games at first base, often serving the team as a designated hitter. Unable to shift his weight and turn his hips as he once did, Mattingly hit only 9 home runs, knocked in just 68 runs, and batted only .288.

Still, the first baseman drew the admiration and respect of all his teammates. Named team captain prior to the start of the season,

Mattingly became more vocal than he had been earlier in his career, taking it on himself to occasionally speak out against team ownership for the manner in which it often mistreated its players. After one particularly unpleasant confrontation with management, Mattingly proclaimed, "The players get no respect around here. [The Yankees] give you money . . . that's it . . . not respect. We get constantly dogged, and players from other teams love to see that. That's why nobody wants to play here."

New York's lack of success on the field and Mattingly's personal struggles with his health increased his level of frustration, often causing him to exchange words through the media with team owner George Steinbrenner. Yet, Steinbrenner chose his words carefully because he knew that Yankee fans adored the captain of their team. As longtime Yankee announcer Michael Kay suggested, "[Mattingly] might be the most revered athlete in New York history. He was the one shining light in a dark tunnel."

Continuing to play through pain, Mattingly posted solid numbers in 1992 and 1993, driving in 86 runs both years while compiling batting averages of .288 and .291, respectively. However, he found himself unable to generate the same kind of power he displayed his first few years in the league, hitting a total of only 31 home runs over the course of those two seasons. Still, the first baseman continued to excel in the field, committing a total of just 7 errors en route to winning his seventh and eighth Gold Gloves.

Although he hit just 6 home runs and knocked in only 51 runs during the strike-shortened 1994 campaign, Mattingly batted .304, reaching the .300 mark for the first time in five years. The Yankee captain found the premature ending to the season particularly frustrating since New York stood in first place in the American League East when play ended in late July.

Mattingly led the Yankees on one final playoff push the following year, with the team successfully earning a postseason berth on the season's final day. The first baseman had one of his least productive offensive seasons, hitting only 7 homers, driving in just 49 runs, and batting .288. But he displayed increased power at the plate over the season's final two months after employing for the first time a high leg kick just as he began striding into the pitcher's offering.

Mattingly took his newfound power stroke into the playoffs, where the Yankees faced the Seattle Mariners. Although New York ended up losing the first round matchup 3–2 after initially taking a 2–0 series lead, Mattingly proved to himself he had the ability to succeed when the games mattered most. Despite striking out a career-high four times against Randy Johnson in game 3, Mattingly finished the series with 10 hits, 1 home run, 6 runs batted in, and a .417 batting average.

Knowing that Mattingly's career was drawing to a close, the Yankees acquired first baseman Tino Martinez from Seattle during the off-season. Mattingly officially announced his retirement one month later, stating that his back problems made it too difficult for him to attempt a comeback. He ended his career with 222 home runs, 1,099 runs batted in, 1,007 runs scored, 2,153 hits, and a .307 batting average. Mattingly ranks in the top 10 in 6 offensive categories on the Yankees' all-time list. He earned 6 selections to the AL All-Star Team and 9 Gold Gloves. His .996 lifetime fielding percentage at first base tied him for the all-time lead at the time of his retirement.

The Yankees defeated the Atlanta Braves in the World Series less than 10 months after Mattingly announced his retirement, leaving the team's former captain to ponder what might have been. Nevertheless, the Yankees relieved some of the angst he must have felt when they retired his number 23 and dedicated his plaque for Monument Park at Yankee Stadium on August 31, 1997. The plaque calls Mattingly "a humble man of grace and dignity, a captain who led by example, proud of the pinstripe tradition and dedicated to the pursuit of excellence, a Yankee forever."

Although Mattingly has since left the Yankee family to manage the Los Angeles Dodgers, he remains a Yankee icon. General manager Brian Cashman, who started out in the organization during the latter stages of Mattingly's career, stated, "Purity. Donnie Baseball is all about the way it's supposed to be."

In discussing his former team captain, the late Yankee owner George Steinbrenner once declared, "He was special. That's the best word you can use for Mattingly because of all the phases of what he meant to me and the Yankees. He was just special."

Mattingly revealed the qualities that made him so popular with Yankee fans when he said, "I never felt I was as talented as some other players. I played from the heart."

CAREER HIGHLIGHTS

Best Season

Mattingly compiled extraordinary numbers in 1985 and 1986, and either of those years would make a solid choice. Donnie Baseball established career highs in home runs (35) and RBIs (145) in his MVP campaign of 1985, and he topped the junior circuit in three offensive categories. However, Mattingly posted better overall numbers the following year, when he led the league in four departments: hits (238), doubles (53), slugging percentage (.573), and total bases (388). His 238 hits and 53 doubles established Yankee single-season records; he also hit 31 homers, drove in 113 runs, and reached career highs in batting average (.352) and runs scored (117). It is a tough decision, but I will go with Mattingly's 1986 campaign, especially since Rickey Henderson played a huge role in enabling Donnie Baseball to drive in a league-leading 145 runs the previous year.

Memorable Moments/Greatest Performances

Mattingly accomplished two historic feats in 1987, tying Dale Long's previous major-league record by homering in eight consecutive games (later matched by Ken Griffey Jr.) and establishing a new major-league mark by hitting 6 grand slams over the course of the season (since tied by Travis Hafner). However, Mattingly's most memorable moment arguably occurred during the Yankees' 15-inning 7–5 victory over the Seattle Mariners in game 2 of the 1995 ALDS. After waiting his entire career to make his first postseason appearance, Donnie Baseball brought the Yankee Stadium crowd to its collective feet by following a Ruben Sierra solo homer with a blast of his own, giving the Yankees a 3–2 lead after six innings.

NOTABLE ACHIEVEMENTS

- Hit more than 30 home runs three times.
- Knocked in more than 100 runs five times.
- Scored more than 100 runs twice.
- Collected more than 200 hits three times.
- Batted over .300 seven times, topping the .340 mark on two occasions.
- Led AL in doubles three times; hits and total bases, twice each; and batting average, RBIs, and slugging percentage, once each.
- AL MVP in 1985.
- 1985 Major League Player of the Year.
- Holds Yankee single-season records for most doubles (53) and hits (238).

- Holds major-league records for most home runs (10) over an eight-game stretch and most consecutive games (10) with an extra base hit.
- Shares major-league records for most consecutive games with a home run (8) and most grand slams in a season (6).
- Four-time *Sporting News* All-Star selection.
- Six-time AL All-Star.
- Nine-time Gold Glove winner.

Bernie Williams

The most recent in a long line of outstanding Yankee center fielders (I will not add Curtis Granderson's name to that list just yet), Bernie Williams manned the same position previously patrolled by Hall of Famers Earle Combs, Joe DiMaggio, and Mickey Mantle for parts of 16 seasons. During that time, Williams carried himself with class, dignity, and elegance, making him one of the most admired and respected players on a Yankees team that captured 10 division titles, 6 American League pennants, and 4 world championships.

Bernie Williams first signed with the Yankees as a 17-year-old amateur free agent in 1985. After spending more than five years in New York's farm system, the native of San Juan, Puerto Rico, finally joined the big club in 1991, batting only .238, with just 3 home runs and 34 RBIs in 85 games. The young outfielder raised his batting average to .280 the following season, but he failed to impress the Yankee front office with his offensive production, hitting only 5 home runs and driving in just 26 runs in almost 300 official plate appearances. American League pitching was not the only obstacle that Williams faced early in his career. He also had to endure an almost endless stream of sarcasm directed his way by some of his teammates, most notably Mel Hall. The boisterous Hall observed the quiet and shy manner with which Williams carried himself, and the veteran outfielder took to derisively referring to his young teammate as "Bambi." Some members of the Yankee hierarchy also believed that Williams had neither the temperament nor the personality to succeed in New York, and they seriously considered including him in a trade for a more established player. Fortunately, such a deal was never consummated, and the switch-hitting outfielder remained with the Yankees.

Williams became the team's starting center fielder in 1993, and he subsequently posted solid numbers in each of the next two seasons, combining for a total of 24 home runs, 125 runs batted in, and 147 runs scored while compiling batting averages of .268 and .289. Nevertheless, the Yankees remained somewhat disappointed in the overall performance of the player they once considered to be the top prospect in their organization. Williams had yet to display the kind of power and run production that they expected from him. Furthermore, he often demonstrated a lack of baseball instincts, particularly on the base paths. Williams had exceptional speed, but he was not a particularly good base runner early in his career, and he combined to steal a total of only 25 bases his first two full seasons.

The 26-year-old Williams finally began to fulfill his great promise in 1995, when he hit 18 home runs, drove in 82 runs, scored 93 others, and batted .307. He became a star the following season, hitting 29 home runs, driving in 102 runs, scoring 108 others, and batting .305 while helping the Yankees to the AL East title. He then batted .467, with 3 home runs and 5 runs batted in against Texas in the ALDS, before capturing ALCS MVP honors by hitting .474, with 2 homers and 6 RBIs during New York's five-game victory over the Baltimore Orioles. The Yankees subsequently won their first world championship since 1978 when they defeated Atlanta in the World Series.

Although the Yankees failed to repeat as American League champions in 1997, Williams had another outstanding year, hitting 21 homers, knocking in 100 runs, scoring 107 others, and batting .328. Williams earned the first of five straight selections to the AL All-Star Team for his efforts; he also won the first of four consecutive Gold Gloves.

The Yankees won the World Series each of the next three seasons, with Williams having arguably his three best years. He hit 26 homers, drove in 97 runs, scored 101 others, and led the AL with a .339 batting average in 1998, helping the Yankees compile 114 victories over the course of the regular season. Williams followed that up by batting a career-high .342 in 1999 while hitting 25 home runs, knocking in 115 runs, scoring 116 others, and collecting 202 hits. He had another outstanding year in 2000, batting .307, scoring 108 runs, and establishing career highs with 30 homers and 121 runs batted in.

One of the American League's most versatile performers throughout the period, Williams usually batted fourth in the Yankee lineup, even though he could hardly be described as a prototypical cleanup hitter. Although he gave the Yankees good power and run production from the number 4 spot in the batting order, he was not a typical "slugger" in that he also hit for a high batting average, drove the ball well to all fields, possessed outstanding speed, and struck out less frequently than most other fourth-place hitters.

The Yankees failed to repeat as world champions in 2001 and 2002. Nevertheless, they captured the AL East title both years, and Williams continued to post outstanding offensive numbers for them. After hitting 26 homers, driving in 94 runs, scoring 102 others, and batting .307 in 2001, Bernie knocked in 102 runs, crossed the plate 102 times, and finished third in the league with a .333 batting average the following year. By the end of that 2002 campaign, Williams had batted over .300 eight straight times, scored more than 100 runs seven straight times, surpassed 20 home runs in six of seven years, and driven in more than 100 runs in five of seven seasons.

Former Yankees manager Joe Torre expressed his admiration for Williams when he said, "He's got a calm about him that I trust, and he's electric at times. . . . I expect big things from him because he doesn't panic. For me, he's in the upper echelon among switch-hitters all-time."

Father Time began to catch up with Williams after the 2002 season, though. He surpassed 20 home runs and 100 runs scored just one time each over the next four years while failing to drive in more than 70 runs or bat any higher than .281 during that same period. New York failed to offer Williams a new contract at the conclusion of the 2006 campaign, forcing the unhappy veteran into an involuntary retirement. He ended his career with 287 home runs, 1,257 runs batted in, 1,366 runs scored, 2,336 hits, 449 doubles, and a .297 batting average. Williams ranks among the all-time Yankee leaders in home runs (seventh), runs batted in (seventh), runs scored (sixth), doubles (third), hits (fifth), and total bases (sixth). Bernie also compiled a .275 career batting average, hit 22 home runs, and knocked in a record 80 runs in postseason play.

CAREER HIGHLIGHTS

Best Season

Although a strong argument could be waged on behalf of either Bernie's 1998 or 2000 campaign, the feeling here is that he had his finest all-around season in 1999. In addition to hitting 25 home runs, knocking in 115 runs, collecting 202 hits, and compiling a .536 slugging percentage, Williams established career highs with 116 runs scored, 100 bases on balls, 317 total bases, a .342 batting average, and a .435 on-base percentage.

Memorable Moments/Greatest Performances

Williams saved his most memorable performance for the 1996 postseason. First, he helped the Yankees eliminate Texas in four games in the ALDS by batting .467, hitting 3 home runs, and knocking in 5 runs. Williams subsequently earned ALCS MVP honors by batting .474, hitting 2 homers, driving in 6 runs, and scoring 6 others during New York's five-game victory over Baltimore. Bernie put an end to game 1 of the ALCS by delivering an 11th-inning walk-off homer against Oriole left-hander Randy Myers.

NOTABLE ACHIEVEMENTS

- Knocked in more than 100 runs five times.
- Scored more than 100 runs eight times.
- Collected more than 200 hits twice.
- Batted over .300 eight straight times.
- 1998 AL batting champion (.339).
- 1996 ALCS MVP.
- Major league record holder for most runs batted in during postseason (80).
- Two-time *Sporting News* All-Star selection.
- Five-time AL All-Star.
- Four-time Gold Glove winner.
- Six-time AL champion.
- Four-time world champion.

12

Alex Rodriguez

One of the most controversial players ever to don the pinstripes, Alex Rodriguez has been a polarizing figure ever since he first joined the Yankees in 2004. While many Yankee fans admire "A-Rod" for his tremendous physical gifts and appreciate the exceptional offensive numbers he has posted for the team over the course of the past eight seasons, many others resent what they perceive to be his superficial and narcissistic nature, and they derive a considerable amount of pleasure from criticizing him for his frequent postseason failures. Nevertheless, the simple facts are that Rodriguez has been one of the most productive offensive players in team history, having won two AL MVP Awards while wearing a Yankee uniform, and he served as the driving force behind New York's successful run to the world championship in 2009.

Alex Rodriguez had already gained widespread recognition as arguably the best all-around player in baseball before he joined the Yankees prior to the start of the 2004 campaign. Originally selected by the Seattle Mariners with the first overall pick of the 1993 amateur draft, Rodriguez wasted little time in establishing himself as a true superstar. After making brief appearances with the Mariners in 1994 and 1995, the 21-year-old shortstop burst onto the scene in 1996, earning a second-place finish in the AL MVP voting by hitting 36 home runs, driving in 123 runs, collecting 215 hits, and topping the junior circuit with 141 runs scored, 54 doubles, 379 total bases, and a .358 batting average. He continued to post exceptional offensive numbers for the Mariners over the course of the next four seasons, annually placing among the league leaders in home runs, RBIs, and runs scored.

After becoming a free agent at the conclusion of the 2000 campaign, Rodriguez signed a huge free-agent contract with the Texas Rangers that made him the highest-paid player in baseball history. A-Rod spent the next three years in Texas, compiling prodigious offensive numbers each season and earning AL MVP honors in 2003 even though the Rangers finished last in the AL West. Despite Rodriguez's tremendous offensive production, the Rangers' last-place finish convinced team management to rid itself of the shortstop's exorbitant contract at the end of the year. That A-Rod subsequently became a member of the Yankees is simply a matter of happenstance.

Seeking to trade their high-priced superstar, the Rangers initially agreed to a deal with the Boston Red Sox. However, the Major League Baseball Players Association vetoed the trade because it called for a voluntary reduction in A-Rod's salary. Taking note of the Rangers' aborted attempt to deal Rodriguez to their archrivals, the Yankees swooped in, offering Texas a package that included star second baseman Alfonso Soriano. The Rangers also agreed to pay $67 million of the $179 million that remained on Rodriguez's contract. Meanwhile, A-Rod paved the way for the deal by agreeing to switch positions from shortstop to third base, in deference to Yankee captain Derek Jeter.

Although Rodriguez posted solid numbers his first year in New York, they failed to approach the figures that he typically compiled for the Rangers. The new Yankee third baseman hit 36 home runs, knocked in 106 runs, scored 112 others, and batted .286 in 2004, earning in the process a spot on the AL All-Star Team and a 14th-place finish in the league MVP voting. However, annoyed by A-Rod's diva reputation that preceded him to New York and angered by a magazine article that came out a few years earlier in which A-Rod seemed to question the overall contributions that the popular Derek Jeter made to the Yankees' success, the majority of Yankee fans searched for flaws in Rodriguez's game. Instead of praising the slugger for the outstanding offensive production that he contributed to the team over the course of the regular campaign, they preferred to focus more on his 131 strikeouts and subsequent failures during the postseason. Rodriguez's inability to hit in the clutch during the Yankees' collapse against Boston in the final four games of the ALCS provided additional fodder to the A-Rod haters, who seemed to dismiss the fact that the rest of the team performed horribly as well in those final four contests.

Rodriguez attempted to win over the fans by significantly improving his numbers in 2005. He batted .321, knocked in 130 runs, and led the league with 48 home runs, 124 runs scored, and a .610 slugging percentage en route to earning AL MVP honors. But when he batted just .133 and failed to drive in a single run against the Angels during the Yankees' five-game ALDS loss, he once again became the object of scorn to the majority of Yankee fans.

The 2006 and 2007 campaigns followed a similar script, with Rodriguez compiling outstanding offensive numbers during the regular season, only to fail during a first-round playoff defeat. A-Rod's performance in 2007 was particularly impressive, as he captured league MVP honors for the second time in three years by batting .314 and topping the circuit with 54 homers, 156 runs batted in, 143 runs scored, 376 total bases, and a .645 slugging percentage. Yet, he again drew the ire of Yankee fans when he batted .267 and drove in just 1 run during New York's first-round playoff defeat at the hands of the Cleveland Indians.

The Yankees failed to advance to the postseason for the first time in 14 years in 2008, and Rodriguez missed a significant amount of playing time due to injury. Yet, he still managed to hit 35 home runs, knock in 103 runs, score 104 others, bat .302, and lead the league with a .573 slugging percentage.

Rodriguez's already tarnished reputation received further damage in February 2009 when his name appeared on a list of 104 players that tested positive for performance-enhancing drugs in a 2003 survey testing conducted by Major League Baseball. A-Rod subsequently attempted to explain his actions by claiming that they were prompted by his desire to prove he was worthy of the exorbitant contract he signed with the Texas Rangers prior to the start of the 2001 season. Admitting during a television interview conducted two days after his name was leaked to the press that he used performance-enhancing drugs from 2001 to 2003, Rodriguez proclaimed, "When I arrived in Texas in 2001, I felt an enormous amount of pressure. I felt like I had all the weight of the world on top of me and I needed to perform, and perform at a high level every day."

Rodriguez accepted full culpability for his actions, claiming he was "young, stupid, and naïve" at the time and stating that he did not use performance-enhancing drugs prior to 2001 and that he had not used them since 2003.

Rodriguez's admission of guilt seemed to lift a huge weight from his shoulders. Although an injured hip forced him to sit out the first month of the season, limiting his total offensive production to some extent, A-Rod ended up surpassing 30 homers and 100 RBIs for the 13th of a major-league record 14 consecutive times. He subsequently helped lead the Yankees to their first world championship in nine years by having the finest postseason of his career. Exorcising any old demons by coming up with one clutch hit after another, Rodriguez batted .455 with 2 home runs and 6 RBIs during New York's three-game sweep of Minnesota in the ALDS. He continued his superlative play against the Angels in the ALCS, batting .429 with 3 more homers and 6 RBIs. Rodriguez capped off his outstanding postseason by hitting 1 home run and driving in 6 runs during New York's six-game World Series victory over the Phillies.

Injuries have slowed Rodriguez in each of the past two seasons, particularly in 2011, when he appeared in only 99 games and failed to reach 30 homers and 100 RBIs for the first time since 1997. Nevertheless, A-Rod still has an excellent chance of reaching several milestones before his playing days are over. With 629 career home runs as of this writing, the 36-year-old Rodriguez appears to be within striking distance of the all-time home run record. His 1,893 runs batted in put him on pace to mount a serious challenge to Hank Aaron's existing RBI mark of 2,297, and his 1,824 runs scored should enable him to pose a threat to Rickey Henderson's current record of 2,295 runs scored. Furthermore, Rodriguez's 2,775 hits have him on pace to eventually join the exclusive 3,000-hit club before he retires. A-Rod's Yankee numbers include 284 home runs, 903 runs batted in, 815 runs scored, 1,240 hits, a .295 batting average, a .391 on-base percentage, and a .550 slugging percentage. In addition to the two MVP trophies that Rodriguez won since coming to New York, he has finished in the top 10 in the balloting two other times. Although Rodriguez clearly is approaching the latter stages of his career, he still has an opportunity to claim an even higher spot in these rankings.

YANKEE CAREER HIGHLIGHTS

Best Season

Rodriguez performed exceptionally well during his MVP campaign of 2005, driving in 130 runs, batting .321, and leading the American League with 48 homers, 124 runs scored, and a .610 slugging percentage. But he surpassed virtually all those marks in 2007, when he compiled a season of historic proportions en route to earning AL MVP honors once again. In easily his finest all-around season since coming to New York, Rodriguez batted .314, posted a .422 on-base percentage, stole 24 bases in 28 attempts, and led the league with 54 home runs, 156 runs batted in, 143 runs scored, 376 total bases, and a .645 slugging percentage.

Memorable Moments/Greatest Performances

Rodriguez had his greatest single day as a Yankee on April 26, 2005, when he hit 3 home runs off Angels pitcher Bartolo Colon and drove in 10 runs. The 10 RBIs were the most by a Yankee since Tony Lazzeri established the American League record by knocking in 11 runs on May 24, 1936.

Rodriguez had another 3-homer day against the Royals on August 14, 2010, reaching Kansas City pitching for 3 home runs and 5 runs batted in.

Rodriguez has also reached several milestones since joining the Yankees in 2004. On August 4, 2007, he hit his 500th career home run against pitcher Kyle Davies of the Kansas City Royals at Yankee Stadium, making him the youngest player ever to reach the 500-home run plateau (32 years, 8 days).

Exactly three years later, on August 4, 2010, Rodriguez became the youngest player in major-league history (and just the seventh player ever) to hit 600 home runs, connecting for number 600 against Shaun Marcum of the Toronto Blue Jays. A little over one month later, on September 6, Rodriguez recorded his 100th RBI, making him the first player ever to drive in as many as 100 runs 14 times.

On October 4, 2009, during the final game of the season, Rodriguez hit 2 home runs in the sixth inning that drove in 7 runs, enabling him to set a new American League record for most RBIs by a batter in a single inning.

However, Rodriguez's most memorable performance, at least as far as Yankee fans are concerned, took place during the 2009 postseason. A-Rod began his extraordinary run by leading the Yankees to victory over the Minnesota Twins in the first game of the ALDS by collecting 2 RBI singles. He followed that up with another RBI single in the sixth inning of game 2, before hitting a game-tying home run off closer Joe Nathan in the bottom of the ninth inning. Game 3 saw him hit another game-tying home run.

Rodriguez continued his heroics in the ALCS, hitting his third game-tying homer of the postseason against Angels closer Brian Fuentes in the bottom of the 11th inning of game 2. He concluded the series with a .429 batting average, 3 home runs, and 6 runs batted in. A-Rod also performed extremely well in the clutch against Philadelphia in the World Series. Facing Phillies closer Brad Lidge, he drove in the go-ahead run with two outs in the ninth inning of game 4. The Yankees went on to win the contest by a score of 7–4 to take a commanding 3–1 lead in the series. Although the Phillies rebounded in game 5, defeating the Yankees 8–6, A-Rod went 2 for 4, with 3 runs batted in. In the series finale back at Yankee Stadium, Rodriguez collected 1 hit in 2 official at bats, walked twice, and scored 2 runs, as the Yankees took game 6 by a final score of 7–3. A-Rod concluded the Fall Classic with a homer, 6 runs batted in, and 5 runs scored.

NOTABLE ACHIEVEMENTS

- Surpassed 30 home runs seven times, topping 40 homers twice and 50 homers once.
- Drove in at least 100 runs seven times, topping 120 RBIs on four occasions.
- Scored more than 100 runs five times.
- Batted over .300 three times.
- Compiled on-base percentage in excess of .400 three times.
- Posted slugging percentage in excess of .600 twice.
- Led AL in home runs and runs scored twice each; RBIs and total bases, once each; and slugging percentage three times.
- Member of 600-home run club.
- Holds major-league records for most home runs in a season by a third baseman (52 in 2007) and most stolen bases by a player in a 50-home run season (24 in 2007).
- AL MVP in 2005 and 2007.
- 2007 *Sporting News* Player of the Year.
- Three-time *Sporting News* All-Star selection.
- Seven-time AL All-Star.
- Won three Silver Sluggers.
- 2009 AL champion.
- 2009 world champion.

⓲ Red Ruffing

Teammates on the Yankees for 13 seasons, Red Ruffing and Lefty Gomez both merited serious consideration for the number 13 spot in these rankings. Gomez had two years in which he reached a level of dominance that Ruffing failed to attain at any point during his career, capturing the pitcher's version of the Triple Crown in 1934 and 1937. Gomez also compiled an almost-identical winning percentage (.652) to the mark that Ruffing posted (.651) during the latter's 15 years in pinstripes. However, the thing that ultimately tipped the scales ever so slightly in Ruffing's favor was his total body of work. While Gomez won 189 games in his 13 years in New York, Ruffing's 231 victories represent the highest total compiled by any Yankee pitcher except Whitey Ford. New York's all-time leader with 261 complete games, Ruffing also ranks either second or third on the team's all-time list in shutouts (40), games started (391), and innings pitched (3,169).

A prime example of how pitching for a contending team can make a good pitcher better, Charles Herbert "Red" Ruffing experienced a renaissance of sorts after the Yankees acquired him from Boston early in 1930 for backup outfielder Cedric Durst and $50,000. After compiling an overall record of just 39–96 and an ERA of 4.61 over parts of seven seasons with the lowly Red Sox, the 25-year-old right-hander posted a mark of 15–5 over the final five months of the 1930 campaign in New York. Although Ruffing compiled a rather mediocre 4.41 ERA the following year, the powerful bats of Babe Ruth, Lou Gehrig, and the other members of New York's potent lineup enabled him to establish a new career high with 16 victories. Ruffing developed into arguably the ace of the Yankee staff the following season, when he finished 18–7, with a 3.09 ERA and a league-leading 190 strikeouts.

Following a subpar 1933 campaign in which he won only nine games, Ruffing began a nine-year stretch during which he never posted fewer than 14 victories. The right-hander compiled a combined record during that time of 161–80. Ruffing had his four best years from 1936 to 1939, helping the Yankees win four consecutive world championships by winning at least 20 games each season. He earned a spot on the *Sporting News* All-Star Team in 1937, 1938, and 1939, posting a combined mark of 62–21 those three years. After placing among the league leaders with 20 wins and a 2.98 ERA in 1937, Ruffing topped the circuit with 21 victories the following year while finishing second in the league with a 3.31 ERA.

Ruffing continued to excel until he entered the military at the conclusion of the 1942 campaign to assist in the war effort. He missed all of the next two seasons and part of 1945 as well, before returning to the Yankees at 40 years of age to post a record of 7–3 and an ERA of 2.89 in his 11 starts. Ruffing spent one more year in New York before ending his career with the Chicago White Sox in 1947. He concluded his 15 years in pinstripes with an overall record of 231–124, a 3.47 ERA, 40 shutouts, 1,526 strikeouts, and an all-time Yankee-record 261 complete games. In addition to surpassing 20 victories on four occasions, Ruffing won at least 15 games seven other times. An exceptional big-game pitcher, Ruffing posted a 7–2 record and a 2.63 ERA in seven World Series with the Yankees, helping them capture six world championships. Commenting on the success that he experienced in the postseason throughout his career, Ruffing suggested, "I always figured World Series games the easiest to pitch. The other team didn't know you . . . and, on the Yankees, we used to figure the National League champion only good enough to finish third or fourth in the American League."

Ruffing accomplished all he did despite losing four toes on his left foot in a mining accident as a teenager. The injury, which caused Ruffing constant pain the remainder of his life, reduced his running speed considerably. It also prompted him to switch positions before his professional playing career got underway. Originally an outfielder, Ruffing ended up becoming one of the best-hitting pitchers in baseball history, compiling a lifetime batting average of .269 and hitting 36 home runs, the third-highest total of any pitcher ever to play the game. He batted over .300 eight times, posting an average of .364 in 1930 that continues to stand as the second-highest single-season mark for a pitcher (Walter Johnson hit .433 for Washington in 1925).

It subsequently took Ruffing a considerable amount of time to gain entrance into Cooperstown, but the members of the Baseball Writers' Association of America finally admitted him in 1967, in his last year of eligibility.

CAREER HIGHLIGHTS

Best Season

Ruffing's 1932 campaign, in which he won 18 games, compiled a 3.09 ERA, tossed 259 innings and 22 complete games, and led all AL pitchers with 190 strikeouts, certainly ranks among his finest. So do each of his 20-win seasons, from 1936 to 1939. The one I ultimately settled on was Ruffing's 1939 campaign. Although he struck out only 95 batters, the right-hander posted a record of 21–7, topped the circuit with 5 shutouts, and finished among the league leaders with a 2.93 ERA, 22 complete games, and 233 innings pitched. Ruffing also batted .307 that year, with a homer and 20 RBIs. He punctuated his outstanding season by allowing just 1 run on 4 hits to the Reds in a complete-game victory during New York's four-game sweep of Cincinnati in the World Series.

Memorable Moments/Greatest Performances

Certainly, Ruffing's outstanding postseason pitching over the course of his career could be considered among his most outstanding achievements. Nevertheless, his greatest individual performance occurred on August 13, 1932, when he threw a complete-game shutout and hit a 10th-inning home run off Washington Senators pitcher Al Thomas to give the Yankees a 1–0 victory. Ruffing remains one of only three pitchers in major-league history to win a game 1–0, hit a home run during the contest, and strike out 10 or more batters.

NOTABLE ACHIEVEMENTS

- Four-time 20-game winner.
- Topped 15 victories seven other times.
- Compiled ERA below 3.00 on four occasions.
- Led AL pitchers in wins, shutouts, and strikeouts once each.
- All-time Yankee leader in complete games (261).
- Second all-time on Yankees in innings pitched (3,169) and shutouts (40).
- Three-time *Sporting News* All-Star selection.
- Six-time AL All-Star.
- Seven-time AL champion.
- Six-time world champion.

14

Lefty Gomez

Known as much for his colorful personality as for his ability to baffle opposing hitters, Vernon "Lefty" Gomez helped anchor the Yankees' starting rotation for nearly a decade. Gomez surpassed 20 victories on four occasions, capturing the pitcher's version of the Triple Crown twice by leading all AL hurlers in wins, ERA, and strikeouts in 1934 and 1937. The lanky left-hander's stellar pitching contributed to 7 Yankee pennants and 6 world championships during his 13 years in pinstripes. An exceptional big-game pitcher throughout his career, Gomez compiled a perfect 6–0 record in the five World Series in which he appeared.

Born in Rodeo, California, Gomez spent his early years in professional baseball pitching for his hometown San Francisco Seals in the Pacific Coast League. After watching the slender 6'2", 175-pound Gomez consistently throw his blazing fastball past Pacific Coast League hitters, the Yankees purchased him from the Seals in 1929 for $35,000. Gomez made his major-league debut with the Yankees the following year, going an unimpressive 2–5 in limited duty. However, the 22-year-old left-hander took the American League by storm in 1931, finishing among the league leaders with 21 wins, a 2.67 ERA, and 150 strikeouts.

Featuring a whiplash delivery and a high leg kick, Gomez continued to thwart AL batters in 1932, compiling a record of 24–7, despite posting a relatively high ERA of 4.21. After winning 16 games the following year, Gomez had arguably his finest season in 1934, leading all AL hurlers with a record of 26–5, a 2.33 ERA, 158 strikeouts, 6 shutouts, 25 complete games, and 282 innings pitched. Gomez's extraordinary performance enabled him to earn a third-place finish in the league MVP voting and a spot on the AL All-Star Team for the second of seven consecutive times. In that year's Midsummer's Classic, the left-hander set a record that still stands, working six full innings in leading the American League to its second straight victory.

As Gomez established himself as one of the sport's premier pitchers, he gradually developed a reputation for being one of its most unique characters. Affectionately nicknamed "Goofy" for his eccentric ways and outrageous sense of humor, Gomez delighted in playing practical jokes on everyone from teammates to umpires. He once stopped a World Series game to watch an airplane fly overhead. On another occasion, he stepped up to the plate to face Bob Feller on a foggy day with a match in his hand. Gomez lit the match before he stepped into the batter's box, prompting the home plate umpire to growl at him, "What's the big idea? Do you think that match will help you see Feller's fast one?" Gomez responded, "No, I'm not concerned about that. I just want to make sure he can see me!"

Another anecdote involving Gomez had him repeatedly shaking off catcher Bill Dickey as the Hall of Fame receiver flashed his signs to the hurler from behind home plate with Jimmie Foxx prepared to face him in a crucial late-game situation at Yankee Stadium. With Foxx having hit a pair of tape measure home runs against the Yankee left-hander earlier in his career, Dickey likely assumed that Gomez felt a need to be extremely careful in his pitch selection to the slugging first baseman. Therefore, Dickey finally approached Gomez on the mound in an attempt to find out what pitch he wished to throw Foxx. Gomez responded by saying, "Nothing. I figure if I wait awhile, maybe he'll get a phone call."

Gomez's bizarre nature notwithstanding, he remained one of the American League's finest pitchers for much of the 1930s. After experiencing slightly subpar seasons in 1935 and 1936, he had another sensational year in 1937, winning the pitcher's Triple Crown for the second time. Gomez posted a record of 21–11 to lead all AL hurlers in victories. He also finished first in ERA (2.33), strikeouts (194), and shutouts (6). Gomez had one more big year left in him, posting 18 victories in 1938, before arm problems began to plague him during the latter stages of the 1939 campaign. He won just 12 games that year, then sat out most of 1940, finishing the season just 3–3. Having developed a beautiful, slow curve during the subsequent off-season, Gomez evolved into more of a finesse pitcher when he returned to the Yankees in 1941. Although Gomez struck out only 76 batters, he concluded the campaign with a record of 15–5. Commenting on his newfound pitching style, Gomez quipped, "I'm throwing as hard as I ever did . . . the ball's just not getting there as fast."

Gomez spent one more year in New York, winning just six games in 1942, before ending his playing career with the Washington Senators the following season. He compiled a lifetime record of 189–101 with the Yankees, along with a solid 3.34 ERA. Gomez's 189 victories place him fourth on the team's all-time win list. He also ranks second in complete games (173), fourth in shutouts (28), and fifth in strikeouts (1,468) and innings pitched (2,498). Gomez's .649 career winning percentage places him 15th on Major League Baseball's all-time list among pitchers with at least 200 decisions, and his 6–0 World Series record gives him the most wins without a loss in the history of the Fall Classic. Gomez also holds the record for most victories in All-Star Game competition (3).

It subsequently took Gomez almost 30 years to gain induction into the Baseball Hall of Fame after his playing career ended. The members of the Veterans Committee finally elected him in 1972.

CAREER HIGHLIGHTS

Best Season

Gomez had outstanding seasons in 1931, 1932, and 1937, surpassing 20 victories each time and capturing the pitcher's version of the Triple Crown in the last of those years. However, he was at his very best in 1934, when he led all AL hurlers in seven pitching categories, including wins (26), ERA (2.33), strikeouts (158), complete games (25), and innings pitched (282).

Memorable Moments/Greatest Performances

Gomez's perfect 6–0 record in World Series competition has to be considered one of his crowning achievements. He also compiled an outstanding 2.86 ERA in his seven World Series starts. However, considering Gomez's reputation for being an exceptionally poor hitter, Major League Baseball's first All-Star Game and game 5 of the 1937 World Series would have to be included among the left-hander's most memorable moments. Gomez served as the winning pitcher and drove in the American League's first run in the inaugural Midsummer's Classic, played in Chicago's Comiskey Park on July 6, 1933. He also starred in the 1937 Fall Classic, tossing two complete-game victories and allowing just three earned runs against the New York Giants, as well as singling home the winning run for the Yankees in their game 5 clincher.

NOTABLE ACHIEVEMENTS

- Four-time 20-game winner.
- Compiled ERA below 3.00 on three occasions.
- Completed at least 20 games four times.
- Won pitcher's Triple Crown twice (1934 and 1937).
- Led AL pitchers in wins, winning percentage, and ERA twice each; shutouts and strikeouts, three times each; and complete games and innings pitched, once each.
- Holds record for most World Series wins without a loss (6).
- Holds record for most wins by a pitcher in All-Star Game competition (3).
- Named to *Sporting News* All-Star Team once (1934).
- Seven-time AL All-Star.
- Seven-time AL champion.
- Six-time world champion.

15

Earle Combs

Earle Combs found himself playing in the shadow of Babe Ruth and Lou Gehrig his entire time in New York. He later had the misfortune of being relegated to second-tier status in the pantheon of great Yankee center fielders by Joe DiMaggio and Mickey Mantle. Yet, Combs was a terrific player in his own right, serving as the center fielder and lead-off hitter for the fabled 1927 New York Yankees "Murderer's Row" squad, which many baseball historians still consider to be the greatest team ever assembled. Combs compiled exceptional numbers for the Yankees out of the leadoff spot that year while doing an outstanding job of patrolling Yankee Stadium's vast expanse in center. A true gentleman as well, Combs was among the most popular players on the Yankee teams for which he played. Yankee manager Joe McCarthy once stated, "They wouldn't pay baseball managers much of a salary if they all presented as few problems as did Earle Combs." Meanwhile, sportswriter and baseball historian Fred Lieb once wrote, "If a vote were taken of the sportswriters as to who their favorite ballplayer on the Yankees would be, Combs would have been their choice."

Nicknamed "the Kentucky Colonel" for his Kentucky roots, Combs was initially discovered by the Louisville Colonels of the American Association in 1922 while playing semiprofessional ball for the Lexington Reos of the Bluegrass League. After signing on to play with the Colonels, Combs spent the next two years in Louisville, posting batting averages of .344 and .380 while developing a reputation for speedy ball hawking in the outfield and running the bases with reckless abandon.

The Yankees acquired the rights to the 24-year-old Combs prior to the start of the 1924 campaign, winning a spirited bidding war by offering the Colonels $50,000 for his services. Combs rewarded the Yankees by playing well for them before fracturing his ankle sliding into home plate at Cleveland's League Park two months into the campaign. Although the outfielder saw no more action the rest of the year, he returned to the Yankees in 1925 to compile exceptional numbers in his first full season. Assigned the job of playing center field and manning the leadoff spot in the Yankee batting order by manager Miller Huggins, Combs batted .342 and placed among the league leaders with 117 runs scored, 203 hits, and 13 triples.

After a solid sophomore campaign that saw him finish fourth in the American League with 113 runs scored, Combs had arguably his finest all-around year in 1927, serving as the offensive catalyst for New York's Murderer's Row team, which dominated the junior circuit with a record of 110–44. In addition to placing among the AL leaders with a .356 batting average, 137 runs scored, 331 total bases, and a .511 slugging percentage, Combs topped the circuit with 231 hits and 23 triples. He also led all AL outfielders in putouts for the first of two straight times. Combs followed that up by batting .310, scoring 118 runs, amassing 194 hits, and collecting a league-leading 21 triples in 1928 en route to earning a sixth-place finish in the AL MVP voting. However, a late-season injury forced him to sit out New York's four-game sweep of St. Louis in the World Series.

Fully healthy again in 1929, Combs had another big year, batting .345 and finishing among the league leaders with 119 runs scored, 202 hits, and 15 triples. He had three more outstanding seasons for the Yankees before injuries began to significantly reduce his playing time and offensive productivity. Combs batted well in excess of .300 and scored well over 100 runs three straight times from 1930 to 1932, establishing a career high with 143 runs scored for New York's 1932 world championship ball club.

After posting solid numbers again in 1933 despite being limited to 122 games by a series of nagging injuries, Combs had his career ended for all intents and purposes in July 1934 when he crashed into the outfield wall at St. Louis's Sportsman's Park chasing after a fly ball. The center fielder suffered a fractured skull, a broken shoulder, and a damaged knee as a result. Placed in intensive care at the hospital for several days immediately thereafter, Combs remained under close watch for another two months before finally being released. He attempted a comeback the following year, but a collision with a fellow Yankee outfielder, coupled with the impending arrival of Joe DiMaggio, prompted Combs to announce his retirement at age 36. Combs ended his playing career with a .325 lifetime batting average, a .397 on-base percentage,

1,186 runs scored, and 154 triples, placing him second in team history only to Lou Gehrig in the last category. His 23 triples in 1927 remain a Yankee single-season record.

The Yankees subsequently offered Combs a coaching job, and he ended up instructing his replacement (DiMaggio) on the nuances of Yankee Stadium's outfield. Combs remained in the Yankee organization until he joined the military a few years later to serve in World War II. He later returned to organized ball to serve as a coach with the Browns, Red Sox, and Phillies. The Veterans Committee inducted Combs into the Hall of Fame in 1970, 35 years after he played his last game. During his induction speech, the former center fielder revealed the humility and graciousness that made him one of the most popular and respected players of his time when he said, "I thought the Hall of Fame was for superstars, not just average players like me."

CAREER HIGHLIGHTS

Best Season

Combs performed brilliantly as a rookie in 1925, when he batted .342, scored 117 runs, and collected 203 hits. He also had big years in 1929, 1930, and 1932. Combs batted .345, scored 119 times, and amassed 202 hits in the first of those seasons. He batted .344 one year later, scored 129 runs, drove in a career-high 82 runs, and led the AL with 22 triples. Combs also batted .321 and scored a career-best 143 runs in 1932. However, Combs had his finest all-around season in 1927, when he scored 137 runs, batted a career-high .356, and led the American League with 231 hits and 23 triples. His 23 triples remain a franchise record, and his 231 hits remained the highest total ever compiled by a Yankee player until Don Mattingly collected 238 safeties for the team in 1986.

Memorable Moments/Greatest Performances

An outstanding postseason player throughout his career, Combs saved some of his finest performances for the World Series. He collected 10 hits and batted .357 in a losing effort against St. Louis in the 1926 Fall Classic. Combs also tormented the Cubs throughout the 1932 series, batting .375, hitting a home run, and driving in four runs during New York's four-game sweep of Chicago. Combs posted a lifetime batting average of .350 in World Series play, along with an exceptional .444 on-base percentage.

Combs also performed some memorable feats during the regular season. On September 22, 1927, he collected three triples in one game, making him one of only three players in team history to do so (Hal Chase and Joe DiMaggio were the others). Combs also fashioned a 29-game hitting streak in 1931 that ties him for the second-longest such streak in franchise history. And Combs took part in a historic event on April 18, 1929, when, batting leadoff against the Red Sox on opening day, his number 1 jersey made him the first member of the Yankees to step to the plate wearing a uniform number.

NOTABLE ACHIEVEMENTS

- Batted over .300 in 10 of 12 seasons, topping the .340 mark five times.
- Scored more than 100 runs eight straight times, surpassing 120 runs scored on four occasions.
- Compiled on-base percentage in excess of .400 seven times.
- Collected more than 200 hits three times.
- Collected more than 20 triples three times.
- Led AL in triples three times and hits once.
- Holds franchise record for most triples in a season (23 in 1927).
- 231 hits in 1927 remained Yankee single-season record for 59 years.
- Four-time AL champion.
- Three-time world champion.

16

Dave Winfield

There will undoubtedly be some Yankee fans who object to the idea of placing Dave Winfield as high as 16th in these rankings. After all, the Yankees advanced to the postseason just once during his eight full years in New York, and Winfield failed miserably in his lone World Series appearance with the club, collecting just 1 hit in 22 official trips to the plate during the team's 1981 series defeat at the hands of the Los Angeles Dodgers. Nevertheless, the fact remains that Winfield performed exceptionally well during his time in New York, compiling impressive numbers on offense while playing right field better than perhaps anyone else in team history. Winfield knocked in more than 100 runs for the Yankees on six occasions, won five Gold Gloves, and earned a spot on the AL All-Star Team eight straight times. It is unfortunate that Winfield's public battles with Yankee owner George Steinbrenner, along with his failures in the 1981 Fall Classic, kept many Yankee fans from fully appreciating everything that the slugging outfielder contributed to the team during his tenure with the ball club.

A tremendous all-around athlete, Dave Winfield spent his first eight major-league seasons with the San Diego Padres after initially being drafted out of college by the NBA's Atlanta Hawks, the ABA's Utah Stars, and the NFL's Minnesota Vikings. Joining the Padres shortly after he graduated from the University of Minnesota in 1973, the 6'6", 220-pound Winfield gradually developed into one of the National League's premier players during his time in San Diego, earning All-Star honors four times. He had his best year for the club in 1979, when he hit 34 homers, batted .308, and topped the senior circuit with 118 runs batted in and 333 total bases en route to earning a third-place finish in the league MVP voting. After another solid year in 1980, Winfield became the game's highest-paid player when he signed a 10-year $23-million contract with the Yankees.

The controversy that Winfield encountered during his time in New York began almost as soon as he signed his record-setting deal. Conflict quickly arose between the outfielder and George Steinbrenner when the Yankee owner realized that he had misinterpreted the contract's cost-of-living escalator clause and that the deal would likely end up costing him closer to $23 million rather than the $16 million he had expected. The misunderstanding caused Steinbrenner to harbor resentment toward Winfield throughout the latter's stay in New York. The Yankee owner consequently attempted to humiliate his star outfielder by frequently berating him in the newspapers.

However, Winfield managed to block out the many distractions that surrounded him and perform exceptionally well throughout the duration of the contract. After being widely criticized for his poor showing in the 1981 World Series, Winfield began a string of five consecutive seasons in which he drove in more than 100 runs. By doing so, he became the first Yankee since Joe DiMaggio to surpass the century mark in RBIs five straight times. Winfield posted outstanding power numbers in 1982 and 1983, combining to hit 69 homers and drive in 222 runs. After Steinbrenner contended at the conclusion of the 1983 campaign that Winfield could not "hit for average," the slugger shortened his swing and compiled a career-high .340 batting average the following year. Yet, in spite of his outstanding performance, Winfield drew the ire of Yankee fans when he challenged popular teammate Don Mattingly for the batting title. Fans of the team cheered wildly every time the young first baseman stepped into the batter's box during the season's latter stages, while Winfield became the object of their scorn. Mattingly ended up winning the batting title by three percentage points, and although Winfield accepted his second-place finish with dignity and class, his relationship with the fans and media soured.

Winfield's lack of rapport with the fans and media could be attributed to a number of other factors as well. In 1983, he accidentally beaned and killed a seagull between innings at a game in Toronto, after which he drew vitriolic criticism from Canadian fans and environmental groups. He also continued to feud with Steinbrenner over money, specifically regarding the owner's allegedly delinquent payments to the Winfield Foundation, Winfield's charitable organization for children. Meanwhile, as Winfield continued to struggle at the plate late in 1985 during the Yankees' unsuccessful run at the AL East title, a bitter Steinbrenner derided his star outfielder by saying to *New York Times* writer Murray Chass, "Where is Reggie Jackson? We need a Mr. October or a Mr. September. Winfield is Mr. May."

Steinbrenner also attempted to malign Winfield's reputation during the latter stages of the 1980s by leaking insulting (and often fictitious) stories about him to the press. The Yankee owner often suggested to his managers that they move Winfield down in the batting order, and he frequently tried to trade him, although Winfield's status as a 10-and-5 player meant that he could not be dealt without his consent.

Yet, through it all, Winfield continued to put up outstanding numbers year after year, hitting 190 home runs and driving in 744 runs between 1982 and 1988. However, back surgery forced Winfield to miss the entire 1989 campaign, and after a slow start in 1990, he accepted a trade to the California Angels for starter Mike Witt. Winfield went on to capture MLB Comeback Player of the Year honors with the Angels, and he later won a world championship as a member of the Toronto Blue Jays.

In just a little over eight full seasons in New York, Winfield hit 205 home runs, knocked in 818 runs, scored 722 others, batted .290, and collected 1,300 hits. More than just an outstanding hitter, Winfield ran the bases extremely well, did an exceptional job of patrolling right field, and totally intimidated opposing base runners with his powerful throwing arm. In addition to his eight nominations to the AL All-Star Team and five Gold Gloves, Winfield earned five Silver Sluggers and four top 10 finishes in the AL MVP balloting. Although Winfield chose to enter the Hall of Fame in 2001 as a member of the San Diego Padres, he had many of his finest seasons for the Yankees. During his induction speech at Cooperstown, Winfield sounded a conciliatory note toward George Steinbrenner, saying, "[Steinbrenner] said he regrets a lot of things that happened. We're fine now. Things have changed."

YANKEE CAREER HIGHLIGHTS

Best Season

Winfield had three of his finest seasons from 1982 to 1984. In the first of those years, he hit a career-high 37 home runs, knocked in 106 runs, and batted .280. Winfield hit 32 homers, drove in 116 runs, scored 99 others, and batted .283 the following year. Although his power numbers fell off somewhat in 1984 to 19 homers and 100 runs batted in, he established new career bests with 106 runs scored and a .340 batting average. Nevertheless, the feeling here is that Winfield had his finest all-around season for the Yankees in 1988—his last full year with the team. The 36-year-old outfielder hit 25 homers, drove in 107 runs, scored 96 others, batted .322, and compiled a career-high .398 on-base percentage en route to earning a fourth-place finish in the league MVP voting.

Memorable Moments/Greatest Performances

Unfortunately, Winfield's accidental beaning of a seagull during a 1983 game in Toronto continues to live on as one of his most memorable moments. However, on a more positive note, Winfield had perhaps his finest stretch as a Yankee from May 22 to June 10, 1984, when he fashioned a 17-game hitting streak during which he collected 34 hits in 74 official trips to the plate, for a .459 batting average. Winfield performed particularly well during the first week of June, when he went 15 for 26, including two 5-hit games over a three-day period at one point.

NOTABLE ACHIEVEMENTS

- Hit more than 30 home runs twice.
- Knocked in more than 100 runs six times.
- Scored more than 100 runs twice.
- Batted over .300 twice.
- Three-time *Sporting News* All-Star selection.
- Eight-time AL All-Star.
- Five-time Gold Glove winner.

❿

Joe Gordon

Fellow Hall of Fame second basemen Tony Lazzeri and Joe Gordon ended up being the leading candidates for the number 17 spot, and either one of them would have made a good choice. Lazzeri spent 12 years in New York, as opposed to Gordon's 7 years, enabling him to compile more impressive totals in most offensive categories than his immediate successor at second for the Yankees. Nevertheless, I elected to go with Gordon due to his superior defensive skills and the greater level of dominance he attained while wearing the pinstripes. Lazzeri earned one *Sporting News* All-Star selection as Yankee second baseman, while Gordon was named to the squad four straight times. Gordon also captured AL MVP honors in 1942; Lazzeri never finished any higher than third in the balloting. In addition, while Lazzeri was considered to be a solid second sacker, Gordon developed a reputation for having more range than any other player at the position throughout most of his career. As much as anything, that last fact enabled Gordon to place one spot higher in these rankings than Lazzeri.

After signing with the Yankees out of the University of Oregon in 1936, Joe Gordon spent two years working his way up the New York farm system, impressing team brass to such an extent that its members elected to release longtime starting second baseman Tony Lazzeri at the conclusion of the 1937 campaign. Gordon made his major-league debut with the Yankees in April 1938, rewarding the faith that team management placed in him by going on to hit 25 home runs and drive in 97 runs in his first big-league season. Gordon's 25 homers set a new American League record for rookie second basemen. He also compiled 450 assists, placing second to Detroit's Charlie Gehringer among AL second sackers. Gordon punctuated his outstanding rookie season by batting .400, hitting a homer, and driving in 6 runs during New York's four-game sweep of the Chicago Cubs in the World Series.

Gordon supplanted Gehringer as baseball's premier second baseman the following year, earning the first of four consecutive selections to the *Sporting News* All-Star Team. In addition to batting .284, scoring 92 runs, and finishing among the AL leaders with 28 home runs and 111 runs batted in, Gordon led all league second basemen in putouts, assists, and double plays. Gordon's outstanding all-around performance helped the Yankees capture their fourth straight world championship and earned him a ninth-place finish in the AL MVP voting and his first trip to the All-Star Game.

Although the Yankees failed to repeat as league champions in 1940, Gordon continued his onslaught against AL pitching, hitting 30 home runs and knocking in 103 runs while batting .281 and scoring a career-high 112 runs. After posting solid numbers again the following year, Gordon had arguably his finest season in pinstripes in 1942, hitting 18 homers, driving in 103 runs, and establishing career bests with a .322 batting average and a .409 on-base percentage. Gordon's exceptional campaign enabled him to edge out Boston's Ted Williams in the AL MVP balloting, in an extremely controversial vote (Williams won the Triple Crown that year).

Perhaps distracted by the events over in Europe, Gordon suffered through a subpar 1943 season that saw him hit only 17 home runs, knock in just 69 runs, and bat only .249. He entered the US Army the following year to assist in the war effort, causing him to miss all of the 1944 and 1945 campaigns. He returned to the Yankees in 1946 to have the poorest season of his career. Sharing time at second base with George "Snuffy" Stirnweiss, who excelled for the team during the war years, Gordon hit only 11 homers, drove in just 47 runs, and batted only .210. Fearful that Gordon might never regain his earlier form, the Yankees traded him to the Cleveland Indians shortly after the regular season for pitcher Allie Reynolds. Gordon departed New York having hit 153 home runs, knocked in 617 runs, scored 596 others, batted .271, and accumulated exactly 1,000 hits in precisely 1,000 games with the team. While Reynolds went on to star for the Yankees over the next several seasons, the Indians never regretted making the deal. Gordon's 32 homers and 124 RBIs in 1948 helped them capture the American League pennant and their first world championship since 1920.

On December 7, 2008, some 30 years after Joe Gordon passed away, the Veterans Committee elected him to the Baseball Hall of Fame. Gordon's only daughter, Judy, gave his induction speech at Cooperstown almost eight months later, saying in her closing remarks,

"[Joe] insisted against having a funeral . . . and, as such, we consider Cooperstown and the National Baseball Hall of Fame as his final resting place to be honored forever."

Almost one year later, on April 29, 2010, *Wall Street Journal* sportswriter Russell Adams wrote a piece entitled "Who Is the Greatest Yankee?" Adams ranked Gordon as the ninth-greatest Yankees position player in franchise history, noting, "Gordon's great strength was defense—his range was the best of any of the 30 candidates we studied."

YANKEE CAREER HIGHLIGHTS

Best Season

It ended up coming down to Gordon's 1940 and 1942 campaigns, and a valid case could be made for either of the two. The second baseman hit 30 homers, drove in 103 runs, scored a career-high 112 others, batted .281, and posted a career-best .511 slugging percentage in the first of those years. In his MVP season of 1942, Gordon hit 18 home runs, knocked in 103 runs, scored 88 times, compiled a career-high .322 batting average, and posted a .491 slugging percentage. The overall numbers would seem to lean slightly toward Gordon's 1940 performance. However, en route to capturing AL MVP honors in 1942, Gordon compiled a .409 on-base percentage—easily the best of his career and 69 points higher than the mark of .340 he posted two years earlier. Gordon finished the 1942 campaign with an on-base plus slugging of .900, which exceeded his 1940 mark of .851 by 49 points. Furthermore, the Yankees won the pennant in 1942, something they failed to do in 1940. And, as Yankee manager Joe McCarthy once said of his second baseman, "All Gordon cares about is winning." That being the case, I will give a slight nod to Gordon's 1942 campaign.

Memorable Moments/Greatest Performances

Aside from being one of the finest defensive infielders of his time, Gordon had a number of memorable days at the plate. On June 28, 1939, he hit 3 home runs during a doubleheader sweep of the Philadelphia Athletics that the Yankees won by a combined score of 33–2. Gordon went 6 for 12 on the day, with 7 runs batted in and 6 runs scored. A little over a year later, on September 8, 1940, Gordon hit for the cycle during a 9–4 victory over the Red Sox at Fenway Park.

Gordon also performed exceptionally well for the Yankees in the 1938 and 1941 World Series. During the 1938 sweep of the Chicago Cubs, he homered once, drove in 6 runs, batted .400, and compiled a .733 slugging percentage. After doubling, driving in a run with a single, and recording the final out in a 3–1 game 1 victory, Gordon doubled in the first two runs in a 6–3 game 2 win. Gordon proved to be the difference in New York's 5–2 win in game 3, hitting a solo home run to tie the score at 1–1 in the fifth inning, and singling home 2 more runs in the sixth. He then capped off his brilliant performance by scoring twice in game 4, to help lead the Yankees to an 8–3 win and their third straight world championship.

Gordon proved to be even more of a factor against Brooklyn in the 1941 Fall Classic, snuffing out Dodger rallies with his glove, while batting .500, hitting a homer, driving in 5 runs, compiling a .667 on-base percentage, and posting a .929 slugging percentage. Gordon started the scoring in game 1 with a solo home run in the second inning. He later drove in another run with an RBI single, walked twice, and turned a double play with the tying run on first base to close out New York's 3–2 win. After the Yankees dropped a close 3–2 decision in the second contest, Gordon led them to victory in game 3 by tripling, walking, and compiling 4 assists, one of which ended the game. Gordon helped secure New York's 7–4 victory in game 4 by doubling in 2 runs in the ninth inning, moments after Dodger catcher Mickey Owen allowed the Yankees to continue batting by allowing a third strike that would have ended the game to elude him. Gordon followed that up by driving in another run in New York's series-clinching 3–1 win in game 5. The second baseman's five double plays (three of them in game 2) remain a record for a five-game series. Yankee manager Joe McCarthy said after the series, "The greatest all-around ballplayer I ever saw, and I don't bar any of them, is Joe Gordon."

NOTABLE ACHIEVEMENTS

- Hit more than 20 home runs four times.
- Knocked in more than 100 runs three times.
- Scored more than 100 runs twice.
- Batted over .300 and compiled on-base percentage in excess of .400 once each.
- Posted slugging percentage in excess of .500 on three occasions.
- Led AL second basemen in putouts once and assists four times.

- 1942 AL MVP.
- Four-time *Sporting News* All-Star selection.
- Six-time AL All-Star.
- Five-time AL champion.
- Four-time world champion.

⒙

Tony Lazzeri

Known as "the quiet man of the Yankees," Tony Lazzeri spent his entire time in New York batting behind such legends as Babe Ruth, Lou Gehrig, Joe DiMaggio, and Bill Dickey. Yet, the second baseman's solid fielding, timely hitting, and outstanding leadership skills enabled him to become a hero in his own right, especially to Italian Americans, who embraced him as baseball's first true star of Italian heritage. Later joined in New York by fellow Italians Joe DiMaggio and Frank Crosetti, Lazzeri helped lead the Yankees to 6 pennants and 5 world championships in his 12 full seasons with the club, serving as one of the key members of 1927's fabled "Murderer's Row" squad.

Born in San Francisco, California, in 1903, Anthony Michael Lazzeri first drew the attention of the Yankees when he batted .355 and set since-broken professional baseball records by hitting 60 home runs and knocking in 222 runs for Salt Lake City in the Pacific Coast League in 1925. Lazzeri also established a record that still stands by scoring 202 runs for the Bees. The fact that the slugging second baseman compiled those extraordinary numbers playing in Salt Lake City's high altitude over the course of a 200-game schedule did not seem to matter to the Yankees, who purchased his contract for $75,000 at the conclusion of the campaign.

Lazzeri made his debut with the Yankees in 1926, taking over the starting second base job from Aaron Ward and appearing in all 155 games for New York. The right-handed hitting Lazzeri had an outstanding rookie season, batting .275, finishing second in the league to teammate Babe Ruth with 114 runs batted in, and placing among the leaders with 18 home runs and 14 triples. Lazzeri's solid performance helped the Yankees claim the first of their three straight American League pennants.

Lazzeri improved his numbers the following season, batting .309, once again placing among the league leaders in home runs (18) and runs batted in (102), and finishing third in the circuit with a career-high 22 stolen bases. In addition, the second sacker helped stabilize the infield of the Murderer's Row ball club by compiling a league-leading 525 assists in the field.

Injuries prevented Lazzeri from appearing in more than 116 games in 1928, limiting him to only 10 home runs and 82 RBIs. Nevertheless, he batted .332 and did an outstanding job in the field, enabling him to earn a third-place finish in the AL MVP balloting. Lazzeri followed that up with two of the most productive seasons of his career. Although the Yankees failed to capture the pennant in either 1929 or 1930, Lazzeri posted exceptional numbers both years. He hit 18 homers, drove in 106 runs, scored 101 others, and established career highs with 193 hits and a .354 batting average in 1929. Lazzeri hit only 9 homers the following season, but he batted .303 and reached career highs in runs batted in (121) and runs scored (109).

After a subpar 1931 campaign, Lazzeri rebounded in 1932 to help lead the Yankees to their first pennant in four years. The second sacker batted .300, collected 16 triples, hit 15 homers, and drove in 113 runs en route to earning an eighth-place finish in the AL MVP voting and his only selection to the *Sporting News* All-Star Team. Lazzeri subsequently helped the Yankees dispose of the Cubs in four straight games in the World Series, hitting 2 homers, driving in 5 runs, and batting .294 against Chicago in the Fall Classic.

Lazzeri spent five more years in pinstripes, knocking in more than 100 runs two more times and helping the Yankees capture back-to-back world championships in 1936 and 1937. However, with Joe Gordon waiting in the wings, the Yankees released Lazzeri at the conclusion of the 1937 campaign. He signed with the Chicago Cubs shortly thereafter, spending the entire 1938 season serving as a backup infielder on Chicago's NL pennant–winning ball club. Released by the Cubs at the end of the year, Lazzeri split the first half of the 1939 campaign between the Dodgers and Giants, before announcing his retirement at midseason.

Tony Lazzeri started at second base for the Yankees for 12 straight years, from 1926 to 1937. During that time, he hit 169 home runs, knocked in 1,154 runs, scored 952 others, collected 1,784 hits, amassed 115 triples, and compiled a batting average of .293. Lazzeri ranks fifth on the Yankees' all-time list in triples; he also ranks in the team's all-time top 10 in runs batted in. Lazzeri earned three top-10 finishes in the AL MVP voting, and he was a member of the junior circuit's inaugural All-Star Team in 1933.

Although Lazzeri gained a reputation during his career as one of the American League's more dangerous batsmen, Yankee manager Miller Huggins chose to focus on his defense when he suggested, "I've seen a few better second basemen, but not many. [Lazzeri] has a phenomenal pair of hands, a great throwing arm, and he covers acres of ground."

An epileptic throughout his life, Lazzeri died at age 42 from a fall caused, according to the coroner, by a heart attack. However, many believe that his fall and premature passing actually resulted from an epileptic seizure. The Veterans Committee elected Lazzeri to the Baseball Hall of Fame in 1991.

YANKEE CAREER HIGHLIGHTS

Best Season

Lazzeri's outstanding rookie campaign of 1926 would have to rank among his very best. So, too, would the exceptional performances he turned in for New York's world championship ball clubs of 1927 and 1932. Still, the feeling here is that Lazzeri had his finest all-around year in 1929, when he hit 18 home runs, knocked in 106 runs, scored 101 others, and established career highs with 193 hits, 37 doubles, 306 total bases, a .354 batting average, a .429 on-base percentage, and a .561 slugging percentage.

Memorable Moments/Greatest Performances

Ironically, the most memorable moment of Lazzeri's career was one that ended up damaging his reputation as a clutch hitter. After performing so well for the Yankees as a rookie throughout the 1926 campaign, Lazzeri stepped to the plate to face the legendary Grover Cleveland Alexander in the bottom of the seventh inning of game 7 of the World Series, with two men out, the bases loaded, and St. Louis leading by a score of 3–2. Alexander, who evened the series at three games apiece one day earlier by tossing a complete-game victory, entered the fray in that precarious situation with the thought in mind of keeping the ball in on Lazzeri to prevent him from fully extending his arms. Lazzeri brought the Yankee Stadium crowd to its feet by driving Alexander's second offering deep down the left-field line, just to the left of the foul pole. After narrowly missing a grand slam that most certainly would have brought the Yankees victory, Lazzeri went down on strikes to Alexander, who pitched two more scoreless innings to give the Cardinals their first world championship. Years later, Alexander continued to suggest, "Less than a foot made the difference between a hero and a bum." Meanwhile, Yankee manager Miller Huggins attempted to defend his second baseman by saying, "Anyone can strike out, but ballplayers like Lazzeri come along once in a generation."

Although Lazzeri failed on that one particular occasion, his career featured a number of momentous moments in which he succeeded in grand fashion. One of only 14 major leaguers to hit for the natural cycle (hitting a single, double, triple, and home run in sequence), Lazzeri became on June 3, 1932, the only player ever to accomplish the feat by completing the cycle with a grand slam.

Playing against the Philadelphia Athletics on May 24, 1936, Lazzeri also became the first major leaguer ever to hit 2 grand slams in one game. In addition to slugging 2 homers with the bases full, Lazzeri left the yard a third time during the contest, concluding the afternoon with an American League record 11 runs batted in. The record-setting performance marked the second time in Lazzeri's career that he hit 3 home runs in a game (he also accomplished the feat in 1927).

Lazzeri's amazing afternoon enabled him to set two other major-league records. His 3 homers gave him a total of 6 over the course of three consecutive games (a mark later surpassed by Shawn Green of the Dodgers in 2002), and his 11 RBIs gave him a total of 15 in two straight games.

NOTABLE ACHIEVEMENTS

- Knocked in more than 100 runs seven times.
- Scored more than 100 runs twice.
- Batted over .300 five times.
- Compiled on-base percentage in excess of .400 once (.429 in 1929).
- Posted slugging percentage in excess of .500 on three occasions.
- Named to *Sporting News* All-Star Team once (1932).
- Named to AL All-Star Team once (1933).
- Six-time AL champion.
- Five-time world champion.

19

Ron Guidry

The author of arguably the greatest single season ever turned in by a Yankees pitcher, Ron Guidry had a year for the ages in 1978. The slightly built left-hander finished the campaign with a record of 25–3, a 1.74 ERA, and 9 shutouts en route to leading American League hurlers in all three categories. Guidry's fabulous performance earned him AL Cy Young honors and a second-place finish in the league MVP balloting and enabled the Yankees to edge out the Boston Red Sox in an extremely hard-fought AL East pennant race. However, "Louisiana Lightning," as he came to be known to Yankee fans, was more than just a one-year wonder. Guidry won more than 20 games three times during his Yankee career, compiling an outstanding overall mark of 170–91 over parts of 14 seasons with the team. He ranks among the franchise's all-time leaders in wins, strikeouts (1,778), shutouts (26), games started (323), and innings pitched (2,392). Yet, in spite of his immense talent that enabled him to carve out a niche for himself in Yankee lore, Guidry almost retired before his career ever truly began.

Ron Guidry traveled a long and arduous road from his birthplace of Lafayette, Louisiana, to the city of New York. After being selected by the Yankees in the third round of the 1971 amateur draft, Guidry spent the better part of six years working his way up through the team's farm system. Yankee management's policy of acquiring veteran pitchers through trades and free agency contributed in large part to the southpaw's lengthy apprenticeship. Also blocking Guidry's path to the majors was the belief held by many within the Yankee organization that the 5'11", 160-pound left-hander lacked the size necessary to compete successfully at the major-league level. Further adding to

Guidry's time in the minors was the lack of success he experienced on those rare occasions he received an opportunity to pitch for the Yankees. Guidry made brief appearances with the club in 1975 and 1976, compiling a record of 0–1, with an ERA in excess of 4.50 and with 35 hits allowed in only 31 2/3 innings of work. Guidry became so discouraged at the conclusion of the 1976 campaign that he seriously considered quitting baseball, before finally electing to give it one more try the following year.

Guidry made the Yankee roster coming out of spring training in 1977, but he started the season working out of the bullpen. It was there that the 26-year-old left-hander perfected the slider—a pitch he learned from Yankee bullpen ace Sparky Lyle. Coupled with his outstanding fastball, the new pitch turned Guidry into a complete pitcher—one of the best the American League had to offer.

After being inserted into the starting rotation early in 1977, Guidry went on to compile a record of 16–7, along with an ERA of 2.82 that placed him fourth in the league rankings. He also finished second in the circuit with five shutouts. Guidry then helped the Yankees capture their first world championship in 15 years by going 2–0 during the postseason, including a complete-game four-hitter against the Dodgers in the World Series.

Guidry followed up his breakout season with an extraordinary 1978 campaign during which he kept the Yankees in the pennant race almost single-handedly while the team battled through injuries and inner turmoil to pursue the Boston Red Sox for the AL East title throughout the summer months. As the Yankees strove to gain their bearings during the season's first half, Guidry practically guaranteed them victory each time he took the mound every fifth day. In addition to leading the league with a record of 25–3, a winning percentage of .893, a 1.74 ERA, and 9 shutouts, Guidry placed among the leaders with 248 strikeouts, 274 innings pitched, and 16 complete games. He earned his 25th victory against the Red Sox in a one-game playoff played at Fenway Park, holding Boston to two runs on six hits over 6 1/3 innings, despite working on only three days' rest. Guidry subsequently posted another two wins during the postseason, limiting Kansas City and Los Angeles to one run apiece in his two starts, as the Yankees captured their second consecutive world championship.

Reggie Jackson later said of Guidry in his autobiography, "This thin, little guy the writers call 'Louisiana Lightning' had been the leader all season. When everything else had fallen apart, he just kept quiet and kept winning. Again, he was the truest Yankee of all."

Jackson added, "The next season, when [Rich] Gossage got hurt in the shower fight with [teammate] Cliff Johnson, Guidry went to the bullpen by choice because he thought he could do the team the most good there. He never got the credit he deserved for that one. He's a winner, and he always managed to get the job done with a great mixture of humility and pride. . . . Gimme the ball. Let me spit a little tobacco. Here comes the fastball and sliders. Hell of a man . . . Ron Guidry."

Guidry did indeed offer to take the injured Gossage's spot in the Yankee bullpen the following year, although he soon returned to the starting rotation. The left-hander ended up going 18–8, with 201 strikeouts, 15 complete games, and a league-leading 2.78 ERA. Although Guidry subsequently found it impossible to match his epic 1978 performance, he remained one of baseball's best pitchers for the next six years, posting a combined record of 154–67 from 1977 to 1985. He surpassed 20 victories two more times, compiling a record of 21–9, an ERA of 3.42, and a league-leading 21 complete games in 1983 and leading all AL hurlers with 22 wins and a .786 winning percentage (22–6) in 1985.

Guidry ended up leading all major-league pitchers with a total of 168 victories from 1977 to 1987, winning at least 14 games in 7 of those 11 seasons. In addition to his outstanding regular-season record, Guidry compiled a lifetime mark of 5–2 in postseason play, along with an impressive 3.02 ERA. He pitched particularly well in the World Series, posting an overall record of 3–1 with a 1.69 ERA and allowing only 20 hits in 32 innings of work. An outstanding all-around athlete, Guidry's quickness and agility enabled him to win five consecutive Gold Gloves at one point. Aside from winning the Cy Young Award in 1978, Guidry earned three other top-5 finishes in the voting, including a second-place finish to Kansas City's Bret Saberhagen in 1985.

Unfortunately, elbow problems plagued Guidry his final three seasons, greatly limiting his effectiveness and forcing him from the Yankees' starting rotation for most of the 1987 and 1988 campaigns. Slow to recover from surgery following the 1988 season, Guidry started 1989 on the disabled list before beginning a rehab assignment in June at Columbus. When he failed to impress Yankee management during his brief stint at the team's Triple-A affiliate, Guidry announced his retirement on July 12, 1989.

The Yankees later retired Guidry's uniform number 49 on "Ron Guidry Day" at Yankee Stadium on August 23, 2003. The team also dedicated a plaque to hang in Monument Park, which calls Guidry "a dominating pitcher and a respected leader . . . a true Yankee."

CAREER HIGHLIGHTS

Best Season

This was a no-brainer. Although Guidry had several other outstanding years, his 1978 campaign is generally considered to be one of the greatest ever compiled by a pitcher in either league. Guidry's 25–3 record gave him a winning percentage of .893, which ranks among the 10 best in baseball history. He led the league with a 1.74 ERA, 9 shutouts, and 6.15 hits allowed per nine innings pitched, and he held opposing batters to a .193 batting average, a .249 on-base percentage, and a .279 slugging percentage. Guidry also placed among the league leaders with 248 strikeouts, 274 innings pitched, and 16 complete games. His 248 strikeouts and 13 consecutive wins at the start of the season remain Yankee records, and his nine shutouts tie him with Babe Ruth for the AL record by a left-hander. Louisiana Lightning earned AL Cy Young honors and finished second to Boston's Jim Rice in the league MVP voting. He called his Yankee-record 18 strikeouts against California on June 17 of that season "perhaps my greatest single thrill." Guidry started the AL East playoff game on October 2 against Boston and won 5–4, in what he suggested was "probably the most tension-packed game I ever played in." Guidry also earned *Sporting News* Player of the Year, Man of the Year, and Associated Press Male Athlete of the Year honors, and he made every all-star team.

Memorable Moments/Greatest Performances

On August 7, 1984, Guidry struck out three batters (Carlton Fisk, Tom Paciorek, and Greg Luzinski) on nine pitches in the ninth inning of a 7–0 win over the Chicago White Sox. In doing so, Guidry became just the eighth American League pitcher and the 20th major-league hurler to accomplish the so-called immaculate inning. However, Louisiana Lightning established himself as the very first pitcher to do so in the ninth inning of a complete game, a feat that has been matched just once since.

Nevertheless, Guidry's greatest and most memorable performance has to be considered the effort he turned in on June 17, 1978, when he allowed just four hits and set a Yankee record that still stands by striking out 18 California Angels during a 4–0 New York win at Yankee Stadium. Guidry's 18-strikeout performance is usually cited as the launching pad of the Yankee Stadium tradition of fans standing and clapping for a strikeout with two strikes on the opposing batter.

Detroit's Alan Trammell later stated,

What comes to mind when I think of Ron Guidry is 1978: 25–3. I think of that slider down and in, and I think of the crowd noise in New York every time he'd get two strikes, which became kind of a thing in New York. . . . The people would get up and, as a hitter, you'd hear that crowd goin' crazy in the background and, ultimately, you'd check-swing and miss at a ball in the dirt. Everybody from the dugout or from the stands would say, "how could you swing at that pitch?" You'd say, "well, when you're 60 feet, 6 inches away, and somebody throws that Steve Carlton–type of slider, it's very hard to lay off of it."

NOTABLE ACHIEVEMENTS

- Three-time 20-game winner.
- Topped 16 victories three other times.
- Compiled ERA below 3.00 on four occasions.
- Completed more than 20 games once (21 in 1983).
- Threw more than 250 innings three times.
- Struck out more than 200 batters twice.
- Led AL pitchers in wins, winning percentage, and ERA two times each and in shutouts and complete games once each.
- Holds American League record for most shutouts in a season by a left-hander (tied with Babe Ruth with nine).
- Holds Yankee record for most strikeouts in a game (18).
- 1978 AL Cy Young Award winner.
- 1978 Major League Player of the Year.
- 1978 *Sporting News* Pitcher of the Year.
- Four-time *Sporting News* All-Star selection.
- Four-time AL All-Star.
- Five-time Gold Glove winner (1982–1986).
- Four-time AL champion.
- Two-time world champion.

20

Graig Nettles

I deliberated long and hard about this selection, trying to decide whether Graig Nettles truly deserved to be ranked as one of the 20 greatest Yankees ever. After all, by placing the All-Star third baseman in the number 20 position, I accorded him a higher ranking than more talented players such as Reggie Jackson and Rickey Henderson. I also placed Nettles ahead of fan favorites such as Thurman Munson and Paul O'Neill—both of whom were more complete hitters than Nettles and meant just as much to the Yankees during their years in pin-stripes. However, when I considered Nettles's total body of work and the integral role he played on four pennant-winning teams and two world championship ball clubs in New York, it seemed appropriate to place him slightly ahead of those other Yankee standouts and assign him the 20th slot in these rankings. Nettles hit 250 home runs in his 11 years as a Yankee, knocked in 834 runs, made 5 AL All-Star teams, won 2 Gold Gloves, and earned 2 top-10 finishes in the league MVP voting. Equally significant is the fact that Nettles started all but 22 games at third base for the Yankees between 1973 and 1978, making him perhaps the team's most indispensable player during that period.

Nettles began his professional baseball career in the farm system of the Minnesota Twins, who selected him in the fourth round of the 1965 amateur draft. After earning brief call-ups by the Twins in 1967 and 1968, Nettles arrived in the majors for good in 1969. However, his stay in Minnesota proved to be a short one, since the Twins included him as part of a six-player deal they completed with the Cleveland Indians at season's end that netted them Luis Tiant.

Nettles ended up having three productive years for the Indians, combining to hit 71 home runs and drive in 218 runs from 1970 to

1972. However, the Yankees had been eyeing Nettles for quite some time, firmly believing that his left-handed power stroke made him a perfect fit for Yankee Stadium's short right-field porch.

The Yankees' quest to land the third baseman finally ended on November 27, 1972, when they traded young outfield prospects Charlie Spikes and Rusty Torres, backup infielder Jerry Kenney, and reserve catcher John Ellis to the Indians for Nettles and backup catcher Gerry Moses. Upon making the deal, Yankee general manager Lee MacPhail stated, "We traded our tomorrow for today. Our fans have waited long enough." As it turned out, the acquisition of Nettles not only improved the Yankees in 1973 but also served as one of the building blocks for the team that won four pennants and two world championships from 1976 to 1981. Nettles evolved into one of the greatest fielding third basemen in baseball history while providing the Yankees with a potent left-handed bat in the middle of their batting order.

Still, while Nettles put up decent power numbers his first two seasons in New York, his overall performance was somewhat lacking. In 1973, he hit 22 home runs and knocked in 81 runs, but he batted only .234 and committed 26 errors in the field. When the team moved to Shea Stadium the following year to accommodate the renovation of Yankee Stadium, Nettles got off to a fast start, hitting 11 home runs in the month of April. However, he hit only 11 more homers the rest of the year, finishing the season with just 22 round-trippers. He also drove in only 75 runs, batted just .246, and committed 21 errors at third base.

In 1975, though, Nettles started to develop into the sort of player the Yankees hoped they had acquired three years earlier. He hit 21 home runs, drove in 91 runs, batted .267, made the All-Star Team for the first time in his career, and was selected to his first *Sporting News* All-Star Team. Nettles had an even better year in 1976 when he helped the Yankees win the pennant by leading the league with 32 homers, driving in 93 runs, and scoring another 88. He also showed marked improvement in his defensive play at third.

Still, the best had yet to come. Nettles had the two greatest seasons of his career in 1977 and 1978, when he established himself as one of the American League's premier players. Nettles finished the first of those years with career highs in home runs (37), runs batted in (107), and runs scored (99) while reducing his error total at third base to just 12. He ended up earning selections to the AL and the *Sporting News* All-Star Teams, winning the first Gold Glove of his career, and finishing fifth in the league MVP voting. Nettles followed that up by hitting 27 homers in 1978, driving in 93 runs, batting a career-high

.276, committing only 11 errors at third, earning selections again to both the AL and the *Sporting News* All-Star Teams, winning his second consecutive Gold Glove, and placing sixth in the league MVP balloting. He capped off his outstanding campaign with a memorable defensive performance against the Dodgers in game 3 of the World Series that completely shifted the momentum of the Fall Classic, helping the Yankees eventually turn a 2–0 series deficit into a six-game victory that brought them their 22nd world championship.

Nettles's tremendous defensive work in the World Series may have amazed baseball fans from around the country, but it really came as no surprise to Yankee fans and Nettles's teammates, who had grown accustomed to seeing him make incredible plays at third with great regularity.

Former Yankee shortstop Bucky Dent said, "He made some plays that were just breathtaking. He was such a quick third baseman on his feet. When he dived, he never missed a ball."

Ron Guidry described what it felt like having Nettles behind him defensively: "Having him back there, you take third base away from the opposing hitters."

Meanwhile, Fred Lynn discussed how he felt as an opposing hitter: "You couldn't get a ball by him. Just couldn't. If there was a runner on, in scoring position, he's knocking it down."

Yet, Nettles's offensive contributions must not be overlooked. He wielded a potent bat that provided the Yankees with a major left-handed power threat for more than a decade.

In discussing Nettles, former Baltimore Orioles catcher Rick Dempsey said, "He would sit back, he'd work the count, get the pitch he wanted, and hit it in the right field seats."

Neil Allen, who pitched against Nettles in the National League, said, "If you made a mistake, he was going to make you pay."

And Gene Michael, who played with and later managed Nettles said, "He could just kill the high fastball."

Another thing that made Nettles so valuable to the Yankees was the fact that he was so durable throughout most of his career. From 1973 to 1978, he never appeared in fewer than 155 games or amassed fewer than 552 at bats. He was a true iron man and one of the primary reasons why New York was able to win three straight pennants and two consecutive world championships.

After another solid season in 1979 in which he earned his fourth selection to the AL All-Star Team, Nettles was diagnosed with hepatitis in July 1980. The illness forced him to sit out 67 games, and he was not quite himself when he returned to the team just prior to New

York's three-game playoff loss to the Royals. He returned to full-time duty in 1981 and was voted ALCS MVP for going 6 for 12, with 1 home run and 9 RBIs in the Yankees' three-game sweep of Oakland. But an injury to his thumb in game 2 of the World Series forced him to sit out the next three contests after the Yankees had taken a 2–0 series lead. By the time Nettles returned for game 6, the Dodgers had already shifted the momentum of the series, and Los Angeles ended up winning the Fall Classic in six games.

The Yankees named Nettles captain prior to the start of the 1982 season, and he remained a productive hitter over the next two years, even as his playing time gradually began to diminish. After hitting 20 home runs, driving in 75 runs, and batting .266 in 462 at bats in 1983, Nettles became disenchanted when he learned that the team intended to platoon him at third base the following year with the newly acquired Toby Harrah. Nettles subsequently asked to be traded, a request the front office became eager to grant after Nettles's book *Balls* was released. The book, a collaborative effort with writer Peter Golenbock, often criticized Yankee owner George Steinbrenner. The Yankees granted Nettles's trade request on March 30, 1984, dealing the disgruntled third baseman to his hometown San Diego Padres for young left-handed pitcher Dennis Rasmussen.

Nettles remained in San Diego three years, helping the Padres capture the 1984 NL pennant, before moving on to Atlanta in 1987. He ended his career the following year as a pinch hitter and backup third baseman with the Montreal Expos. Nettles retired from the sport with 390 home runs (the fifth-highest total by any third baseman in history) and 1,314 runs batted in. He earned six All-Star selections (five of those coming as a member of the Yankees) and three selections to the *Sporting News* All-Star Team (all as a Yankee).

YANKEE CAREER HIGHLIGHTS

Best Season

Although Nettles also performed exceptionally well in 1976 and 1978, leading the AL with 32 homers in the first of those years and batting a career-high .276 in the second of those campaigns, he had his best statistical season in 1977. Neither Nettles's .255 batting average nor his .333 on-base percentage that year was particularly impressive. However, he reached career bests in home runs (37), runs batted in (107), runs scored (99), and slugging percentage (.496). Nettles also earned a fifth-place finish in the AL MVP voting and won the first of his two straight Gold Gloves.

Memorable Moments/Greatest Performances

Nettles established a new American League record (since broken) by hitting 11 home runs during the month of April 1974. He also excelled at the plate throughout the 1981 ALCS, leading the Yankees to a three-game sweep of Oakland by batting .500, homering once, and driving in 9 runs.

Nevertheless, even though he posted a batting average of just .160 over the course of the 1978 World Series, Nettles is probably remembered most for the incredible defensive exhibition he put on in game 3 that helped the Yankees completely shift the momentum of the Fall Classic to their side.

With the Yankees trailing the Dodgers two games to none, the series shifted back to New York for the next three contests. In game 3, the Yankees sent 25-game winner Ron Guidry to the mound in the hope that he might help get them back in the series. However, the Yankee lefthander did not have his best stuff that day, and while he pitched well, it was Nettles's defensive heroics that turned the tide. Guidry pitched much of the game with Dodger runners on base, and Los Angeles had men in scoring position on at least three occasions when Nettles snuffed out potential rallies with his fabulous glove work. Whether lunging to his glove side or diving to his backhand, Nettles put on a clinic at third, spearing several hot smashes by Dodger batters and turning them into outs. His performance preserved the Yankees' 5–1 victory, completely changing the momentum of the series and giving New York the impetus to go on and win the next three games as well as capture their second consecutive world championship.

Guidry later recalled his teammate's performance that day: "Even though I didn't have the greatest stuff, I knew that, if I'm gonna have them hit a ball somewhere, let them hit it to Graig. He'll make the play."

Dodger Manager Tommy Lasorda later said of Nettles's performance, "That was one of the greatest exhibitions of playing third base I've seen in all my career."

Dusty Baker, a Dodger outfielder and one of Nettles's victims, was even more effusive in his praise, saying, "If it wasn't for him, there's a good chance we would have won that World Series. That was the best fielding performance I've ever seen."

NOTABLE ACHIEVEMENTS

- Hit more than 30 home runs twice.
- Knocked in more than 100 runs once (107 in 1977).
- Led AL with 32 home runs in 1976.
- Three-time *Sporting News* All-Star selection.
- Five-time AL All-Star.
- Two-time Gold Glove winner.
- Four-time AL champion.
- Two-time world champion.

21

Paul O'Neill

Considered by many to be the "heart and soul" of the Yankee dynasty of the late 1990s, Paul O'Neill helped lead the team out of one of the darkest periods in franchise history into its next period of greatness. Frequently referred to as a "warrior" by Yankee owner George Steinbrenner due to his love and passion for the game, O'Neill became a favorite of Yankee fans shortly after he joined the team in 1993 as a result of the tremendous intensity that he brought with him to the ball field each day. An outstanding hitter and a solid outfielder as well, O'Neill topped the .300 mark in batting in six of his nine seasons in New York, and he surpassed 100 RBIs on four occasions. O'Neill's potent bat and exceptional on-field leadership enabled the Yankees to win four World Series and advance to the postseason in each of his final seven years with the team.

A native of Columbus, Ohio, Paul O'Neill grew up during the 1970s a huge fan of Cincinnati's "Big Red Machine." That last fact made being selected by the Reds in the fourth round of the 1981 amateur draft a dream come true. O'Neill progressed slowly through Cincinnati's farm system, receiving brief call-ups in 1985 and 1986, before joining the big-league club for good in 1987. The left-handed swinging O'Neill became Cincinnati's starting right fielder in 1988, a role he maintained the next five seasons.

O'Neill posted solid numbers his first three full years with the Reds, averaging 16 home runs and 75 runs batted in while consistently batting close to the .270 mark. However, the 6'4", 220-pound outfielder ultimately fell out of favor with Cincinnati manager Lou Piniella after the Reds' skipper suggested that he try to hit more home runs. O'Neill hit a career-high 28 homers for the Reds in 1991, and he drove in 91 runs. But the emphasis on the long ball came at the expense of the 28-year-old's development as an all-around hitter. O'Neill's batting average dropped to .256, and he struck out a career-high 107 times. When he slipped to .246 with just 14 home runs in 1992, the Reds and Piniella became convinced that his best days were already behind him.

O'Neill's career took a dramatic turn on November 3, 1992, when Cincinnati GM Jim Bowden traded him to the Yankees for outfielder Roberto Kelly. The Yankees had posted a losing record in each of the previous four seasons, but with O'Neill joining Don Mattingly and the hard-hitting Mike Stanley and Danny Tartabull in the middle of the team's batting order, New York finished second in the AL East with a mark of 88–74. No longer asked to swing for the fences, O'Neill flourished at the plate, establishing a new career high by batting .311 while hitting 20 homers and driving in 75 runs. Furthermore, O'Neill, whom the Yankees viewed primarily as a platoon player when he first arrived, demonstrated he had the ability to hit left-handers as well as righties.

His confidence buoyed by the success that he experienced his first year in pinstripes, O'Neill embarked on the greatest season of his career in 1994. Wresting away from Don Mattingly the Yankee captain's cherished number 3 spot in the batting order, O'Neill led the American League with a .359 batting average. He also finished among the league leaders with a .460 on-base percentage and a .603 slugging percentage en route to earning AL All-Star honors for the first of four times and a fifth-place finish in the league MVP voting. The Yankees also had quite a year, posting a league-best 70–43 record before the season ended prematurely as the result of a players' strike.

Neither O'Neill nor the Yankees performed quite as well when the players returned to their jobs the following year. Nevertheless, they both put together solid seasons, with the Yankees sneaking into the playoffs as the AL wild card and O'Neill hitting 22 homers, driving in 96 runs, and batting an even .300. The Yankees subsequently lost their first-round playoff matchup with the Seattle Mariners in five games, but O'Neill acquitted himself extremely well, hitting 3 home runs, knocking in 6 runs, and batting .333.

The Yankees began their extraordinary postseason run the following year, winning four of the next five World Series and advancing to the Fall Classic in all but one of the next six seasons. O'Neill proved to be one of the team's most significant contributors throughout that period, providing numerous clutch hits and driving in countless key runs from his number 3 spot in the lineup, consistently batting in excess of .300, and hitting the ball out of the park when a need for the long ball arose. Particularly effective from 1997 to 2000, O'Neill knocked in more than 100 runs each of those years; he also batted well over .300 in 1997 and 1998.

However, O'Neill's contributions to the success the Yankees experienced during that time could not be measured by statistics alone. He inspired his teammates with his selfless approach to the game, and the intensity he brought with him to the ballpark each day rubbed off on everyone else who wore the pinstripes. His own worst critic, O'Neill never seemed satisfied with his performance, causing him to frequently attack water coolers or destroy his batting helmet. Dissatisfaction with an umpire's decision often prompted him to toss equipment onto the field. Although some fans and members of the media criticized O'Neill for his antics, others praised him, believing that his quest for perfection helped lead the Yankees to their record-setting 1998 performance. Also contributing greatly to that memorable campaign was the selfless attitude that the members of the team took with them to the park each day, one that O'Neill put into words when he said, "You play the game to win the game, and not to worry about what's on the back of the baseball card at the end of the year."

The Yankees found it difficult to replace O'Neill's leadership when he officially announced his retirement at the conclusion of the 2001 campaign. After capturing four of the previous six world championships, it took them eight years to win another World Series. The Yankees have also had a hard time finding anyone capable of posting the type of offensive numbers O'Neill consistently compiled for them during his time in New York. In his nine years as a Yankee, O'Neill hit 185 home runs, knocked in 858 runs, scored 720 others, and batted .303. He also hit 10 homers and drove in 34 runs in 76 postseason games.

YANKEE CAREER HIGHLIGHTS

Best Season

A strong case could be made for O'Neill's 1997 or 1998 campaign. In the first of those years, he hit 21 homers, drove in a career-high 117 runs, batted .324, compiled a .399 on-base percentage, and posted a .514 slugging percentage. One year later, O'Neill hit 24 home runs, knocked in 116 runs, batted .317, finished with a .372 on-base percentage and a .510 slugging percentage, and established career bests with 95 runs scored and 191 hits.

Still, it is difficult to go against O'Neill's fabulous 1994 performance. Although the season ended prematurely, limiting the right fielder to 103 games, 21 home runs, and 83 runs batted in, he posted career highs in batting average (.359), on-base percentage (.460), and slugging percentage (.603). Although there is no way of knowing with any amount of certainty how O'Neill would have fared had the season been allowed to run its natural course, he was on pace to establish career highs with 30 homers, 120 RBIs, and 100 runs scored.

Memorable Moments/Greatest Performances

Although O'Neill hit three home runs in one game for the Yankees on August 31, 1995, he created the most indelible images of himself in the minds of most Yankee fans with his heroic postseason performances.

The first such effort took place in game 5 of the 1996 World Series against the Atlanta Braves. Although O'Neill found himself slowed by a sore hamstring throughout the entire postseason, Yankee manager Joe Torre continued to go with his starting right fielder the full nine innings of every contest, believing that doing so gave him the best chance of winning. With the series tied at two games apiece and the Yankees clinging to a 1–0 lead in the bottom of the ninth inning, New York closer John Wetteland faced Braves pinch hitter Luis Polonia with two men out and runners on first and third. Torre's strategy appeared to have backfired when Polonia ripped a Wetteland offering deep into the right-center-field power alley. However, O'Neill justified the faith his manager placed in him by willing himself into the ball's path and fully extending his arm at the last moment to snare Polonia's drive and preserve New York's 1–0 victory. With the ball tucked safely in his glove, O'Neill pounded the outfield wall and emitted a primal scream of exultation as his teammates mobbed him.

Fully healthy the following year, O'Neill did all he could to lead the Yankees to victory over Cleveland in the ALDS. Although the Indians eventually eliminated the Yankees from the postseason tournament in five games, O'Neill put on a memorable performance, batting .421, hitting 2 home runs, and knocking in 7 runs. In game 1 at Yankee Stadium, he followed circuit blasts by teammates Tim Raines and Derek Jeter with a home run of his own, marking the first time in postseason history that a team hit three consecutive round-trippers. In game 3 at Jacobs Field, he drove in 5 of the Yankees' 6 runs and smashed a game-breaking grand slam off Chad Ogea in the fourth inning.

Yet most memorable was O'Neill's at bat in the top of the ninth inning of the decisive fifth contest. With two men out and the Yankees trailing by a score of 4–3, O'Neill drove a Jose Mesa fastball deep to straightaway center field. The ball hit high off the center field wall, failing to leave the ballpark by less than a foot. Cleveland center fielder Marquis Grissom fielded the ball quickly and threw a strike to second base that appeared to beat O'Neill to the bag. However, O'Neill slid deftly around the tag of shortstop Omar Vizquel and stretched out his hand to reach the far side of the base. His face bloodied from the slide, O'Neill subsequently left the game for a pinch runner despite his fervent objections, after which Bernie Williams lofted a long fly ball to end the game and the Yankees' season. Nevertheless, the sequence of O'Neill bludgeoning the pitch and somehow eluding Vizquel's tag has become the enduring character portrait of the ferocity with which he played.

Yankee fans shared one final memorable moment with O'Neill in game 5 of the 2001 World Series, bidding their "warrior" a fond fare-well. With the remaining games of the Fall Classic scheduled to be played in Arizona and with O'Neill having indicated earlier he likely planned to retire at the end of the year, Yankee fans began chanting his name when he took his spot in right field in the top of the ninth inning. They continued to cheer him even as the Yankees came off the field to bat in the bottom of the inning, prompting a teary-eyed O'Neill to tip his cap in appreciation. The Yankees ended up overcoming a 2–0 deficit to win the game in extra innings, although they eventually lost the series in seven games. True to his word, O'Neill announced his retirement at the conclusion of the Fall Classic. Since his retirement, his number 21 has not been worn by any Yankee player, leading to speculation that it will be officially retired at some point in the future.

NOTABLE ACHIEVEMENTS

- Knocked in more than 100 runs four times.
- Batted over .300 six straight times.
- Compiled on-base percentage in excess of .400 twice.
- Posted slugging percentage in excess of .600 once (.603 in 1994).
- 1994 AL batting champion (.359).
- Holds AL record for most stolen bases in final season (22 in 2001).
- Four-time AL All-Star.
- Five-time AL champion.
- Four-time world champion.

Roger Maris

Although Yankee fans ended up burning him in effigy, Roger Maris was a terrific all-around ballplayer who made huge contributions to five consecutive pennant-winning teams and two world championship ball clubs during his time in New York. Remembered mostly as the man who broke Babe Ruth's single-season home run record, Maris accomplished so much more after he arrived in the Bronx in 1960. The slugging right fielder captured AL MVP honors his first two years in pinstripes, won a Gold Glove for his outstanding play in the outfield, and inspired teammates with his aggressive base running. Yet, due to his inaccurate portrayal by the media, Maris left New York a hated man at the end of 1966, likely wishing he never had the temerity to challenge the great Bambino's long-standing mark.

An outstanding all-around athlete, Roger Eugene Maris originally signed with the Cleveland Indians right out of high school in 1953. After spending his early days in Cleveland's farm system primarily as a line-drive hitter, the left-handed-hitting Maris eventually learned to pull the ball under the tutelage of manager Jo Jo White while playing at Keokuk in 1954. Maris spent four years in the minor leagues before he joined the Indians as a 22-year-old outfielder in 1957. He had a solid rookie season, hitting 14 home runs and knocking in 51 runs in 116 games, but after alienating the Cleveland front office by refusing to play winter ball at the end of the year, Maris found himself jettisoned to Kansas City early in 1958.

The quiet and shy Maris thrived in Kansas City, hitting 28 home runs, driving in 80 runs, and scoring 87 others in his first year with his new team. Although injuries forced him to miss more than a month of the following campaign, the right fielder played well enough to make the All-Star Team for the first time.

Maris was quite happy playing in the small Midwestern town, and he fully expected to spend the remainder of his career there. The outfielder needed to alter his mind-set, though, when he learned he had been traded to New York for a package of four players, which included veterans Don Larsen and Hank Bauer, journeyman first baseman Marv Throneberry, and promising young outfielder/first baseman Norm Siebern. The Yankees actually had their eyes on Maris for quite some time before making the deal, believing that the outfielder's compact yet powerful left-handed swing made him a perfect fit for Yankee Stadium's short right-field porch. However, the extremely forthright Maris alienated much of the New York press corps upon his arrival in the big city by revealing to them the displeasure he felt over having to leave Kansas City.

Nevertheless, the lopsided deal paid huge dividends for the Yankees, with their new right fielder proving to be the perfect complement to Mickey Mantle in the middle of their batting order. Maris hit 39 home runs in his first year in pinstripes, finishing just one homer behind Mantle in the race for the league's home run crown. The right fielder also placed second in the circuit with 98 runs scored while leading the league with 112 runs batted in and a .581 slugging percentage and winning a Gold Glove for his outstanding work in the outfield. Maris's exceptional all-around year helped lead the Yankees to the first of five straight pennants and enabled him to edge out Mantle by three points in the league MVP voting.

Even though Maris's contributions to the success of the team over the course of the season were undeniable, Yankee fans grew somewhat resentful toward him as he continued to challenge Mantle for the league lead in home runs. They cheered Mantle wildly every time he stepped into the batter's box, while Maris barely elicited any sort of response from them.

The feelings of the fans toward Mantle and Maris gradually intensified the following year, as the two sluggers drew closer and closer to Babe Ruth's single-season home run record. Since the mark was held by a Yankee, New York fans felt that Mantle should be the one to break it. Furthermore, many people believed that Maris's .269 batting average made him unworthy of eclipsing the great Ruth's longstanding record. The fans subsequently cast Maris as an outsider and a usurper, and nothing he might have done from that point on would have been good enough to please them.

Displaying their indifference toward Maris, fewer than 15,000 fans showed up at Yankee Stadium on the season's final day to see the slugger establish a new single-season record. Yet, the importance of the right fielder to the success of the team was once again indisputable. Maris not only led the American League with 61 home runs but also topped the circuit with 141 runs batted in, 132 runs scored, and 366 total bases en route to capturing his second consecutive MVP Award. However, many people considered his record-breaking performance to be something of a fluke, and when Maris hit "only" 33 home runs the following year, his critics felt vindicated, making him the object of their wrath. Still, there were other factors that greatly contributed to the lack of popularity that Maris experienced with the fans of New York.

Adding to the furor surrounding Maris was the negative image that the New York media created of him in the local newspapers. As Maris drew closer and closer to Ruth's cherished record during the 1961 campaign, the pressure he endured intensified greatly, and the number of interview requests with which he had to comply became almost unbearable. Shy, quiet, unassuming, and uncharismatic, Maris never felt comfortable being in the spotlight. He tended to give short, honest answers to reporters' questions, and if he considered a question to be a stupid one, he said so. Maris felt extremely uncomfortable being questioned by large groups of reporters, and he conducted himself much better in one-on-one interviews. But, he always remembered if a reporter wrote something about him that he felt either misquoted or misrepresented him. In such instances, Maris invariably chose to stop dealing with the writer. As a result, some members of the media began portraying him as a sullen and moody snob.

To make matters worse, the Yankees found themselves completely unprepared for the media circus. As a result, they failed to assist Maris in any way, offering him nothing in the way of protection and setting no guidelines. As Maris said in later years, the Yankee public relations department essentially hung him out to dry. The stubborn and suspicious Maris simply did not know how to handle his newfound celebrity. As he grew increasingly suspicious and irritable over the course of the season, he granted fewer and fewer interview requests. However, when he snubbed powerful and influential sportswriter Jimmy Cannon, the latter wrote a scathing article on Maris that caused much of the public to view the outfielder in an unfavorable light.

Therefore, Yankee fans found it quite easy to question the severity of Maris's injuries. The right fielder broke his hand sliding into home plate in June 1965, causing him to lose much of the strength in the hand. X-rays taken failed to reveal the break, though, prompting the Yankees to subsequently list Maris on their injury report as day-to-day. As Maris continued to sit on the bench unable to play, fans of the team began to question his heart and desire. The already antagonistic press literally added insult to injury by questioning the outfielder's mettle. Maris later revealed that he also felt that club officials minimized the severity of the injury and that they sometimes acted as if they, too, considered him well enough to play.

Another X-ray was finally taken, which showed a small fracture of a bone in the hand. Although the hand was surgically repaired at the end of the season, the damage to Maris's reputation was irreparable. His tenuous relationship with the fans, the media, and the Yankee front office worse than ever, Maris spent his remaining time in New York being treated as an object of scorn.

However, Maris's teammates had a different perception of the man. Bobby Richardson, who played with Maris for seven seasons, said, "He was the most reserved, quiet individual I think I ever knew, so the press' portrayal of him was not the real Roger Maris."

Clete Boyer said of his former teammate, "The guy was a great player. They like to say that 1961 was a fluke, but Roger hit 39 homers and was the American League MVP in 1960. Not too many stiffs become back-to-back MVPs."

Whitey Ford discussed Maris in his book *Few and Chosen*: "He was fast, and he was a great base-runner with excellent instincts when it came to taking the extra base. And he was as good as I've seen at breaking up the double play."

Moose Skowron said of Maris, "He could run, he could throw, he could hit . . . great defensive outfielder. He did the little things to win a ballgame . . . and the writers crucified him . . . no way."

In speaking of Maris, Mickey Mantle said, "When people think of Roger, they think of the 61 home runs, but Roger Maris was one of the best all-around players I ever saw. He was as good a fielder as I ever saw, he had a great arm, he was a great base-runner—I never saw him make a mistake on the bases—and he was a great teammate. Everybody liked him."

Perhaps Gil McDougald said it best when he said, "Roger was the everyday ballplayer that every manager would like to see on a ball-club."

Maris was also a winner. He played in more World Series than any other player in the 1960s. In addition to his five World Series appearances with the Yankees, he helped the St. Louis Cardinals capture the NL pennant in 1967 and 1968, after the Yankees dealt him to the Cardinals for journeyman third baseman Charley Smith at the conclusion of the 1966 campaign. Maris ended his seven-year stay in New York with 203 home runs, 547 runs batted in, 520 runs scored, a .265 batting average, a .356 on-base percentage, and a .515 slugging percentage.

Maris left New York despondent and disappointed that things could not have been different between himself and Yankee fans. After retiring from baseball at the end of the 1968 season, he opened a Budweiser Beer distributorship in Gainesville, Florida, where he resided following his playing career. Maris stayed away from Yankee Stadium for more than a decade, declining numerous invitations to Old-Timer's Day. However, he finally agreed to come back when George Steinbrenner offered to donate money to build a stadium in Gainesville. Maris made his return on opening day 1978, fittingly raising the Yankees' 1977 championship flag with Mickey Mantle and being given a standing ovation when he received his introduction to the crowd.

The fans at Yankee Stadium again cheered Maris loudly when he returned to the ballpark in 1984 to have his old number 9 retired, along with the number 32 worn by his deceased teammate Elston Howard. Maris displayed the kind of emotions during his acceptance speech that he previously failed to show the public—the sort of emotions that Yankee fans had longed to see from him during his tenure with the team.

Roger Maris passed away just one year later from lymph gland cancer. Shortly before his death on December 14, 1985, he said, "I always came across as being bitter. I'm not bitter. People were very reluctant to give me any credit. I thought hitting 60 home runs was something. But everyone shied off. Why, I don't know. Maybe I wasn't the chosen one, but I was the one who got the record."

YANKEE CAREER HIGHLIGHTS

Best Season

Was there ever any doubt? Maris's 1961 campaign was easily the greatest of his career. He captured AL MVP honors for the second consecutive year by leading the league with 61 home runs, 141 runs batted in, 132 runs scored, and 366 total bases—all career highs. Although Maris batted just .269, he walked 94 times, enabling him to compile a very respectable .372 on-base percentage (also the highest mark of his career). His .620 slugging percentage also represented the best figure he ever posted.

Memorable Moments/Greatest Performances

Mickey Mantle often said that Roger Maris eclipsing Babe Ruth's single-season home run record was the greatest feat he ever saw anyone accomplish in baseball. The pressure that Maris endured as he moved inexorably closer to Ruth's mark indeed made his performance that much more amazing. For one specific moment, though, I will opt for Maris's record-setting 61st homer, a blast immortalized over the air waves by a screaming Phil Rizzuto—another Yankee legend.

NOTABLE ACHIEVEMENTS

- Held Major League Baseball's single-season home run record (61 in 1961) for 37 years.
- Hit more than 30 home runs three times.
- Knocked in more than 100 runs three times.
- Scored more than 100 runs once (132 in 1961).
- Compiled slugging percentage in excess of .600 once (.620 in 1961).
- Led AL in home runs, runs scored, total bases, and slugging percentage once each and in RBIs twice.
- AL MVP in 1960 and 1961.
- Two-time *Sporting News* All-Star selection (1960 and 1961).
- Three-time AL All-Star.
- 1960 Gold Glove winner.
- Five-time AL champion.
- Two-time world champion.

23

Jack Chesbro

If any Yankee pitcher ever put together a season capable of rivaling the one Ron Guidry compiled for the team in 1978, that hurler was Jack Chesbro. Pitching for the New York Highlanders (who eventually became the Yankees) in 1904, the spitballing right-hander recorded a season of historic proportions, winning a 20th-century record 41 games while tossing 455 innings and 48 complete games. Almost single-handedly, Chesbro came within a hair of leading the franchise to its first American League pennant, failing to do so on the season's final day when he uncorked a wild pitch that haunted him the rest of his life.

Nicknamed "Happy Jack" for his pleasant demeanor, John Dwight Chesbro originally broke into the major leagues as a 25-year-old with the National League's Pittsburgh Pirates in 1899. After experiencing a moderate amount of success his first two years in Pittsburgh, Chesbro developed into one of the senior circuit's better pitchers in 1901, when he finished 21–10, with a 2.38 ERA, 26 complete games, and a league-leading 6 shutouts. The 28-year-old right-hander evolved into a full-fledged star the following year, when, pitching for a Pirates team that captured the National League pennant by a record 27 1/2 games, he finished 28–6 to lead all NL hurlers in wins and winning percentage (.824). He also topped the circuit with 8 shutouts, compiled a 2.17 ERA, and threw 31 complete games.

Offered a lucrative contract by the newly formed New York Highlanders of the upstart American League at the conclusion of the campaign, Chesbro jumped to the rival league, where he immediately established himself as the ace of New York's pitching staff. The Highlanders won 72 games in their inaugural season, and Chesbro posted

21 of those victories. He ended the year with a record of 21–15, a 2.77 ERA, 33 complete games, and 325 innings pitched.

Although Chesbro featured the usual assortment of pitches, he relied heavily on the spitball to thwart opposing batters. Highlander manager Clark Griffith, a fine pitcher in his own right, discussed Chesbro's use of the pitch, which remained legal until 1920: "I still remember the first day he threw the spitball in a regular game. We were playing Cleveland. He had a tough first inning. They hit him for three runs. He came back to the bench and said, 'Griff, I haven't got my natural stuff today. I'm going to give 'em the spitter the next inning, if it's all right with you.' I told him to go to it, and you know what? He fanned 14. They didn't get another run and we won the game 4 to 3."

Chesbro exceeded all expectations the following year, when he compiled one of the most amazing seasons in major-league history. In addition to leading all American League pitchers with a record of 41–12, Chesbro topped the circuit with 51 starts, 48 complete games, and 455 innings pitched. He also finished among the leaders with a 1.82 ERA, 6 shutouts, and 239 strikeouts. Chesbro incredibly completed his first 30 starts, failing to go the distance only three times the entire year. Yet, tarnishing Chesbro's brilliant performance was a single pitch he replayed in his mind for years to come.

Primarily because of Chesbro, the Highlanders entered the season's final week with an opportunity to overtake the Boston Americans for first place in the standings. New York faced Boston in a critical five-game series at season's end, with the AL pennant at stake. Chesbro defeated the Americans in the first contest, giving the Highlanders a slim half-game lead. Boston won each of the next two games, though, retaking first place by a margin of 1 1/2 games. Chesbro returned to the mound for the first game of a season-ending doubleheader, which the Highlanders needed to sweep to finish atop the AL standings. The score remained tied at 2–2 heading into the top of the ninth inning, when Boston placed a runner at third base with two men out. At that juncture, Chesbro unleashed a spitball on a 0–2 count to Freddy Parent. Reports conflict whether the pitch sailed over the head of catcher Deacon McGuire or if McGuire reacted slowly to Chesbro's offering. Regardless of who was primarily at fault, the Boston runner scored from third as the ball rolled to the backstop, giving the Americans the victory and the AL pennant. New York had to settle for a close second-place finish, ending the year with a record of 92–59.

Chesbro spent four more full seasons in New York, never again coming close to matching his record-setting performance. However, he remained an effective pitcher, winning 23 games once and posting

19 victories another time, while compiling an ERA below 3.00 all four years. Chesbro moved on to Boston in 1909, where he ended his career as a member of the Red Sox. Chesbro concluded his time in New York with an overall record of 128–93, a 2.58 ERA, 227 starts, 168 complete games, and 1,952 innings pitched. He ranks third in team history in complete games, fifth in earned run average, and tenth in innings pitched. Although Chesbro pitched for two pennant-winning clubs in Pittsburgh, surpassed 20 victories on five occasions, and compiled a lifetime record of 198–132 over 11 major-league seasons, he gained admittance to the Baseball Hall of Fame through the Old Timers Committee in 1946 primarily on the strength of his remarkable 1904 campaign.

YANKEE (HIGHLANDER) CAREER HIGHLIGHTS

Best Season

Another no-brainer. Chesbro's 1904 season not only easily ranks as the best of his career but arguably as one of the 10 greatest seasons by a pitcher in baseball history. His 41 victories remain the most wins compiled by a hurler in a single season since 1893, standing as the "modern day" record for well over 100 years.

Memorable Moments/Greatest Performances

On April 22, 1903, Chesbro pitched the very first game in the history of the franchise that eventually came to be known as the New York Yankees, losing a 3–1 decision to the Washington Senators.

Yet, in spite of his fabulous performance over the course of the 1904 campaign, Chesbro pitched his most memorable game for the Highlanders on the final day of that unforgettable season, dropping a 3–2 decision to Boston that gave the Americans the AL pennant. The stigma attached to the loss and what was officially labeled a wild pitch marred the remainder of Chesbro's life. More than his modern-record 41 wins, that game came to be the most vivid memory of Chesbro's playing career. Long after his death in 1931, his widow continued her futile efforts to have the official scorer's decision on the pitch changed to a passed ball.

NOTABLE ACHIEVEMENTS

- Holds modern day record with 41 wins in 1904.
- Three-time 20-game winner.

- Compiled ERA below 2.00 once (1.82 in 1904).
- Completed at least 30 games twice.
- Threw more than 300 innings four times, tossing more than 400 frames once.
- Struck out more than 200 batters once (239 in 1904).
- Led AL pitchers in wins (41), winning percentage (.774), complete games (48), and innings pitched (455) in 1904.

㉔

Thurman Munson

Although his career numbers fail to approach the figures compiled by some of the Yankee immortals who precede him on this list, Thurman Munson gained icon-like status among Yankee fans during his relatively brief time in New York with his clutch hitting, tremendous work ethic, exceptional leadership ability, and hard-nosed style of play. The first player to be named Yankee captain since Lou Gehrig during the 1930s, Munson played the game with grit and determination, epitomizing Yankee pride and perseverance. Under his leadership, the franchise emerged from one of its darkest periods into its next era of greatness. The Yankees won three straight American League pennants and two world championships with Munson stationed behind the plate, bringing 11 years of futility to an end.

A rich tradition of outstanding receivers already existed on the Yankees by the time that Thurman Lee Munson assumed the team's starting catching duties in 1970, with Bill Dickey, Yogi Berra, and Elston Howard taking turns manning the position for the ball club the previous 40 seasons. However, unlike his three exceptional predecessors, Munson arrived in New York brimming with so much self-confidence that he not only annoyed many opposing players but also surprised some of his own teammates. Within a few years, though, Munson established himself as one of the American League's most admired and respected players and as one of the most beloved figures in New York sports history.

Born in Akron, Ohio, on June 7, 1947, Munson starred in baseball, football, and basketball in high school before attending Kent State University on a baseball scholarship. Upon his graduation, the 21-year-old Munson was selected by the Yankees with the fourth overall pick of the 1968 amateur draft. Ascending rapidly through the New York farm system, Munson appeared in fewer than 100 minor-league games before he earned a permanent call-up to the majors in August 1969. In 86 at bats with New York over the season's final two months, Munson batted .256 and hit his first major-league home run. His performance so impressed the members of the Yankee front office that they traded away incumbent receiver Frank Fernandez during the off-season, all but handing the starting job to Munson.

Still, the trust that the Yankee front office placed in Munson failed to exceed the amount of confidence the young man had in his own abilities. Former teammate and close friend Bobby Murcer, who was in his first full major-league season himself when Munson joined the team in 1969, said of the receiver, "He felt like he belonged the first time he stepped on the field here at Yankee Stadium. . . . The late '60s and early '70s, rookies were supposed to be seen and not heard. Thurman was a different kind of rookie—he was seen and heard."

Fellow Kent State alumnus Gene Michael, who roomed with Munson during the latter's first few years in the league, suggested, "Thurman got away with more things as a rookie than most players would. For some reason, they accepted Thurman quickly . . . his brashness and that. But he really wasn't that way. He was very concerned and compassionate in a lot of ways."

The confidence that Munson had in himself helped him make it through the difficult early days of his 1970 rookie season. Off to a terrible start, he continued to believe in himself, as did manager Ralph Houk, who stuck with the struggling rookie despite his early slump. Munson rewarded Houk by finishing the season with a .302 batting average and winning American League Rookie of the Year honors. Although his average dropped to .251 the following season, Munson made the All-Star Team for the first of seven times, beginning a long-time rivalry shortly thereafter with Boston's Carlton Fisk, who captured AL Rookie of the Year honors the following year.

More than just a solid hitter, Munson displayed remarkable quickness and agility behind the plate his first few years in the league. While he lacked Johnny Bench's powerful throwing arm, Munson had perhaps the quickest release in baseball, and he displayed an extraordinary amount of agility coming out from behind the plate on slowly hit balls.

Mel Stottlemyre, who pitched to Munson in the latter's early years on the team, stated, "He was so sure of himself, and so sure of what he could do behind the plate. He was known for his quickness behind the plate. He was as quick as anybody I've ever seen coming out from behind that crouch on bunted balls and on his throws to second base."

Although Munson's throwing efficiency suffered in later years due to the constant pounding that he endured behind the plate, he excelled as a defender early in his career. In addition to his tremendous quickness, Munson had an accurate throwing arm, committing only 1 error throughout the entire 1971 campaign.

Munson neither hit for much power nor drove in a lot of runs during the early stages of his career. He failed to hit more than 10 home runs or drive in more than 53 runs in any of his first three seasons. Primarily an opposite-field line-drive hitter at that juncture, Munson generally chose not to challenge old Yankee Stadium's "Death Valley" in left-center and center field. As a result, he usually batted second in the Yankee lineup. However, Munson began to find his power stroke in 1973, when he simultaneously improved his technique at turning on inside pitches and relaxing when he stepped into the batter's box with men on base. In his first truly productive offensive season, Munson hit 20 home runs, knocked in 74 runs, and batted .301.

In addition to increasing his offensive productivity, Munson became more of a team leader. Extremely competitive and possessing a burning desire to win, he challenged his teammates to work as hard as they possibly could, always seeking to bring out the best in them.

Outfielder Elliott Maddox, who had his best major-league season in his first year with the team in 1974, spoke of the kind of leader Munson was and of the influence he had on him: "If Thurman was on your case and telling you, 'You have to apply yourself more, you have to do this, or you have to do that because you know you're capable of it,' it meant he liked you. So, he loved me because he never gave me a moment's peace. . . . So, you would want to do it, just to get him off your back."

Munson reached his peak during the mid-1970s, batting over .300 and driving in more than 100 runs three straight times, from 1975 to 1977. After batting a career-high .318 in the first of those seasons, he captured AL MVP honors in 1976 by hitting 17 home runs, driving in 105 runs, batting .302, and leading the Yankees to their first pennant in 12 seasons. The following year, Munson hit 18 homers, knocked in 100 runs, and batted .308. However, due to the number of injuries that he sustained over the years from catching more than 130 games virtually every season, Munson's productivity began to decline in 1978. Although he batted .297, he hit only 6 home runs and knocked in just 71 runs. Yet, he helped lead his team to the world championship for the second straight season with his clutch hitting, superb handling of pitchers, and tremendous leadership qualities. In fact, many of his teammates considered Munson to be the most important and indispensable player on the team—in essence, the glue that held the rest of the ball club together.

Ron Guidry, who became a regular member of the starting rotation in 1977, said, "Having him there, everybody kind of revolved around him, because you could take me out of a game and they could still play and win. You could take somebody else out and they could probably still win. But, if you took Thurman out, our chances of winning were half as good."

Guidry also spoke of the confidence that Munson instilled in his pitchers:

> Pitching was made easier because I got to throw to a guy like Thurman. He made pitchers that were average ones good. He made them win a lot of games because of his ability to take all the pressure and call the game. We all felt like: "That's the best pitch to throw. I'm not gonna second-guess it and say it's not." I could have thrown a guy 20 sliders and made him look foolish, but, if he called for a fastball, that's what I threw.

Willie Randolph, who joined the Yankees in Munson's MVP season of 1976, discussed the catcher's all-around ability:

> When you think of Thurman Munson, you think about the total package. This man could even run. Most catchers back then would just go base to base. Thurman would take you first to third in a minute. If you needed an RBI, he could hit that patented line drive to right to drive in runs. If you needed a home run, he could turn on you and take you deep; the total package. I don't think, even when you talk about the great catchers of the game—and he was obviously up there—none of those guys really did everything well like Thurman did. He did everything that was necessary to win.

While Munson's offensive production began to decline his final two seasons, he nevertheless accomplished enough his first several years in the league to be grouped with the great Yankees catchers who preceded him. In fact, Munson was quite proud of his linkage to Bill Dickey, Yogi Berra, and Elston Howard. Like Berra and Howard, he earned AL MVP honors. He also finished in the top 10 in the voting two other times. In addition to being named to the American League All-Star Team a total of seven times, Munson earned four selections to the *Sporting News* All-Star Team and three Gold Gloves.

After struggling somewhat with men on base early in his career, Munson gradually developed into one of the finest clutch performers of his time. Longtime Kansas City Royals batting coach Charlie Lau commented, "Of all the Yankee hitters, Thurman Munson was the one that scared me the most when he came up. He had that swing and that heart, he was just totally clutch."

Lau's statement was well founded. In 14 ALCS games, Munson hit 2 home runs, knocked in 10 runs, and batted .339. In 16 World Series contests, he hit 1 homer, drove in 12 runs, and batted .373. Even though the Yankees were swept by Cincinnati in the 1976 World Series, Munson batted .529 and had 6 hits in his final 6 at bats.

Demonstrating the admiration and respect that many of Munson's opponents had for him, Reds catcher Johnny Bench stated, "I was always totally amazed at Thurman. I thought he was one of the greatest competitors I've ever known."

Munson's competitive spirit prompted Reggie Jackson to write of his former teammate in his autobiography, "Had he lived, I bet we would have won two more World Series in New York, both in 1980 and in 1981."

Unfortunately, Munson was not a member of the Yankees in either of those years since his life tragically ended on August 2, 1979. While practicing takeoffs and landings in his private plane in Akron, Ohio, Munson perished when his aircraft hit a tree. Munson's tragic death stunned his teammates and Yankee fans alike, leaving everyone associated with the ball club in a state of shock. Perhaps Ron Guidry expressed everyone's feelings best when he said, "I had the feeling that it would never be the same. I said to myself: 'I'm gonna win games, but it will never be the same again, because you can't replace him.' There was no way to replace that man."

Thurman Munson's career ended with him having hit 113 home runs, driven in 701 runs, scored 696 others, collected 1,558 hits, and batted .292. More than 30 years have now passed since Munson played his last game for the Yankees. Nevertheless, he continues to remain a prominent figure in the hearts and minds of Yankee fans and players alike. Munson's locker remained empty in the old Yankee Stadium clubhouse—unused by anyone since his death. It has since been moved to the new Yankee Stadium to serve as a reminder of the team's fallen captain.

Joe Torre, who managed the Yankees to 4 world championships and 12 consecutive playoff appearances during his 12 seasons in the Bronx, once suggested, "The way [Munson] played the game exemplifies what we have been about. . . . I just sense that Thurman is in everybody's ear during the course of the season. There's no question his presence in the clubhouse is felt because of his locker."

CAREER HIGHLIGHTS

Best Season

Munson had four truly outstanding seasons, any of which could be classified as the finest of his career. Although he knocked in only 74 runs in 1973 due primarily to a rather mediocre supporting cast, Munson batted .301, compiled a .362 on-base percentage, and established career highs with 20 home runs, 29 doubles, and a .487 slugging percentage. He posted extremely comparable numbers in each of the three years in which he batted over .300 and drove in more than 100 runs. Since Munson captured AL MVP honors in 1976 and performed extraordinarily well during the postseason, I will go with that campaign. In addition to hitting 17 homers, batting .302, and knocking in a career-high 105 runs, Munson batted .435 against Kansas City in the ALCS, before posting a batting average of .529 against Cincinnati in the World Series.

Memorable Moments/Greatest Performances

Certainly, Munson's exceptional hitting against the Reds during Cincinnati's four-game sweep of the Yankees in the 1976 World Series has to rank among his greatest performances. The catcher's 6 hits in his final 6 plate appearances demonstrated his grittiness, determination, and unyielding nature, since he refused to admit defeat even as Cincinnati's powerful "Big Red Machine" continued to overwhelm the Yankees.

Nevertheless, the one moment that perhaps defined Munson more than any other occurred during game 3 of the 1978 ALCS against the Kansas City Royals. With the series knotted at a game apiece and the Yankees trailing by a run late in the contest, Munson stepped to the plate with one man on base, not having homered in more than two months due to a badly damaged shoulder and bruised and battered body. Yet, the Yankee captain somehow summoned the strength to hit a ball some 30 feet over the 430-foot sign in deepest left-center field at Yankee Stadium to win the game. The blow enabled the Yankees to overcome a 3–home run performance by George Brett and take a 2–1 lead in the series. They finished off the Royals the next evening and went on to capture their second straight world championship by defeating the Los Angeles Dodgers in the World Series.

NOTABLE ACHIEVEMENTS

- Knocked in more than 100 runs three times.
- Batted over .300 five times.
- Compiled lifetime batting average of .357 in postseason play, with 3 home runs and 22 RBIs in 30 games.
- Hit safely in all but 1 of 16 World Series games in which he played.
- 1970 AL Rookie of the Year.
- AL MVP in 1976.
- Four-time *Sporting News* All-Star selection.
- Seven-time AL All-Star.
- Three-time Gold Glove winner.
- Three-time AL champion.
- Two-time world champion.

25

Reggie Jackson

The fact that the Yankees eventually retired Reggie Jackson's number 44 seems to indicate that the slugging right fielder deserves a higher place in these rankings. Also supporting that notion are the enormous contributions that Jackson made to four division-winning teams, three pennant winners, and two world championship ball clubs during his years in pinstripes. Nevertheless, the simple facts are that "Mr. October" spent just five years in New York and that he was a productive player in only four of those. As a result, Jackson must settle for the number 25 spot, instead of the higher ranking that many Yankee fans likely would accord him.

Reginald Martinez Jackson had already established himself as one of baseball's premier players by the time he joined the Yankees in 1977. The boastful outfielder helped to foster that notion by announcing shortly after he signed with the team, "I didn't come to New York to be a star . . . I brought my star with me."

While Jackson's braggadocio and narcissistic tendencies tended to rub many people the wrong way, he undoubtedly felt that he earned the right to make such proclamations due to the body of work he produced as a member of the Oakland A's. Jackson helped lead Oakland to five straight AL West titles from 1971 to 1975 and consecutive world championships in 1972, 1973, and 1974. During that time, Jackson proved to be the A's most dynamic offensive player, frequently leading the team in home runs and runs batted in, while exciting fans around the league with his awesome power at the plate and colorful persona. Jackson had his two best years in Oakland in 1969 and 1973. In the first of those campaigns, he batted .275, compiled a .410 on-base percentage, hit 47 homers, drove in 118 runs, and led the American

League with 123 runs scored and a .608 slugging percentage. Reggie earned AL MVP honors in 1973 by batting .293 and topping the circuit with 32 home runs, 117 runs batted in, 99 runs scored, and a .531 slugging percentage.

Although Jackson led the A's to their fifth straight AL West title in 1975 by driving in 104 runs, scoring 91 others, and hitting a league-leading 36 homers, he left Oakland at the end of the year. With free agency looming for the outfielder at the conclusion of the 1976 campaign, controversial A's owner Charlie Finley elected to deal his most prominent player to the Baltimore Orioles. Jackson spent one year in Baltimore, finishing among the league leaders with 27 home runs and 91 runs batted in and topping the circuit with a .502 slugging percentage.

The American League's most charismatic player began courting potential suitors shortly after the 1976 campaign ended. Although Jackson received substantial offers from several other teams, he eventually chose to sign with the Yankees. Explaining his decision, Jackson stated that he selected the Yankees because "George Steinbrenner simply out-hustled everyone else." The Yankee owner's persistence certainly made a favorable impression on the market's most sought-after free agent. There also is little doubt that the five-year deal worth almost $3 million helped the slugger make up his mind.

The marriage of Jackson and the Yankees seemed to be a natural: the American League's most flamboyant player performing on the world's largest stage. While still a member of the A's in 1973, Jackson once boasted, "If I was playing in New York, they'd name a candy bar after me."

Jackson's boastful manner alienated him from several of his new teammates before he even joined the club in spring training. Particularly resentful of the slugger was New York's emotionally fragile manager Billy Martin, who viewed Jackson as a threat to his relationship with Steinbrenner. Nevertheless, Jackson's reputation and immense talent forced even his harshest critics to acknowledge the importance of his acquisition. Jackson, though, created additional feelings of animosity when he made several ill-advised comments during a supposedly off-the-record conversation with *SPORT* magazine writer Robert Ward during spring training.

As the two men sat together having drinks at a local bar, the subject of Jackson's potential contributions to the team arose. According to Jackson, he noted that the Yankees had won the pennant the previous year but subsequently lost the World Series to the Cincinnati Reds in four straight games. The team's new right fielder then suggested that New York needed one more thing to win it all, and he pointed out the various ingredients in his drink. Ward suggested that Jackson might be "the straw that stirs the drink," a notion with which the slugger found no fault. However, when the story appeared in the May 1977 issue of *SPORT*, Ward quoted Jackson as saying, "This team, it all flows from me. I'm the straw that stirs the drink. Maybe I should say me and [Thurman] Munson, but he can only stir it bad."

Although Jackson has continued to suggest that his comments were taken out of context and that he never said anything negative about Munson during the interview, Ward has maintained through the years that he quoted Jackson accurately. Giving further credence to Ward's version of the story is an article that later appeared in the *New York Times* in which writer Dave Anderson revealed that the slugger made similar comments to him during a July 1977 conversation. Anderson suggested that Jackson told him, "I'm still the straw that stirs the drink. Not Munson, not nobody else on this club."

Munson's status as team captain and arguably the most beloved player on the Yankees caused virtually all his teammates to develop a dislike for Jackson. Several of them never forgave the slugger, while others eventually learned to accept his boastful manner as a necessary evil. Jackson later attempted to explain his actions by saying, "I wanted to be part of the Yankee family, and when everyone didn't greet me with open arms, I drew back, got more insecure, and started running my mouth a little."

Jackson's braggadocio made his first several months in New York extremely difficult ones, especially since it further intensified manager Billy Martin's feelings of resentment toward him. Martin refused to bat Jackson in the prestigious cleanup spot in the batting order, choosing instead to place him in the fifth or sixth slot. The relationship between the two men grew increasingly contentious over the course of the season, until their anger finally boiled over on June 18 during a 10–4 loss to the Boston Red Sox in a nationally televised game at Fenway Park. Feeling that Jackson failed to properly charge a bloop hit by Red Sox slugger Jim Rice, Martin immediately replaced his right fielder with Paul Blair. When Jackson arrived at the Yankee dugout, Martin confronted him at the top step, yelling that Jackson had shown him up. As the two men continued to argue, Jackson claimed that Martin's heavy drinking had impaired his judgment. Despite being 18 years older, 2 inches shorter, and some 40 pounds lighter than Jackson, the irate Yankee manager lunged at the superstar outfielder, prompting coaches Yogi Berra and Elston Howard to quickly restrain him.

Even though Jackson experienced a tremendous amount of adversity during his first year in pinstripes, he ended up having a very productive season. The 31-year-old outfielder batted .286, scored 93 runs, stole 17 bases, and led New York with 32 home runs and 110 runs batted in. Particularly effective after team leaders Munson and Lou Piniella convinced Martin to bat Jackson cleanup, he hit 13 home runs and knocked in 49 runs over his final 50 games. Jackson's strong second-half performance helped the Yankees win the AL East by a margin of 2 1/2 games over Boston and Baltimore. They then faced Kansas City in the ALCS for the second straight year, once again coming out on top in a hard-fought five-game series. Although Jackson struggled terribly at the plate against the Royals, he delivered a huge hit during New York's late-inning, come-from-behind rally in the decisive fifth game. His greatest heroics, though, had yet to come.

The Yankees took a 3–2 lead against the Dodgers in the World Series, which returned to Yankee Stadium for game 6. Jackson, who hit a home run in each of the previous two contests, drew a four-pitch walk in his first plate appearance. In a truly amazing performance, he then proceeded to hit three consecutive home runs, each on the first pitch, against three different Dodger pitchers. The last blast, a towering drive into the black-painted batter's-eye seats well beyond the center-field wall, some 475 feet from home plate, enabled Jackson to join Babe Ruth as the only players ever to hit 3 home runs in one World Series game (Albert Pujols later accomplished the feat as well). Since Jackson also homered off Don Sutton in his final at bat in game 5, he accomplished the remarkable feat of hitting 4 home runs on four consecutive swings of the bat against four different Dodger pitchers. Leading New York to victory almost single-handedly in game 6, Jackson earned series MVP honors, becoming the first player to do so with two different teams. Mr. October finished the Fall Classic with 5 home runs, 8 runs batted in, 10 runs scored, a .450 batting average, a .542 on-base percentage, and a .755 slugging percentage.

The toast of New York following his incredible 1977 World Series performance, Jackson nevertheless continued to experience problems with Billy Martin the following year, until the manager finally resigned under a cloud of controversy midway through the campaign. Buoyed by the confidence placed in him by new Yankee manager Bob Lemon, Jackson helped New York overcome a 14-game deficit to first-place Boston over the season's final two months, finishing the year with 27 home runs and 97 runs batted in. He then lived up to his Mr. October billing by batting .462 against the Royals in the ALCS, before hitting 2 home runs, driving in 8 runs, and batting .391 during New York's six-game World Series triumph over Los Angeles.

Jackson spent three more years in New York, having his best season in 1980, when he led the American League with 41 home runs, knocked in 111 runs, scored 94 others, and batted a career-high .300 to earn a second-place finish to George Brett in the league MVP voting. A subpar 1981 campaign by Jackson prompted George Steinbrenner to allow the right fielder to leave via free agency at season's end. The 36-year-old outfielder ended up signing with the California Angels, for whom he had his last big year. Jackson finished the 1982 season with 101 runs batted in, 92 runs scored, a .275 batting average, and a league-leading 39 home runs, prompting Steinbrenner to later admit that "letting Reggie go was the biggest mistake I ever made." Jackson spent four more years with the Angels, never again approaching those numbers, before ending his career back in Oakland in 1987.

Jackson left the game with 563 career home runs, 1,702 runs batted in, 1,551 runs scored, and 2,584 hits. He hit 144 of those home runs as a member of the Yankees; he also knocked in 461 runs, scored 380 others, collected 661 hits, and batted .281 while wearing the pinstripes. Jackson earned AL All-Star honors in each of his five seasons in New York.

After his retirement as an active player, Jackson pursued numerous business ventures before returning to the game, first as an advisor to the Oakland A's and, later, to the Yankees.

YANKEE CAREER HIGHLIGHTS

Best Season

Although Jackson arguably had one or two better years in Oakland, he had his finest season for the Yankees in 1980, when he helped lead them to their best record in 17 years. The Yankees finished first in the AL East with a mark of 103–59, with Jackson earning a second-place finish in the league MVP voting by topping the circuit with 41 home runs, knocking in 111 runs, scoring 94 others, batting .300 for the only time in his career, and compiling a .398 on-base percentage and a .597 slugging percentage.

Memorable Moments/Greatest Performances

Jackson's unfortunate altercation with Billy Martin in the Yankee dugout during that 10–4 loss to the Red Sox at Fenway Park on June 18,

1977, came to symbolize in many ways the tumultuous nature of the enigmatic slugger's five-year stay in New York. Nevertheless, Jackson's greatest performance and clearly his most memorable moment in a Yankee uniform took place in game 6 of the 1977 World Series, when he hit three consecutive home runs against the Dodgers to give the Yankees their first world championship in 15 years. Jackson's extraordinary effort remains one of the most amazing performances in the history of the Fall Classic.

NOTABLE ACHIEVEMENTS

- Hit more than 30 home runs twice.
- Knocked in more than 100 runs twice.
- Batted .300 once.
- One of only 3 players in major-league history to hit 3 home runs in 1 World Series game (game 6 of 1977 series).
- 1977 World Series MVP.
- 1980 *Sporting News* All-Star selection.
- Five-time AL All-Star.
- Three-time AL champion.
- Two-time world champion.

Herb Pennock

A couple of Hall of Fame pitchers take up the next two spots in the rankings, with Herb Pennock and Waite Hoyt compiling numbers so similar during their years in pinstripes that their places here are almost interchangeable. Pennock posted a record of 162–90 and an ERA of 3.54 over the course of 11 seasons with the Yankees, while Hoyt finished 157–98 with an ERA of 3.48 in his 10 seasons in the Bronx. The two men finished extremely close in most other statistical categories as well, making it quite difficult to rank one ahead of the other. In the end, I elected to place Pennock one spot ahead of Hoyt due to the former's perfect 5–0 record in World Series play (Hoyt compiled a mark of 6–3 for the Yankees in the Fall Classic).

Known for his effortless pitching style and ability to win big games, Herb Pennock was one of many players that Yankees owner Jacob Ruppert literally stole from the Boston Red Sox. After originally signing with Connie Mack's Philadelphia Athletics as an 18-year-old in 1912, Pennock joined the Red Sox midway through the 1915 campaign. The left-hander subsequently spent parts of the next seven seasons in Boston, compiling a rather mediocre 62–59 record while in Beantown. With Boston owner Harry Frazee making it a regular practice to sell many of his best players to the Yankees, Pennock found himself dealt to New York on January 30, 1923, for three nondescript players and $50,000.

Pennock thrived in New York, employing his two principles of pitching—"observing the enemy" and "conserving the energy"—to post a regular-season record of 19–6 in 1923, which enabled him to lead all American League pitchers with a .760 winning percentage. He then began to establish his reputation as an outstanding "big game" pitcher by defeating the Giants twice in the World Series, giving the Yankees their first world championship in the process.

Pennock followed that up with arguably his finest all-around season in 1924. Although the Yankees failed to capture their fourth straight American League pennant, finishing second to the Washington Senators, Pennock compiled a record of 21–9, along with a 2.83 ERA and a career-high 25 complete games. The crafty southpaw had another big year in 1926, posting 23 victories and tossing 19 complete games en route to helping the Yankees edge out Cleveland for the league championship. The Yankees subsequently lost the World Series to the Cardinals in seven games, but Pennock pitched exceptionally well during the Fall Classic, tossing two complete game victories, throwing four scoreless innings in relief, and compiling an ERA of 1.23 over 22 total innings of work.

Pennock continued his outstanding work in each of the next two seasons, posting a combined record of 36–14 while compiling earned run averages of 3.00 and 2.56. He also led all AL hurlers with 5 shutouts in 1928. However, the 1928 campaign turned out to be Pennock's last season as a top-notch starter. After shutting out Boston on three hits on August 12, the 34-year-old left-hander found himself unable to raise his arm to comb his hair. Listed as day-to-day, Pennock missed the rest of the season, including the World Series. He never again returned to top form, hanging on with the Yankees as a fifth or sixth starter until 1932, when he moved to the bullpen. Nevertheless, Pennock continued to excel in big-game situations, saving games 3 and 4 of the Yankees' 1932 World Series sweep of the Chicago Cubs. After Pennock limited Chicago to two singles over four innings of work, the newspapers dismissed the Cubs as "young fellows taking lessons from an artist."

It was Pennock's effortless style of pitching that enabled him to garner such praise. He had a graceful, almost languid pitching motion, threw mostly breaking pitches, and never seemed to exert himself. Longtime Yankee receiver Bill Dickey once stated, "You can catch Pennock sitting in a rocking chair."

Following his outstanding performance against the Cubs in the 1932 World Series, Pennock spent only one more year in New York. Released by the Yankees at the conclusion of the 1933 campaign, he returned to Boston, where he ended his playing career the following season. Pennock retired from baseball with an overall record of 241–162 and a 3.60 ERA. In addition to compiling a mark of 162–90 and an ERA of 3.54 with the Yankees, he threw 164 complete games and 2,203 innings while wearing the pinstripes. Pennock ranks in the team's all-time top 10 in wins, complete games, and innings pitched. The members of the Baseball Writers Association of America elected Pennock to the Hall of Fame in 1948, shortly after he passed away at the age of 53.

YANKEE CAREER HIGHLIGHTS

Best Season

Pennock won a career-high 23 games for the Yankees in 1926, and he threw 19 complete games and 266 innings. However, Pennock's 3.62 ERA failed to earn him a top-10 finish in the league rankings, and he benefited greatly from pitching for easily the circuit's top offensive team. That being said, I will opt instead for Pennock's 1924 campaign. Pitching for a ball club that finished second in the American League in runs scored, the left-hander compiled a record of 21–9 that placed him second among AL hurlers in victories. Pennock also finished third in the league with a 2.83 ERA, 286 innings pitched, 25 complete games, and four shutouts. His 25 complete games and 286 innings pitched both represented career highs.

Memorable Moments/Greatest Performances

Pennock had perhaps his greatest stretch of pitching during the second half of the 1924 campaign. With the Yankees pursuing the first-place Washington Senators, Pennock defeated Walter Johnson 2–0 on July 5. Although the Senators ended up edging out the Yankees for the American League pennant, Pennock went on to win 15 of his last 18 decisions.

Still, Pennock usually saved most of his finest pitching performances for the postseason. Compiling a lifetime 5–0 record in World Series play, along with an exceptional 1.95 ERA, Pennock rarely disappointed when the stakes were highest. In his first World Series appearance with the Yankees on October 11, 1923, he snapped the Giants' eight-game series winning streak at the Polo Grounds by defeating the crosstown rivals 4–2. Pennock went the distance despite being so injured in the lower spine by a fourth inning Jack Bentley pitch that it took him 10 minutes to reach first base. Pennock returned to the mound just two days later to save the Yankees' game 4 victory, working out of a bases-loaded jam in the eighth inning by inducing Frankie Frisch to pop out. Pennock subsequently gave the Yankees their first world championship by starting and winning game 6, despite pitching on only one day of rest. Home plate umpire Billy Evans called Pennock's effort "the greatest pitching performance I have ever seen," noting that the weary southpaw defeated the Giants even though he "had nothing."

However, Pennock may well have saved his two best games for the 1926 and 1927 World Series. He started game 1 of the 1926 Fall Classic against St. Louis, defeating the Cardinals, 2–1, on a three-hitter. Pennock fared even better against Pittsburgh in game 3 the following year. Facing a Pirates team that had forged an .833 winning percentage against left-handed starters over the second half of the season, Pennock held Pittsburgh hitless until Pie Traynor singled safely with one man out in the top of the eighth inning. Pennock went on to record a complete-game 8–1 victory for New York, allowing the Pirates just 3 hits.

NOTABLE ACHIEVEMENTS

- Two-time 20-game winner.
- Won 19 games two other times.
- Compiled ERA below 3.00 on three occasions.
- Completed more than 20 games three times.
- Led AL pitchers in winning percentage, shutouts, and innings pitched once each.
- 1926 *Sporting News* All-Star selection.
- Five-time AL champion.
- Four-time world champion.

Waite Hoyt

Herb Pennock's teammate in New York for seven seasons, Waite Hoyt won more games for the Yankees during the 1920s (157) than any other pitcher. After being acquired from the Red Sox prior to the start of the 1921 campaign, Hoyt went on to pitch for six pennant-winning teams and three world championship ball clubs in New York, serving as staff ace on most of those squads. He won at least 16 games in seven of his nine full years with the Yankees, surpassing 20 victories twice and posting 19 wins on two other occasions. Hoyt teamed with Pennock to head the pitching staff of the Yankees' 1927 "Murderer's Row" club, still considered by many baseball historians to be the greatest team ever assembled.

Born in Brooklyn, New York, on September 9, 1899, Waite Charles Hoyt acquired the nickname "Schoolboy" after he signed with John McGraw's New York Giants at the tender age of 15 in 1915. After three years in the minors, Hoyt made his lone appearance for the Giants midway through the 1918 campaign, working one scoreless inning and striking out two batters. Returned to the minor leagues for more seasoning, the 19-year-old right-hander reemerged as a member of the Boston Red Sox the following year. Hoyt spent two years in Boston, compiling an overall record of 10–12, before being sent to New York as part of a huge eight-player deal.

Hoyt's acquisition paid immediate dividends for the Yankees, as the 21-year-old hurler finished among the league leaders with 19 wins, a 3.09 ERA, 21 complete games, and 282 innings pitched in his first year in pinstripes. Hoyt's outstanding performance helped the Yankees capture their first American League pennant. Although they subsequently lost their best-of-nine World Series match-up with the rival New York Giants in eight games, Hoyt pitched exceptionally well, tossing three complete games, compiling a record of 2–1, and allowing John McGraw's ball club just 18 hits and no earned runs over 27 innings of work.

Hoyt had another big year in 1922, winning 19 games for the second consecutive time and helping the Yankees repeat as American League champions. Although the Yankees again came up short against the Giants in the World Series, Hoyt pitched well in his lone start, allowing just one earned run in seven innings of work.

Hoyt combined to win a total of 35 games over the course of the next two seasons, before his performance slipped somewhat in 1925 and 1926. However, after posting a composite record of 27–26 those two years, Hoyt had arguably his best season in 1927. Pitching for the Yankees' fabled Murderer's Row ball club, the 27-year-old right-hander led all AL hurlers with a record of 22–7. He also placed among the league leaders with a 2.63 ERA, 23 complete games, and 256 innings pitched. Although Hoyt subsequently struggled somewhat in his lone World Series start against Pittsburgh, he emerged victorious in game 1, working 7 1/3 innings and surrendering 4 runs on 8 hits to the Pirates during a 5–4 Yankee win.

Hoyt followed that up by posting a career-best 23–7 record for New York's 1928 world championship ball club. In addition to finishing third in the league with 23 victories, Hoyt ranked among the league leaders with a 3.36 ERA, 19 complete games, and 273 innings pitched. He also topped the circuit with eight saves. Hoyt then hurled two complete-game victories against St. Louis in the World Series, limiting the Cardinals to just 3 earned runs and 14 hits over 18 innings of work.

However, the 1928 campaign turned out to be Hoyt's last big year. After going just 10–9 with a 4.24 ERA for the Yankees in 1929, the veteran right-hander found himself traded to the Detroit Tigers early in 1930 for a package of three players. Hoyt remained in Detroit for two years, before splitting his final eight seasons between four other teams. He ended his career back in New York with the Brooklyn Dodgers in 1938. Hoyt left the game with an overall record of 237–182 and an ERA of 3.59. In addition to compiling a record of 157–98 and an ERA of 3.48 during his time in New York, Hoyt tossed 156 complete games and 2,272 innings. He ranks in the Yankees' all-time top 10 in wins, complete games, and innings pitched. Hoyt eventually gained induction into the Baseball Hall of Fame through the Veterans Committee in 1969.

YANKEE CAREER HIGHLIGHTS

Best Season

Although Hoyt pitched exceptionally well in 1921 and 1928, his 1927 campaign would have to be considered the finest of his career. In addition to leading all American League pitchers with 22 victories and a .759 winning percentage, Hoyt placed second in the league with a 2.63 ERA and 3 shutouts. He also finished third with 23 complete games and ranked fifth with 256 innings pitched.

Memorable Moments/Greatest Performances

An outstanding postseason performer, Hoyt compiled an overall record of 6–3 with a sub-2.00 ERA in six World Series with the Yankees. He pitched particularly well in the 1921 Fall Classic against the Giants. Although the Yankees ended up losing their first World Series to their National League counterparts in eight games, Hoyt put on a memorable performance. After hurling a complete-game 2-hit shutout in game 2, he returned to the mound for game 5, giving the Yankees a 3–2 lead in the series by tossing another complete game victory, this time defeating the Giants by a score of 3–1. The Giants came back to win the next two contests, thereby going up 4–3 in the series. With his team facing elimination in game 8, Hoyt pitched another gem, battling Giants starter Art Nehf the full nine innings before dropping a heartbreaking 1–0 decision. The Giants scored their only run of the contest on an error in the top of the first inning. Hoyt concluded the series with a record of 2–1, an ERA of 0.00, and 3 complete games, having surrendered just 18 hits in 27 total innings of work.

NOTABLE ACHIEVEMENTS

- Two-time 20-game winner.
- Won 19 games two other times.
- Compiled ERA below 3.00 once (2.63 in 1927).
- Completed more than 20 games twice.
- Led AL pitchers in wins, winning percentage, and saves once each.
- 1928 *Sporting News* All-Star selection.
- Six-time AL champion.
- Three-time world champion.

28

Phil Rizzuto

A New York icon as both a player and an announcer, Phil Rizzuto spent virtually his entire adult life in the Yankee organization. After a stellar 13-year playing career that landed him in Cooperstown, Rizzuto spent 40 years in the broadcast booth, entertaining Yankee fans with his uninhibited, unpretentious, and self-deprecating style of announcing. Had the decision been made here to include "the Scooter's" broadcasting career during the formulation of these rankings, he undoubtedly would have finished higher on this list. Nevertheless, the man generally considered to be the second-greatest shortstop in team history clearly earned the 28th spot with his exceptional base running, outstanding fielding ability, and extraordinary bunting skills that helped the Yankees win nine pennants and seven world championships in his 12 full years with the team.

Having grown up in Brooklyn, New York, as a fan of the Dodgers, Philip Francis Rizzuto tried out for his favorite team in 1935. However, Dodger manager Casey Stengel did all he could to discourage the 5'6", 150-pound 17-year-old shortstop from pursuing a career in professional baseball when he advised the youngster to "go get a shoeshine box." Undeterred by Stengel's harsh words, Rizzuto signed with the Yankees as an amateur free agent two years later, after which he went on to earn *Sporting News* Minor League Player of the Year honors as a member of the Kansas City Blues in 1940.

Promoted to the majors at the start of the 1941 campaign, Rizzuto initially had a difficult time gaining acceptance by the veteran core of Yankee players, which preferred that the popular Frank Crosetti retain the team's starting shortstop job. However, Rizzuto's spirited play eventually earned him not only the starting assignment but also the admiration and respect of all his teammates. The rookie shortstop helped lead the Yankees to the American League pennant by batting .307 and swiping 14 bases, topping the club in steals for the first of eight times. Rizzuto improved on his overall numbers the following year, earning the first of his five All-Star selections by batting .284, driving in a career-high 68 runs, scoring 79 others, finishing third in the league with 22 stolen bases, and leading all AL shortstops in put-outs for the first of two times.

Rizzuto found his major-league career put on hold for the next three years while he served in the US Navy during World War II. From 1943 to 1945, he played third base on a Navy baseball team managed by Yankees catcher Bill Dickey that featured Brooklyn's Pee Wee Reese at shortstop.

After returning to the Yankees in 1946, Rizzuto put together three solid seasons before having his best year to date in 1949. The diminutive shortstop earned a second-place finish to Ted Williams in the AL MVP voting by batting .275, knocking in 65 runs, scoring 110 others, and finishing second in the league with 18 stolen bases. Rizzuto followed that up with the finest season of his career in 1950, when he helped lead the Yankees to their second of an all-time record five consecutive world championships. The Scooter earned AL MVP and *Sporting News* Major League Player of the Year honors by batting .324, compiling a .418 on-base percentage, driving in 66 runs, and placing among the league leaders with 125 runs scored, 200 hits, and 36 doubles. He also led all league shortstops in putouts and fielding percentage, establishing in the process a new record for players at his position (since broken) by handling 238 consecutive chances without an error. Rizzuto also set a new mark for AL shortstops (later broken) by playing 58 straight errorless games from September 18, 1949, through June 7, 1950.

Although Rizzuto failed to compile a similarly impressive stat line the following year, he ended up winning World Series MVP honors by leading the Yankees to a six-game triumph over the crosstown rival Giants. In addition to excelling in the field throughout the Fall Classic, Rizzuto collected 8 hits in 25 times at bat for a .320 batting average.

Rizzuto had two more good years for the Yankees, helping them win the World Series again in 1952 and 1953, before his skills began to diminish. After batting just .195 in 1954, the Scooter assumed a part-time role with the team the following year. Rizzuto subsequently appeared in only 31 games for New York over the course of the first five months of the 1956 campaign before the team released him on August 25. Rizzuto ended his 13-year playing career with 877 runs scored, 1,588 hits, 149 stolen bases, and a .273 batting average. At the time of his retirement, his 1,217 career double plays ranked second in major-league history, trailing only Luke Appling's total of 1,424, and his .968 career fielding percentage trailed only Lou Boudreau's mark of .973 among AL shortstops. Rizzuto also ranked among the all-time leaders in games played at shortstop (1,647), putouts (3,219), assists (4,666), and total chances (8,148).

Although Rizzuto compiled only moderately impressive offensive numbers over the course of his career, Ty Cobb once mentioned him with Stan Musial as "two of the few modern ball players who could hold their own among old timers." Another all-time great, Ted Williams, once suggested that the Red Sox would have replaced the Yankees as AL champions several times during the 1940s and early 1950s had his team had Rizzuto as its shortstop. Meanwhile, Casey Stengel, who ended up managing Rizzuto for eight seasons after he so callously dismissed him when Rizzuto tried out for his Dodger team in 1935, later proclaimed, "[Rizzuto] is the greatest shortstop I have ever seen in my entire baseball career, and I have watched some beauties."

Shortly after the Yankees released Rizzuto as a player, they hired him to be an announcer. The Scooter joined the Yankees' broadcast team in 1957, after which he spent the next 40 years entertaining Yankee fans with his unique and often comical broadcasting style. A "homer" in the truest sense of the word, Rizzuto made no attempt to conceal his loyalties during his radio and television broadcasts. He rooted openly for the Yankees, often expressing his glee when they succeeded and his dissatisfaction when they failed. Nevertheless, even the staunchest Yankee haters found it impossible to dislike Rizzuto due to his warm and unpretentious nature. Whether referring to someone as a "huckleberry," praising a restaurant at which he recently dined, wishing a listener a happy birthday or anniversary, or sending get-well wishes to someone in the hospital, Rizzuto endeared himself to Yankee fans, making them feel as if he was a member of their own family. As a result, Rizzuto became a true Yankee icon, reaching a level of popularity as an announcer that surpassed the one he attained as a player. That is what made saying goodbye to the Scooter so difficult when he passed away one month shy of his 90th birthday on August 13, 2007.

Fortunately, the Yankee organization took the opportunity to honor Rizzuto several years earlier, retiring his number 10 and awarding him a plaque in Yankee Stadium's Monument Park on August 4, 1985. After a long wait, Rizzuto also gained admittance to the Baseball Hall of Fame, being inducted by the Veterans Committee in 1994.

CAREER HIGHLIGHTS

Best Season

Although Rizzuto had very good years in 1949 and 1951, the 1950 campaign was clearly his best. Starting all 155 games at shortstop for the Yankees, Rizzuto knocked in 66 runs and established career highs with 125 runs scored, 200 hits, 36 doubles, 7 homers, 92 bases on balls, a .324 batting average, a .418 on-base percentage, and a .439 slugging percentage. He did not come close to matching most of those numbers in any other season. Rizzuto earned AL MVP and *Sporting News* Major League Player of the Year honors; he also was awarded the Hickok Belt as the top professional athlete of the year.

Memorable Moments/Greatest Performances

Rizzuto excelled for the Yankees during the 1951 World Series, leading them to a six-game victory over the Giants by collecting 8 hits, batting .320, driving in 3 runs, and scoring 5 others. The highlight of the Fall Classic for the Scooter occurred in the top of the fourth inning of game 5 when he gave the Yankees a 7–1 lead by hitting a 2-run homer into the short right-field porch at the Polo Grounds. The Yankees went on to win the contest by a score of 13–1, and they took the next game as well, to capture the third of their record five straight world championships.

Nevertheless, the event with which Rizzuto is perhaps most closely associated took place with him in the broadcast booth. Working the final game of the 1961 campaign for WCBS radio, Rizzuto called the action as Roger Maris stepped to the plate with a chance to break Babe Ruth's single-season home run record:

"Here's the windup; fastball . . . hit deep to right . . . this could be it! Way back there! Holy cow, he did it! 61 for Maris! And look at the fight for that ball out there! Holy cow, what a shot! Another standing ovation for Maris . . . and they're still fighting for that ball out there, climbing over each other's backs. One of the greatest sights I've ever seen here at Yankee Stadium!"

NOTABLE ACHIEVEMENTS

- Batted over .300 twice.
- Scored more than 100 runs twice.

- Surpassed 200 hits once.
- AL MVP in 1950.
- 1950 *Sporting News* Major League Player of the Year.
- 1950 Hickok Belt winner.
- 1951 World Series MVP.
- Four-time *Sporting News* All-Star selection.
- Five-time AL All-Star.
- Nine-time AL champion.
- Seven-time world champion.

29

Mel Stottlemyre

Perhaps the most overlooked and underrated pitcher in the rich history of the Yankees, Mel Stottlemyre had the misfortune of spending virtually his entire career pitching for losing or mediocre teams. After first arriving in the Bronx in August 1964, Stottlemyre excelled during the final two months of the season, enabling New York to edge out Chicago and Baltimore for the American League pennant. However, the 1964 World Series turned out to be Stottlemyre's only trip to the postseason, since the Yankees found themselves mired in mediocrity the remainder of his career. New York finished with a losing record in 5 of Stottlemyre's 10 remaining years with the team, seriously contending for the pennant just once. Through it all, though, the slender right-hander remained one of the American League's top hurlers, earning All-Star honors five times, surpassing 20 victories on three occasions, and serving as the ace of New York's pitching staff.

Born in Hazleton, Missouri, on November 13, 1941, Melvin Leon Stottlemyre grew up in the state of Washington, graduating from Mabton High School before attending Yakima Valley Community College. After signing with the Yankees as an amateur free agent in 1961, Stottlemyre spent parts of four seasons in the New York farm system, excelling at every level. The right-hander established himself as arguably the team's top prospect in 1964 when he earned International League Pitcher of the Year and Minor League Player of the Year honors while at Richmond. Stottlemyre posted a record of 13–3 and an ERA of 1.42 over the season's first four months, prompting the Yankees to summon him to the big leagues in early August. In the midst of a pennant race, New York desperately needed another reliable starter to complement Whitey Ford, Jim Bouton, and Al

Downing. The 22-year-old rookie quickly demonstrated that he was up to the task, handling himself like a veteran after being inserted into the starting rotation upon his arrival. Following his debut on August 12, Stottlemyre proceeded to compile a 9–3 record in his 12 starts while posting an outstanding 2.06 ERA. His exceptional performance helped the Yankees capture their fifth consecutive American League pennant.

Apparent immediately upon Stottlemyre's arrival was the outstanding movement he had on his sinkerball. While he also featured an excellent slider and an above-average fastball, Stottlemyre's sinker looked like it fell right off a table, breaking almost straight down as it approached home plate. Correspondingly, the young right-hander induced an inordinate number of ground ball outs when he had his best stuff. Since the downward movement of his sinkerball tended to increase when his arm grew tired, he seemed to pitch more effectively during the latter stages of contests.

Also evident from the very beginning was Stottlemyre's tremendous poise. The youngster always maintained his composure, conducting himself like a wily veteran in the middle of an extremely close pennant race. The maturity with which Stottlemyre carried himself prompted Yankee manager Yogi Berra to hand him the ball three times against the Cardinals in the World Series. Starting game 2 against Bob Gibson, Stottlemyre went the distance in pitching the Yankees to an 8–3 victory. Squaring off against Gibson again in game 5, the rookie right-hander held the Cardinals to just 1 earned run over seven innings, before leaving the contest for a pinch hitter in the bottom of the seventh frame with the Yankees trailing by a score of 2–0. Although New York eventually lost the game in extra innings, Tom Tresh prevented Stottlemyre from being charged with the loss when he tied the contest in the bottom of the ninth inning with a 2-run homer. Stottlemyre subsequently found himself pressed into duty on just two days' rest in game 7 when Whitey Ford's ailing shoulder left him unable to start the decisive contest for New York. The rookie did his best to keep the Yankees in the game, but he ended up taking the loss to Gibson and the Cardinals after he surrendered 3 runs in the fourth inning. Little did Stottlemyre know at the time that he would never again make a postseason start for the team. Yet, no matter how poorly the Yankees played the remainder of his career, Stottlemyre continued to stand out as a true professional and link to the championship ball clubs the team fielded in the past.

The Yankees finished sixth in the American League in 1965, but Stottlemyre compiled a record of 20–9 and an ERA of 2.63 in his sophomore campaign. He placed second in the league in wins and shutouts (4), and he topped the circuit with 291 innings pitched and 18 complete games. The right-hander's outstanding performance earned him a spot on the AL All-Star Team and his only selection to the *Sporting News* All-Star squad.

Stottlemyre pitched less effectively in 1966, losing a league-leading 20 games for the last-place Yankees. However, he rebounded the following year, compiling a 2.96 ERA and a record of 15–15 despite receiving little in the way of run support from ninth-place New York. The right-hander followed that up with two of his finest seasons, surpassing 20 victories in 1968 and 1969 despite pitching for a team that featured one of baseball's most anemic offenses. Stottlemyre finished 21–12 with a 2.45 ERA in the first of those campaigns while throwing 19 complete games, 279 innings, and 6 shutouts. He posted a record of 20–14 in 1969, with a 2.82 ERA, 303 innings pitched, and a league-leading 24 complete games.

Stottlemyre also pitched well in 1971 and 1973, but poor run support from his teammates enabled him to compile a combined record of only 32–28 those two years. In fact, a weak Yankee lineup resulted in Stottlemyre posting a career record of just 164–139—a mark that does not come close to reflecting just how effectively he pitched for the team much of the time.

Nevertheless, Stottlemyre still amassed some fairly impressive numbers. In addition to winning more than 20 games three times, he surpassed 15 victories on four other occasions. He ended his career with an outstanding 2.97 ERA. Stottlemyre threw at least 250 innings in each of his nine full seasons, tossing as many as 303 frames in 1969. He completed at least 18 games five times, and he threw at least 6 shutouts three times, tying Red Ruffing for second place on New York's all-time list with 40 career shutouts (Whitey Ford is first with 45). Stottlemyre also ranks among the Yankees' all-time leaders in wins, innings pitched (2,661), complete games (152), strikeouts (1,257), and ERA (for pitchers with over 800 innings). Yet, Stottlemyre's name rarely comes up when the finest pitchers ever to wear a Yankee uniform are mentioned.

Whitey Ford is one former Yankee who considers the exclusion of Stottlemyre's name during such discussions to be an injustice. Ford, who was in the latter stages of his Hall of Fame career when Stottlemyre joined the Yankees in 1964, said in his book *Few and Chosen*, "If [Stottlemyre] had been with the teams I played on, he would have been a 20-game winner several more times and might have been regarded as the greatest right-handed pitcher in Yankees history."

Outfielder Roy White, who spent parts of 10 seasons playing behind Stottlemyre in New York, said of his former teammate,

I think Mel's been very underrated. He was really a dominant pitcher for the Yankees until he got hurt. He broke more bats than anybody. He had that great sinkerball, a good slider, and good control. He was a big-game pitcher. He was a lot like Catfish Hunter, personality-wise, in that he was always the same. After a game, you couldn't tell whether he won or lost. He was one of those guys who wouldn't go into a shell after he lost a game, get mad, and not talk to the press, or anything like that. He was the same guy all the time. But, when you talk about great Yankee pitchers, he's usually never mentioned. People have kind of forgotten about him, but this guy was really tough.

Unfortunately, the workload that Stottlemyre carried for the Yankees his first 10 seasons in the Bronx took its toll on his right arm. The right-hander tore the rotator cuff in his pitching shoulder early in 1974, bringing his pitching career to a premature end at the age of 32. Stottlemyre attempted to rehabilitate his ailing shoulder during the off-season, but the Yankees released him in the spring. Claiming that management lied to him about giving him more time to come back from his injury, Stottlemyre vowed to never have anything to do with the team as long as George Steinbrenner remained in charge. The pitcher's feelings of animosity toward Steinbrenner intensified when the Yankee owner subsequently reneged on a promise he made to pay Stottlemyre $40,000, whether he could pitch again or not, if he went to rehab his shoulder with a kinesiology professor he knew at Michigan State.

Stottlemyre received an offer from his former manager Ralph Houk to join the Detroit Tigers in spring training, but he found himself unable to pitch again. After officially retiring from the game, Stottlemyre went 20 years without having any contact with the Yankees, annually tearing up his invitation to the Old Timers' Game.

After spending more than 17 years serving as pitching coach for three major-league teams, Stottlemyre elected to return to the Yankees when he received a telephone call from George Steinbrenner shortly after the hiring of Joe Torre to be the new manager in the fall of 1995. Recalling his telephone conversation with the Yankee owner, Stottlemyre said, "He never really apologized for what happened years earlier, but I could tell he felt badly about it. When I got off the phone, I said to my wife, 'If he had the nerve to call me, I guess I've got enough nerve to go to work for him.'"

Stottlemyre joined Joe Torre's staff for the start of the 1996 campaign, proving to be an integral member of the coaching staff that helped New York capture four world championships in the next five years. However, Steinbrenner's demanding and impulsive nature eventually began to wear thin on Stottlemyre, who later admitted he became aware that the owner criticized him privately after the Yankees stopped winning championships under Torre. Stottlemyre resigned as New York's pitching coach after 2005, later revealing, "I felt I might be pushed out the door if I didn't go out on my own. I didn't want to hold a grudge again, so I decided it was time."

Although Stottlemyre often objected to the callous manner with which Steinbrenner sometimes treated his employees, he very much appreciated the kindness the Yankee owner showed him during one of the most difficult periods of his life. After being diagnosed in 2000 with multiple myeloma—a life-threatening blood disorder—Stottlemyre had to endure weeks of chemotherapy administered to him at New York's Sloan-Kettering Hospital. He later recalled, "I had my ups and downs with [Steinbrenner], and I didn't always like the way he did things, but I'll never forget how much he did for me when I was sick." Stottlemyre eventually recovered from the illness and is currently in remission.

CAREER HIGHLIGHTS

Best Season

Stottlemyre's 1965 or 1968 campaign would have made a solid choice. The right-hander won a career-high 21 games and compiled his lowest single-season ERA (2.45) in the second of those years. He also completed 19 games, threw 279 innings, and tossed 6 shutouts en route to earning a 10th-place finish in the AL MVP voting. But 1968 became known as the Year of the Pitcher due to the level of dominance that hurlers displayed in both leagues. Although Stottlemyre placed among the AL leaders in virtually every major statistical category, he failed to top the junior circuit in any. Furthermore, Detroit's Denny McLain (31–6, 1.96 ERA, 28 complete games, 336 innings pitched) and Cleveland's Luis Tiant (21–9, 1.60 ERA, 19 complete games, and a league-leading 9 shutouts) had significantly better years for their teams.

Meanwhile, Stottlemyre posted extremely comparable numbers in 1965, when he finished 20–9, with a 2.63 ERA, 18 complete games, 291 innings pitched, and 4 shutouts. In addition to placing near the top of the league rankings in wins, ERA, and shutouts, he topped the circuit in complete games and innings pitched. Stottlemyre was arguably the American League's best pitcher, earning a spot on the *Sporting News* All-Star Team. That last fact pushed 1965 just barely ahead of 1968 as his finest season.

Memorable Moments/Greatest Performances

With 40 career shutouts, Stottlemyre pitched a number of outstanding games. Among his more notable efforts were the consecutive shutouts that he tossed at the start of the 1967 campaign. After blanking the Senators on just 2 hits on opening day in Washington, the Yankee ace defeated the Red Sox at Yankee Stadium just five days later by a final score of 1–0, limiting Boston to only 4 hits.

Stottlemyre saved many of his finest performances for those occasions when he squared off against the opposing team's best pitcher. On April 12, 1969, he threw a one-hitter against Detroit at Tiger Stadium, defeating in the process reigning AL MVP Denny McLain by a score of 4–0. Stottlemyre hurled another gem against the A's at Oakland-Alameda County Stadium on August 24, 1971, allowing just 2 hits en route to beating eventual Cy Young and MVP Award winner Vida Blue 1–0.

Stottlemyre had arguably his most memorable game against the Red Sox at Yankee Stadium on July 20, 1965, when he not only pitched the Yankees to a 6–3 victory over Boston but also became the first pitcher in 55 years to hit an inside-the-park grand slam. Stottlemyre recalled years later, "I remember a lot about it. It was in the [Yankee] Stadium, the ball was hit to left-center field, against Boston, a real hot day in July. The pitcher was Bill Monbouquette. Those things you don't forget."

Still, Stottlemyre had probably his finest all-around performance as a rookie when, on September 26, 1964, he threw a 2-hit shutout against the Senators in Washington and collected 5 hits in five trips to the plate during a 7–0 victory.

NOTABLE ACHIEVEMENTS

- Three-time 20-game winner.
- Topped 15 victories four other times.
- Compiled ERA below 3.00 in 6 of 11 seasons.

Jack Chesbro won a 20th-century record 41 games for the New York Highlanders in 1904. Bain News Service collection at the Library of Congress.

Bob Meusel warming up his rifle arm. Bain News Service collection at the Library of Congress.

They called old Yankee Stadium "The House That Ruth Built." Bain News Service collection at the Library of Congress.

The American League fielded a powerful team at the 1937 All-Star Game, which included Yankee sluggers Lou Gehrig, Bill Dickey, and Joe DiMaggio (left to right: Lou Gehrig, Joe Cronin, Bill Dickey, Joe DiMaggio, Charlie Gehringer, Jimmie Foxx, Hank Greenberg). The Harris & Ewing Collection at the Library of Congress.

Mickey Mantle hit more home runs during his 18 years with the Yankees than any other switch hitter in baseball history.

Elston Howard earned AL MVP honors in 1963, becoming in the process the first African American player to win the award.

Don Mattingly's passion for the game earned him the nickname "Donnie Baseball" during his career in pinstripes. Photo courtesy of Jim Accordino.

Derek Jeter—"The Captain." Photo courtesy of Keith Allison.

(left to right) Lou Gehrig, Babe Ruth, Earle Combs, and Tony Lazzeri formed the nucleus of the Yankees' Murderer's Row squad of 1927. Copyright Leslie Jones Collection, courtesy of the Trustees of the Boston Public Library, Print Dept.

Red Ruffing (left) and Lefty Gomez (middle) served as co-aces of the Yankee pitching staff for much of the 1930s. They are joined here by George Selkirk, the man who took over for Babe Ruth in right field in 1935. Copyright Leslie Jones Collection, courtesy of the Trustees of the Boston Public Library, Print Dept.

Bill Dickey began the Yankee legacy of exceptional catchers behind home plate. Copyright Leslie Jones Collection, courtesy of the Trustees of the Boston Public Library, Print Dept.

Joe DiMaggio and Lou Gehrig with Yankee manager Joe McCarthy. Copyright Leslie Jones Collection, courtesy of the Trustees of the Boston Public Library, Print Dept.

Yankee manager Joe McCarthy flanked by Lou Gehrig and a very young Tommy Henrich. Copyright Leslie Jones Collection, courtesy of the Trustees of the Boston Public Library, Print Dept.

(left to right) Joe Gordon, Bill Dickey, and Charlie Keller combined with Joe DiMaggio to give the Yankees the American League's most powerful lineup during the late 1930s and early 1940s. Copyright Leslie Jones Collection, courtesy of the Trustees of the Boston Public Library, Print Dept.

Joe Gordon and Phil Rizzuto (both in the center) gave the Yankees outstanding defense up the middle during their relatively brief time together. They are flanked by Johnny Sturm on the left and Red Rolfe on the far right. Copyright Leslie Jones Collection, courtesy of the Trustees of the Boston Public Library, Print Dept.

Yogi Berra (left), here with Gus Niarhos, helped lead the Yankees to 14 American League pennants and 10 world championships. Copyright Leslie Jones Collection, courtesy of the Trustees of the Boston Public Library, Print Dept.

Allie Reynolds, Vic Raschi, and Ed Lopat (left to right) gave the Yankees a "Big Three" in their starting rotation that helped lead them to a record five straight world championships from 1949 to 1953. Copyright Leslie Jones Collection, courtesy of the Trustees of the Boston Public Library, Print Dept.

Whitey Ford, Mickey Mantle, and Billy Martin made headlines both on and off the field during their time together in New York.

Mel Stottlemyre

Mel Stottlemyre won 20 games, three times pitching for mediocre Yankee teams during the 1960s.

An extremely consistent and reliable performer, Roy White bridged the gap between two distinct eras of Yankee excellence.

Roy White

Bobby Murcer had thrust upon him the unenviable task of trying to replace Mickey Mantle as the Yankees' marquis player. Photo courtesy of Jim Accordino.

Thurman Munson served as the heart and soul of the Yankees' world championship teams of 1977 and 1978. Photo courtesy of Ryan Barber.

Graig Nettles helped turn around the 1978 World Series with his miraculous glove work at third base. Photo courtesy of Jim Accordino.

Reggie Jackson helped lead the Yankees to four division titles, three A.L. pennants, and two world championships in his five years in New York. Photo courtesy of Jim Accordino.

Willie Randolph played more games at second base than any other Yankee in history. Photo courtesy of © Arlene Schulman

Dave Winfield and Don Mattingly teamed up to give the Yankees one of the American League's most formidable lineups for much of the 1980s.

Andy Pettitte ranks third all-time among Yankee pitchers in wins. Photo courtesy of Keith Allison.

Mike Mussina proved to be one of the best free-agent signings in team history. Photo courtesy of Keith Allison.

Hideki Matsui spent seven productive seasons in New York, earning World Series MVP honors in 2009 by batting .615, with 3 home runs and 8 RBIs. Photo courtesy of Keith Allison.

Robinson Cano has established himself in recent years as arguably the best all-around second baseman in the Major Leagues. Photo courtesy of Keith Allison.

- Tossed more than 20 complete games once, completing 19 games three other times.
- Threw more than 250 innings nine straight times, surpassing 300 mark once (303 in 1969).
- Led AL pitchers in complete games twice and in innings pitched once.
- Tied for second all-time on Yankees with 40 shutouts.
- 1965 *Sporting News* All-Star selection.
- Five-time AL All-Star.
- 1964 AL champion.

30

Bob Meusel

Spending 10 full seasons in New York playing in the shadow of the great Babe Ruth prevented Bob Meusel from ever gaining the sort of recognition that he likely would have received had he played almost anywhere else. The fact that Lou Gehrig joined Meusel in the Yankee lineup for his final five years with the team further reduced the amount of credit the outfielder received for the overall contributions he made to the success of the ball club. Nevertheless, Meusel served as an integral member of six pennant-winning teams and three world championship ball clubs during his time in New York, providing the Yankees with outstanding production in the middle of their lineup and a powerful and accurate throwing arm in their outfield. Meusel knocked in more than 100 runs five times for the Yankees; he also compiled more than 20 outfield assists for them twice, leading all American League outfielders in the last category both times. Still, the general consensus was that Meusel never lived up to his full potential. Yankee manager Miller Huggins called him "indifferent," pointing to his lazy attitude, which often manifested itself when he refused to run out ground balls.

After starting his professional baseball career at the age of 20 with the Vernon Tigers of the Pacific Coast League in 1917, Robert William Meusel joined the US Navy during World War I. He spent his time in the military playing for the navy's baseball team, before returning to the Tigers for the 1919 season. The Yankees purchased Meusel's contract prior to the start of the 1920 campaign, and the right-handed hitting slugger spent his first year in New York splitting his time between third base and the outfield. The 23-year-old Meusel had a solid rookie season, batting .328, driving in 83 runs, and collecting 40 doubles in only 119 games.

Meusel became a full-time outfielder the following year, spending most of his time in right field, before moving over to the more spacious left field two years later to take better advantage of his outstanding speed. In his breakout season, Meusel hit 24 homers; drove in 135 runs; scored 104 others; accumulated 16 triples, 40 doubles, and 190 hits; stole 17 bases; batted .318; and led all AL outfielders with 28 assists. Meusel's outstanding performance helped the Yankees capture their first American League pennant and gained him general recognition as one of the junior circuit's best all-around players. The Yankees subsequently lost the World Series to the Giants, after which Meusel and teammate Babe Ruth were suspended by baseball commissioner Kenesaw Mountain Landis for the first five weeks of the ensuing campaign for participating in a barnstorming tour during the off-season.

Despite missing more than 30 games in 1922, Meusel had another solid season, batting .319, placing among the league leaders with 16 home runs, and topping circuit outfielders with 24 assists. The Yankees won the pennant again, and although they ended up losing the World Series to the Giants for the second straight time, Meusel performed well, leading the team with a .300 batting average.

Meusel had another good year for New York's 1923 world championship ball club, driving in 91 runs and batting over .300 for the fourth consecutive season. Although the outfielder subsequently batted just .269 against the Giants in the World Series, he led all players on both teams with eight runs batted in.

After batting .325, knocking in 120 runs, and stealing a career-high 26 bases in 1924, Meusel had arguably his finest all-around season in 1925. With Babe Ruth missing two months of the campaign due to a serious illness, Meusel assumed the mantle of offensive team leader. Despite playing his home games in Yankee Stadium, with its distant outfield fences in left and left center, the right-handed-hitting Meusel led the league with 33 home runs and 138 runs batted in. He also batted .290 and scored 101 runs.

Meusel continued to post solid offensive numbers in each of the next three seasons, including driving in 103 runs and establishing career highs with a .337 batting average and 47 doubles for the Yankees' legendary 1927 "Murderer's Row" ball club. However, his performance slipped in 1929, prompting the Yankees to deal him to Cincinnati at the end of the year. Meusel spent just one year with the Reds before returning to the minor leagues for two seasons and eventually announcing his retirement at the conclusion of the 1932 campaign. In his 10 full seasons with the Yankees, Meusel hit 146 home runs, knocked in 1,005 runs, scored 764 others, collected 1,565 hits, accumulated 338 doubles and 87 triples, and compiled a batting average of .311. His 1,005 RBIs during the 1920s were the fourth most by any major leaguer. Meusel ranks in the Yankees' all-time top 10 in batting average, doubles, and triples.

Perhaps noted even more for his powerful throwing arm, Meusel drew raves from everyone who saw him patrol the outfield. Babe Ruth claimed, "I never saw a better thrower." Bob Quinn, who served as president for both the Boston Red Sox and the Boston Braves, suggested, "Meusel's arm was the best I ever saw. And I'm talking about strong arms, not merely accurate ones. Meusel threw strikes to any base from the outfield."

Meanwhile, Miller Huggins, who Meusel frequently exasperated with his apathetic attitude, noted, "There is one thing fans don't get about Meusel; the number of runs he prevents by just standing out in left field. Coaches will not send many in when a ball is hit to him."

Discussing the outfielder's all-around skills, Huggins added, "I know of no hitter who can hit the ball harder than Meusel—excepting, of course, Babe Ruth. He had everything to make him great: a good eye at bat, strength, a natural, easy swing, and that wonderful steel arm."

CAREER HIGHLIGHTS

Best Season

Although Meusel had an outstanding year for the fabled 1927 Yankees, knocking in 103 runs and establishing career highs with 47 doubles, a .337 batting average, and a .393 on-base percentage, the ultimate decision here was to go with his 1921 or 1925 campaign. In the first of those years, Meusel batted .318, hit 24 homers, drove in 135 runs, amassed 40 doubles, and reached career bests in runs scored (104), hits (190), triples (16), and slugging percentage (.559). He posted comparable numbers in 1925, hitting 33 home runs; knocking in 138 runs; scoring 101 others; batting .290; accumulating 181 hits, 34 doubles, and 12 triples; and compiling a .542 slugging percentage. But with Babe Ruth hitting immediately in front of Meusel in 1921 and having arguably the greatest offensive season in baseball history, the strong-armed outfielder had a better supporting cast than in 1925, when Ruth appeared in only 98 games, batted just .290, and drove in only 66 runs. Meusel served as New York's primary offensive threat for the only time in his career in 1925, making that his best all-around season.

Memorable Moments/Greatest Performances

Meusel served as one of the primary combatants in one of the most notorious brawls in baseball history on June 13, 1924. With the Yankees holding a 10–6 lead over the Tigers in the top of the ninth inning, Detroit player/manager Ty Cobb gave pitcher Bert Cole the signal to hit Meusel with a pitch. Babe Ruth noticed the sign and warned his teammate, who rushed to the mound to fight the Tiger hurler after being struck in the back with the pitch. Both benches subsequently emptied, with numerous individual battles breaking out and a riot developing when over a thousand fans also rushed onto the field. The police finally managed to control the brawl, arresting several fans in the process. Meanwhile, the umpire of the game, Billy Evans, pushed Meusel out of Navin Field to safety. American League president Ban Johnson punished Meusel and Cole by fining them and issuing a 10-day suspension.

On a more positive note, Meusel had a number of outstanding days on the ball field that earned him a considerable amount of notoriety during his playing days. He remains one of only three players in baseball history to hit for the cycle three times during his career. Meusel accomplished the feat for the first time during a win against the Washington Senators on May 7, 1921. He duplicated his earlier effort in a win over the Detroit Tigers on July 21, 1922. Meusel victimized the Tigers again on July 26, 1928.

An outstanding base runner as well, Meusel accomplished the rare feat of stealing second, third, and home in the same game on May 16, 1927. He also swiped home twice in World Series play.

However, Meusel's most memorable World Series performance took place in the 1923 Fall Classic, when the outfielder helped lead the Yankees to their first world championship. Meusel's 2-run triple in the second inning of game 4 helped key a 6-run Yankee rally that led to an 8–4 win. He followed that up by going 3 for 5 and driving in three runs in game 5, before putting the Yankees ahead to stay in game 6 with a 2-run single. Meusel ended up leading both teams with 8 runs batted in.

Meusel also had a historic day in the outfield on September 5, 1921, tying a major-league record for outfielders by recording 4 assists in one game.

NOTABLE ACHIEVEMENTS

- Batted over .300 seven times, topping the .320 mark on three occasions.
- Hit more than 20 home runs twice, surpassing 30 homers once.
- Knocked in more than 100 runs five times.
- Scored more than 100 runs twice.
- Accumulated at least 40 doubles five times.
- Stole more than 20 bases twice.
- Led AL with 33 home runs and 138 RBIs in 1925.
- Led all AL outfielders in assists twice.
- One of only three players in major-league history to hit for the cycle three times during career.
- Six-time AL champion.
- Three-time world champion.

Elston Howard

The first African American player to don a New York Yankees uniform, Elston Howard traveled a long and arduous road while working his way up the Yankee farm system. Although Howard first joined the Yankee organization in 1950, he had to overcome many obstacles, including a considerable amount of racial prejudice, before he finally found himself wearing pinstripes at the major-league level. Yet, through it all, Howard carried himself with the same class and dignity on which he built his reputation.

After graduating from Vashon High School in his hometown of St. Louis in 1948, Elston Gene Howard received numerous athletic scholarship offers from Big Ten universities. However, the 19-year-old multisport star instead elected to join the Kansas City Monarchs of the Negro Leagues. Howard played the outfield for three years in Kansas City, performing under the tutelage of manager Buck O'Neil and rooming with Ernie Banks. The Yankees, who had been extremely slow to sign black players, offered Howard a contract on July 19, 1950, and subsequently assigned the talented youngster to their farm team at Muskegon, Michigan. Howard spent the next four years in the minors, having his path to the big-league club blocked as much by the organization's unwillingness to promote him as by the level of talent on the Yankee roster.

In a move designed to prolong Howard's minor-league career, the Yankee front office first decided to convert the 24-year-old into a catcher in 1953, after he had already worked his way up to the Triple-A level. The New York hierarchy not only knew that the transition would be a difficult one for Howard but figured that he would eventually have to contend with future Hall of Fame catcher Yogi Berra for playing time once he arrived in New York. Nevertheless, Howard took the move in stride because he had a tremendous desire to play for the Yankees.

It was Howard's desire to play for New York and his calm demeanor that made him the perfect man to break the color barrier for the Yankees. While other dark-skinned players, such as former Yankee prospect Vic Power, had been dealt to other teams due to their more outspoken and confrontational personalities, Howard preferred to walk away from controversy and keep his emotions to himself. Although Howard's disposition had to make his career with the Yankees extremely unpleasant at times, he always carried himself with pride and dignity, never revealing to others the degree to which the injustices he frequently endured bothered him inside.

Still, as hard as the members of the Yankee front office tried, they found themselves unable to further delay Howard's arrival to the major-league club by 1955. Playing for Toronto of the International League the previous year, Howard hit 22 home runs, drove in 109 runs, and batted .330 en route to capturing league MVP honors. Howard finally joined the Yankees in the spring of 1955, making his major-league debut with the team on April 14, and singling in his first at bat. A 1955 Bowman company baseball card elaborated on the reputation that the 26-year-old rookie had established for himself around baseball: "Elston comes to the Yankees as one of the most heralded rookies in many years. Although he has been a catcher, and is carried on the roster as a catcher, it is thought that he may be converted into an outfielder. It seems he is just too good not to play regularly in major-league ball, and yet it is hard to displace a veteran as good as Yogi Berra."

Howard did indeed find it extremely difficult to displace Yogi Berra behind the plate for the Yankees. Berra remained the team's primary receiver through 1960, with Howard splitting time his first six seasons among catcher, first base, and the outfield. Yet, even though Howard failed to attain full-time status at any point during that period, he remained a key contributor to New York's five pennant-winning and two world championship teams, earning AL All-Star honors each year from 1957 to 1960. After batting .314 and knocking in 66 runs in only 376 at bats in 1958, Howard established new career highs with 18 home runs and 73 RBIs the following year.

The fact that Howard accumulated as many as 400 official at bats just once in his first six seasons prevented him from posting the type of offensive numbers he undoubtedly would have compiled under different conditions. Nevertheless, his teammates were keenly aware of

the kind of ability he possessed, and they knew how good he would
have been had he been given more of an opportunity to showcase his
talents. Bobby Richardson, who spent his entire career playing with
Howard, said, "I knew that Elston would have been a star on any
other ballclub. When I first saw Elston and saw the tools that he had, I
thought to myself, 'My goodness, the Yankees are certainly fortunate
to have him.'"

Howard finally supplanted Yogi Berra as the team's number one
catcher in 1961. Although the New York media focused primarily on
the exploits of Roger Maris and Mickey Mantle over the course of the
campaign, Howard had an exceptional year in his own right. In addition to hitting 21 home runs and driving in 77 runs in 446 at bats, he
batted a career-high .348 and finished 10th in the league's MVP voting.
The following year, Howard hit another 21 home runs and knocked in
a career-best 91 runs.

Howard established himself as one of the leaders on the Yankees
by 1963, having gained the admiration and respect of everyone on the
team. The members of the Baseball Writers' Association of America
recognized Howard's leadership qualities when they made him the
first black player to be named the American League's Most Valuable Player for his role in helping the Yankees win the AL pennant.
Despite losing Mantle and Maris for much of the season due to injuries, New York still managed to finish first in the junior circuit, due
largely to the efforts of Howard. In addition to providing leadership
on the field and in the clubhouse, he hit 28 home runs, knocked in
85 runs, and batted .287. Howard also finished third in the voting the
following year, when he batted .313, drove in 84 runs, and won his
second consecutive Gold Glove for establishing new AL records for
receivers, with 939 putouts and 1,008 total chances. Howard earned
his third selection in four seasons to the *Sporting News* All-Star Team
and the eighth of his nine consecutive selections to the AL All-Star
squad.

Injuries severely limited Howard's playing time and offensive
productivity from 1965 to 1967, prompting the Yankees to part ways
with the popular receiver on August 3, 1967, when they dealt him to
the arch-rival Boston Red Sox for two nondescript players. Howard
left New York having hit 161 home runs, driven in 733 runs, collected
1,405 hits, and compiled a .279 batting average over 13 seasons. His
lifetime fielding percentage of .993 remained the major-league record
for catchers until 1973.

Even though Howard batted only .147 for the Red Sox the final
two months of the season, his ability to handle a pitching staff shone

through. In fact, he received much of the credit for stabilizing Boston's pitching staff, enabling his new team to edge out three other clubs for the American League pennant.

Tony Conigliaro, the former Boston outfielder who played with Howard briefly, said, "I don't think I ever saw a pitcher shake off one of his signs. They had too much respect for him."

Former Yankee relief pitcher Hal Reniff said of Howard, "Unless you pitched to him, you didn't know how good he was . . . how agile he was behind the plate."

Ex-reliever Bill Fischer said, "Ellie Howard was a winning player, an All-Star. He was probably overlooked because of those great Yankee teams he played on. He was a leader; he took charge."

Perhaps more than anything, Elston Howard was a man of great inner strength, possessing an ability to deal with all kinds of adversity. Several years after he joined the Yankees, Howard and his wife attended a dinner with Jackie and Rachel Robinson. Jackie, who always resented the Yankees for their lack of interest in signing black players, told Howard that he considered the Yankees to be a bigoted organization. Robinson also suggested that, in some ways, Howard experienced more difficulties in New York than he himself encountered during his time in Brooklyn. Robinson claimed that the Dodger front office had always given him its full support, while Yankee management had displayed a considerable amount of resistance toward Howard as he made his way up the organizational ladder.

After ending his career with Boston in 1968, Howard returned to the Yankees, serving as their first base coach from 1969 to 1979. In the last of those years, Howard was diagnosed with myocarditis, a rare heart disease that causes rapid heart failure. Howard initially considered a heart transplant, but his condition quickly deteriorated. After staying a week at New York Presbyterian Hospital in New York City, Howard died of the heart ailment in 1980 at just 50 years of age. Upon learning of his passing, *New York Times* columnist Red Smith wrote, "The Yankees organization lost more class on the weekend than George Steinbrenner could buy in 10 years."

Dick Howser, the Yankee manager at the time, played and coached with Howard in New York. Howser, who passed away prematurely himself just a few years later, paid tribute to his friend and former colleague by saying, "Elston exemplified the Yankee class of the 1950s and 1960s. Class was the way to describe the guy. He epitomized the Yankee tradition. Everybody in baseball respected him."

On July 21, 1984, the Yankees retired Howard's uniform number 32 and dedicated a plaque in his honor for Monument Park at Yankee

Stadium. The plaque describes him as "a man of great gentleness and dignity" and "one of the truly great Yankees."

YANKEE CAREER HIGHLIGHTS

Best Season

It was difficult not to select 1961 based on the career-high .348 batting average that Howard posted for the Yankees that magical season. He also compiled his highest on-base percentage (.387) and slugging percentage (.549) for the team that year. But Howard posted better numbers in virtually every other offensive category in 1963, when he batted .287, knocked in 85 runs, and established career highs with 28 home runs and 75 runs scored. More important, he assumed the role of team leader in the absence of Mickey Mantle and Roger Maris for much of the year. Injuries limited Mantle to only 65 games and 213 total plate appearances, while Maris found himself able to suit up for only 90 contests. Although the statistics that Howard compiled over the course of the campaign were hardly overwhelming, his leadership proved vital to the success of the team. The members of the Baseball Writers' Association of America recognized that last fact by naming Howard the American League's Most Valuable Player.

Memorable Moments/Greatest Performances

Howard had the most productive offensive game of his career in Kansas City on August 19, 1962, when he went 4 for 6, with 2 home runs and 8 runs batted in during a 21–7 Yankee victory. However, Yankee fans that followed the team during Howard's 13-year stay in New York are more likely to remember the many clutch hits he delivered in postseason play.

Howard accomplished the rare feat of hitting a home run in his first World Series at bat, connecting for a 2-run blast against Dodger right-hander Don Newcombe in the second inning of game 1 in the 1955 Fall Classic. Howard's blow, which tied the contest 2–2, gave the Yankees their first 2 runs in a 6–5 victory.

Howard connected against Newcombe again in game 7 of the following year's World Series, hitting 1 of 4 round-trippers that the Yankees collected during their 9–0 championship-clinching win.

The Yankees ended up losing the 1957 World Series to the Milwaukee Braves in seven games, dropping game 4 in the process by a final score of 7–5 in 10 innings. Nevertheless, Howard delivered argu-ably the most memorable hit of the series when he hit a 3-run homer off Warren Spahn with 2 outs in the top of the ninth inning of game 4, which tied the score at 4–4.

The Yankees turned the tables on the Braves in the 1958 World Series, overcoming a 3–1 deficit to defeat Milwaukee in seven games. Howard proved to be a huge factor in the Yankees' come-from-behind victory, playing a key role in each of the final three contests. Playing left field in game 5, Howard helped preserve a 1–0 Yankee lead when he caught a sinking fly ball in the sixth inning and made a throw to first base that doubled up Milwaukee speedster Bill Bruton. Again playing the outfield in game 6, Howard threw out Andy Pafko at the plate in the second inning, before singling and scoring what turned out to be the game-winning run in the top of the 10th inning of a 4–3 Yankee victory. Howard was at it again in game 7, singling in Yogi Berra with the go-ahead run in the bottom of the eighth inning, as the Yankees completed their comeback with a 6–2 win. Although team-mate Bob Turley earned official World Series MVP honors, Howard's outstanding all-around performance earned him recognition as series MVP by the New York chapter of the Baseball Writers' Association of America, which presented him with the Babe Ruth Award.

NOTABLE ACHIEVEMENTS

- Hit more than 20 home runs three times.
- Batted over .300 three times.
- 1958 Babe Ruth Award winner as World Series MVP.
- 1963 AL MVP.
- Three-time *Sporting News* All-Star selection.
- Nine-time AL All-Star.
- Two-time Gold Glove winner.
- Nine-time AL champion.
- Four-time world champion.

Jorge Posada

Yankee fans less than 40 years of age—especially those who closely follow sabermetrics—might well object to the idea of placing Jorge Posada 32nd in these rankings. They likely will feel that the longtime Yankee catcher deserves a higher spot, especially since his final ranking has him trailing fellow receivers Elston Howard and Thurman Munson. After all, Posada compiled significantly better offensive numbers than both Howard and Munson during his 17 seasons in New York. Posada's 275 home runs exceeded Howard's total by more than 100 and more than tripled Munson's output. He also finished well ahead of Howard and Munson in runs batted in, runs scored, hits, doubles, and slugging percentage. The only offensive categories in which Posada trailed his two predecessors were triples and batting average. However, while Posada's career average of .273 fell short of the marks posted by both Howard (.279) and Munson (.292), his greater ability to draw bases on balls enabled him to compile a significantly higher on-base percentage (.374) than either man (Howard's was .324 while Munson's was .346).

Nevertheless, the feeling here is that Munson and Howard both deserve to be ranked ahead of Posada due to their superior all-around skills. During his time with the Yankees, Posada never developed into anything more than a marginal signal caller, and he remained a below-average defensive receiver his entire time in pinstripes (he finished either first or second in the AL in passed balls a total of seven times). Furthermore, Posada was a poor base runner, displaying a complete lack of instincts on the base paths. Meanwhile, Howard's exceptional baseball acumen and outstanding quickness behind the plate helped compensate for his lack of foot speed. Munson also had exceptional agility and intelligence; he was also blessed with good running speed for a catcher. Of even greater significance is the fact that Howard and Munson were both tremendous field generals who took control of games from behind home plate. They were exceptional team leaders who earned the complete respect and trust of the members of their respective pitching staffs. More than anything, that innate quality ended up pushing both men ahead of Posada, who frequently butted heads with Yankee pitchers during his time in New York.

Yet, all the negatives notwithstanding, Posada established himself as one of the finest offensive receivers in team history during his years in pinstripes. A five-time Silver Slugger winner and five-time member of the AL All-Star and *Sporting News* All-Star Teams, Posada surpassed 20 home runs eight times, 90 RBIs five times, and 90 runs scored and 40 doubles two times each. He also batted over .300 once, compiled an on-base percentage in excess of .400 four times, and posted a slugging percentage in excess of .500 on four occasions. Posada amassed more doubles (379) and drew more bases on balls (936) than any other Yankee receiver, and he hit more home runs (275) than any other player who manned the position for the team, with the exception of Yogi Berra. His many accomplishments helped the Yankees capture 12 division titles, 7 American League pennants, and 5 world championships.

Originally a second baseman when the Yankees first selected him in the 24th round of the 1990 amateur draft, Jorge Rafael Posada spent the better part of six years working his way up through the team's farm system, being converted into a catcher in his second minor-league season. After brief call-ups in 1995 and 1996, the 26-year-old receiver joined the Yankees for good in 1997, batting .250, hitting 6 home runs, and driving in 25 runs, serving primarily as Joe Girardi's backup behind home plate. Posada continued to split playing time with Girardi the next two seasons, working on his defensive skills under the tutelage of the veteran catcher while displaying glimpses of his offensive prowess by combining for a total of 29 homers and 120 RBIs. The Yankees finally elected to turn over the full-time starting-catching duties to Posada in 2000, a season in which the receiver earned AL All-Star honors for the first of four consecutive times by hitting 28 home runs, driving in 86 runs, scoring 92 others, batting .287, compiling a .417 on-base percentage, and posting a .527 slugging percentage.

After totaling 42 home runs and 194 RBIs over the course of the next two seasons, Posada had the most productive year of his career in 2003, earning a third-place finish in the AL MVP voting by batting .281 and establishing career highs with 30 homers and 101 runs batted in. He followed that up with three more productive years, before having arguably his finest all-around season at the age of 36. Posada concluded the 2007 campaign with 20 home runs, 90 runs batted in, 91 runs scored, and a career-high .338 batting average, .426 on-base percentage, and .543 slugging percentage.

Posada's outstanding performance earned him a new four-year $52-million contract to remain with the Yankees. However, he spent much of 2008 on the disabled list, eventually requiring surgery to repair his injured right shoulder. Posada returned to the team in 2009, helping the Yankees capture their first AL East title in three years by hitting 22 homers, knocking in 81 runs, and batting .285. He also performed well during the subsequent postseason, homering twice and driving in eight runs, as the Yankees won their first world championship since 2000.

Advancing age caused Posada's offensive production and playing time to diminish in each of the next two seasons, prompting him to announce his retirement when he became a free agent at the end of the 2011 campaign. Posada concluded his 17 seasons in New York with 275 home runs, 1,065 RBIs, 900 runs scored, 1,664 hits, 379 doubles, a .273 batting average, a .374 on-base percentage, and a .474 slugging percentage. He ranks 8th in team history in home runs, 7th in doubles and walks, and 10th in total bases (2,888). Posada is one of only two Yankee catchers to hit as many as 30 home runs in a season (Yogi Berra is the other).

CAREER HIGHLIGHTS

Best Season

Posada earned a third-place finish in the AL MVP balloting in 2003, when he established career highs with 30 home runs and 101 runs batted in. He also scored 83 runs, batted .281, compiled a .405 on-base percentage, and posted a .518 slugging percentage. However, his overall offensive numbers were slightly better in 2007, a season in which he finished sixth in the MVP voting. In addition to compiling the highest batting average (.338), on-base percentage (.426), and slugging percentage (.543) of his career, Posada hit 20 homers, knocked in 90 runs, scored 91 others, and reached career bests in hits (171), doubles (42), and total bases (275). Posada finished near the top of the league rankings in batting average (fourth), on-base percentage (third), slugging percentage (eighth), and doubles (eighth). His outstanding performance made him the only catcher in major-league history to bat over .330 and surpass 20 home runs, 40 doubles, and 90 RBIs in the same season.

Memorable Moments/Greatest Performances

Posada experienced the first of several memorable moments as a member of the Yankees on May 17, 1998, when he caught David Wells's perfect game against Minnesota at Yankee Stadium. The Yankee catcher received another honor some 10 years later, on September 21, 2008, when he caught the ceremonial first pitch prior to the start of the final game played at the original Yankee Stadium. The pitch was thrown to Posada by Julia Ruth Stephens—the only living daughter of Babe Ruth. Posada made history the following season, when he hit the first regular-season home run in the new Yankee Stadium against Cleveland's Cliff Lee on April 16, 2009.

Posada had the most productive offensive day of his career against Detroit on September 10, 2003, when he hit a grand slam and drove in seven runs during a 15–5 Yankee rout of the Tigers. He also had big games against the Houston Astros on consecutive days in June 2010, becoming the first Yankee since Bill Dickey in 1937 to hit grand slams in back-to-back games.

Still, Yankee fans are likely to think of Posada most kindly when they recall the many times he delivered for the team in postseason play.

Posada got one of his biggest hits for the Yankees on October 13, 2001, when his fifth-inning solo homer provided all the scoring in the club's 1–0 victory over Oakland in game 3 of the ALDS. The win helped the Yankees overcome a 2–0 deficit in a series they eventually went on to win in five games.

Posada delivered another huge hit in game 7 of the 2003 ALCS against Boston. Facing Pedro Martinez in the bottom of the eighth inning with the Red Sox leading 5–3, Posada stroked a double to short center field that drove home Bernie Williams and Hideki Matsui with the game-tying runs. The Yankees eventually won the contest in the 11th inning on a walk-off homer by Aaron Boone.

Posada continued to come up big in the clutch during the Yankees' successful run to the world championship in 2009. After hitting a tie-breaking home run in the seventh inning of New York's series-clinching game 3 win over Minnesota in the ALDS, Posada tied up game 3 of the ALCS against the Angels with a solo homer in the top of the eighth.

Although the Yankees eventually lost the 2011 ALDS in five games to Detroit, Posada ended his career in pinstripes in style, collecting 6 hits in 14 official trips to the plate en route to compiling a .429 batting average, a .579 on-base percentage, and a .571 slugging percentage.

NOTABLE ACHIEVEMENTS

- Hit 30 home runs once.
- Surpassed 20 homers seven other times.
- Knocked in more than 100 runs once.
- Batted over .300 once.
- Topped 40 doubles twice.
- Compiled on-base percentage in excess of .400 four times.
- Posted slugging percentage in excess of .500 four times.
- Only catcher in major-league history with more than 20 home runs, 40 doubles, 90 RBIs, and .330 batting average in same season.
- Third in 2003 AL MVP voting.
- Won 5 Silver Sluggers.
- Five-time *Sporting News* All-Star selection.
- Five-time AL All-Star.
- Seven-time AL champion.
- Five-time world champion.

③

Andy Pettitte

Just as younger Yankee fans will likely find fault with Jorge Posada's placement in these rankings, they too are likely to object to Andy Pettitte's assignment to the number 33 position. After all, Pettitte ranks third in team history in wins (203), second in strikeouts (1,823) and games started (396), and fourth in innings pitched (2,536). He won more postseason games (19) than any other pitcher in major-league history (18 of those coming as a Yankee), and with a total of 148 victories (111 of those coming as a Yankee), he posted more wins between 2000 and 2009 than any other hurler in either league.

However, supporters of Pettitte who routinely suggest that he was a tremendous big-game pitcher who deserves serious consideration for the Hall of Fame tend to look at the left-hander through rose-colored glasses. Although Pettitte was indeed a fine pitcher who generally performed well during the postseason, he turned in several poor performances. Before pitching a gem in game 5 of the 1996 World Series, Pettitte surrendered 7 runs to the Braves in only 2 1/3 innings in the opening contest. One year later, he allowed the Indians 7 runs on 9 hits in only five innings of work in game 2 of the ALDS. In his lone start against Cleveland in the 1998 ALCS, Pettitte surrendered 6 runs on 8 hits in only 4 2/3 innings. He also allowed the Braves 5 runs on 10 hits in just 3 2/3 innings in his lone start in the 1999 World Series. Pettitte was also hit extremely hard by Arizona in the 2001 World Series and by Anaheim in the 2002 ALDS. Pettitte's career record of 19–10 in postseason play is quite impressive. But he compiled a very mediocre 3.83 ERA in his 42 starts, clearly indicating that he does not deserve to be mentioned in the same breath with postseason legends such as Sandy Koufax (0.95), Bob Gibson (1.89), and Curt Schilling (2.23). Pettitte also posted a less-than-stellar regular-season ERA of 3.88 over the course of his career, including a mark of 3.98 in his 13 seasons with the Yankees, which represents a rather high figure for someone deemed to be Hall of Fame worthy.

Also working against Pettitte is his admission of guilt to the use of performance-enhancing drugs. On December 15, 2007, Pettitte verified the claim made by former Yankees trainer Brian McNamee that he injected the left-handed pitcher with HGH on two to four occasions in 2002 to allow Pettitte to heal quickly from an elbow injury. Although Pettitte denied at the time having used HGH or any other performance-enhancing drug at any other time during his career, it later surfaced that he received at least two additional injections of HGH in 2004. That being the case, we are left wondering to what extent Pettitte enhanced his performance by artificial means during his playing days. Although Pettitte likely would not have finished any higher than 33rd in these rankings anyway, it consequently became impossible for me to seriously consider moving him up any further on this list. Nevertheless, Pettitte's outstanding career accomplishments as a member of the Yankees most certainly earned him a spot somewhere in the top 50.

Selected by the Yankees in the 22nd round of the 1990 amateur draft, Andrew Eugene Pettitte spent four long years working his way up the organizational ladder before finally earning a spot on New York's major-league roster in 1995. Joining the Yankees' starting rotation early in the year, the 23-year-old left-hander had a solid rookie campaign, compiling a record of 12–9 en route to earning a third-place finish in the AL Rookie of the Year balloting. Pettitte developed into the ace of the Yankees' pitching staff the following year, when he finished 21–8, to lead all American League pitchers in wins. The 6'5", 235-pound southpaw's outstanding performance earned him a second-place finish in the AL Cy Young voting and spots on the AL and *Sporting News* All-Star Teams.

Pettitte followed that up with arguably his finest season in pinstripes in 1997, posting a record of 18–7 and an exceptional 2.88 ERA, which helped lead the Yankees into the playoffs for the third straight time. Pettitte led all AL pitchers with 35 games started; he also finished among the leaders in wins, ERA, winning percentage (.720), and innings pitched (240). Although Pettitte's earned run average jumped to well over 4.00 in each of the next three seasons, the left-hander continued to serve as one of the anchors of a Yankee pitching staff that helped lead the team to three consecutive world championships. Pettitte posted a combined record of 49–31 from 1998 to 2000, earning a fourth-place finish in the Cy Young balloting in the last of those years, when he compiled a mark of 19–9. He also began to establish his reputation as an outstanding big-game pitcher during that time, compiling a composite record of 6–1 in postseason play. Pettitte performed particularly well against Texas and San Diego during the 1998 postseason, limiting the Rangers to 1 run on 3 hits in seven innings of work in the ALDS, before shutting out the Padres on only 5 hits in 7 1/3 innings in his lone World Series start.

The Yankees failed to win another world championship in any of the next three seasons, losing the World Series in 2001 and 2003 and being eliminated by the Anaheim Angels in the first round of the postseason tournament in 2002. Nevertheless, Pettitte remained a consistent winner for the club, combining for another 49 victories, including a 21-win effort in 2003. Yet, never fully satisfied with Pettitte's performance, Yankee management allowed the 31-year-old hurler to leave via free agency at the conclusion of the 2003 campaign. Pettitte ended up signing a three-year $31.5-million contract with the Houston Astros, with whom he remained until he became a free agent again at the end of 2006.

Upon the termination of his three-year deal with the Astros, Pettitte elected to return to New York when the Yankees expressed interest in bringing him back to the Bronx for a second tour of duty. Pettitte subsequently spent the final four years of his career pitching for the team that originally signed him almost two decades earlier. He posted at least 14 victories in three of those seasons, concluding the 2009 campaign with an exceptional postseason run during which he became the first pitcher in Major League Baseball history to start and win three series-clinching playoff games in the same year. Although still extremely effective in 2010, Pettitte decided to announce his retirement during the subsequent off-season, expressing an interest in spending more time with his family. Pettitte ended his playing career with a lifetime record of 240–138. He posted an overall mark of 203–112 for the Yankees. Pettitte's postseason record with the Yankees was 18–9. In addition to winning more postseason games than any other pitcher in baseball history, Pettitte holds the all-time record for most starts (42) and innings pitched (263). He pitched for eight division-winning, seven pennant-winning, and five world championship teams in New York.

YANKEE CAREER HIGHLIGHTS

Best Season

Pettitte had arguably the best year of his career for Houston in 2005, when he finished 17–9 with a 2.39 ERA for the light-hitting Astros.

However, his finest season in New York could be narrowed down to either 1996 or 1997. Pettitte led all AL hurlers with 21 wins in the first of those years, while losing only eight times and compiling a 3.87 ERA en route to earning a second-place finish in the league Cy Young balloting. But other than wins and winning percentage, he did not finish among the AL leaders in any major statistical category. Meanwhile, Pettitte placed near the top of the league rankings in five categories in 1997, when he compiled a record of 18–7, for a winning percentage of .720, along with a 2.88 ERA, 240 innings pitched, and a league-leading 35 starts. He also allowed fewer hits (233) than innings pitched for one of only three times as a member of the Yankees. Although Pettitte won three more games the previous year, he pitched more effectively in 1997. That was his finest season in pinstripes.

Memorable Moments/Greatest Performances

Pettitte's outstanding performance during the 2009 postseason certainly ranks among his greatest accomplishments. The left-hander compiled a postseason record of 4–0, en route to becoming the first pitcher to start and win three series-clinching games in the same year. After helping the Yankees complete their three-game sweep of Minnesota in the ALDS by limiting the Twins to just 1 run on 3 hits over 6 1/3 innings in New York's 4–1 game 3 victory, Pettitte posted another strong effort against Anaheim in game 6 of the ALCS, holding the Angels to only 1 run over 6 1/3 innings. Pettitte subsequently completed his trifecta by defeating Philadelphia twice in the World Series, including a 7–3 victory in the series clincher.

Still, Pettitte turned in his most memorable performance in game 5 of the 1996 World Series against the Braves. With the Fall Classic tied at two games apiece, Pettitte engaged NL Cy Young Award winner John Smoltz in a classic pitcher's duel in Atlanta that ended in a 1–0 Yankee victory. Displaying tremendous will and determination throughout the tension-filled contest, Pettitte worked 8 1/3 scoreless innings, allowing the Braves just 5 hits, in making the lone run his teammates scored in the fourth inning stand up as the game winner. The Yankees subsequently won their first World Series in 18 years when the two teams returned to New York for game 6.

NOTABLE ACHIEVEMENTS

- Two-time 20-game winner.
- Won at least 14 games 10 other times.

- Compiled ERA below 3.00 once (2.88 in 1997).
- Led AL pitchers in wins once and games started three times.
- Third all-time on Yankees in wins (203), second in strikeouts (1,823) and starts (396), and fourth in innings pitched (2,536).
- Major League Baseball's all-time postseason wins leader with 19 (18 with Yankees).
- Only pitcher ever to start and win 3 series-clinching playoff games in same year.
- 2001 ALCS MVP.
- Two-time *Sporting News* All-Star selection.
- Three-time AL All-Star.
- Seven-time AL champion.
- Five-time world champion.

34

Bob Shawkey

Rivaling Mel Stottlemyre as arguably the most overlooked and under-appreciated of all Yankee pitchers was Bob Shawkey, who had the misfortune of coming to New York before the Yankees became perennial pennant contenders during the 1920s. Acquired from Connie Mack's Philadelphia Athletics midway through the 1915 campaign, Shawkey spent his first few years in pinstripes pitching for a team that found itself mired in mediocrity much of the time. Nevertheless, the hard-throwing right-hander stood out as one of the American League's finest hurlers, annually placing among the circuit leaders in wins, complete games, innings pitched, shutouts, and strikeouts. And after Babe Ruth arrived in New York in 1920, Shawkey continued to pitch at an extremely high level, winning at least 16 games five straight times and helping the Yankees capture their first five American League pennants and first two world championships.

After beginning his career in professional baseball with the Harrisburg Senators of the Tri-State League in 1911, James Robert Shawkey made his major-league debut with the Philadelphia Athletics midway through the 1913 campaign. The 23-year-old right-hander became a regular member of the A's starting rotation the following year, compiling a record of 15–8, a 2.73 ERA, and 18 complete games for the American League champions. However, when Philadelphia lost the World Series to the light-hitting Boston Braves in four straight games, A's owner/manager Connie Mack began disassembling his team during the subsequent off-season, selling most of his best players to other ball clubs. After breaking up his "hundred thousand-dollar infield," which included Hall of Fame second baseman Eddie Collins, Mack peddled Shawkey to the Yankees for the sum of $18,000 on June 28, 1915.

Pitching for a team that finished 14 games under .500 in 1915, Shawkey struggled somewhat in his first year in New York, winning just 4 of his 11 decisions. However, he helped the Yankees post their first winning record in six seasons the following year, going 24–14, with a 2.21 ERA, 21 complete games, 277 innings pitched, and a league-leading 8 saves. Although Shawkey pitched well again in 1917, compiling an ERA of 2.44 and tossing 16 complete games, poor run support from New York's feeble lineup limited him to a record of 13–15.

After missing virtually all of the 1918 season while serving in the Navy during World War I, Shawkey returned to the Yankees in 1919 to begin an exceptional stretch during which he won 20 games in three of the next four seasons. He posted marks of 20–11, 20–13, 18–12, and 20–12 from 1919 to 1922 while compiling an ERA below 3.00 and tossing more than 20 complete games in three of those four years. His 2.45 ERA in 1920 led the American League, as did his 5 saves in 1919. The Yankees won their first two American League pennants in 1921 and 1922, losing the World Series to the Giants both times. Although they failed to earn a victory in the 1922 Fall Classic, Shawkey pitched extremely well in his lone start, holding the National League champions to 3 runs on 8 hits over 10 innings.

Shawkey had another solid year for the Yankees' 1923 world championship ball club. After making history by starting the first game ever played at Yankee Stadium, he went on to compile a record of 16–11 for the first of two consecutive seasons. Shawkey moved to the Yankee bullpen in 1925, spending the final three years of his career working as a spot starter/long reliever. He finished his 13 seasons in New York with a record of 168–131 and a 3.12 ERA. Shawkey's 168 victories place him sixth on the Yankees' all-time list. He also ranks in the team's all-time top 10 in innings pitched (2,489), complete games (164), shutouts (26), and strikeouts (1,163). Shawkey's seven 1–0 victories remain a Yankee record.

A student of the mental aspects of pitching, Shawkey studied the great hitters of his era to analyze the success they experienced against him so that he might vary his pitches accordingly. Shawkey's intellectual approach to his craft enabled him to transition into coaching when his playing career ended. He served in that capacity under Miller Huggins in 1929, until the Yankee manager passed away late in the year. Shawkey assumed the team's managerial reins in 1930, leading the Yankees to a third-place finish before being replaced at the helm by Joe McCarthy prior to the start of the 1931 campaign. Shawkey subsequently began a long career of minor league managing, coaching in the Pittsburgh and Detroit farm systems. He returned to Yankee Stadium in 1976, though, to throw out the ceremonial first pitch at the opening day festivities for the renovated Yankee Stadium. Shawkey passed away four years later at the age of 90, on New Year's Eve 1980.

YANKEE CAREER HIGHLIGHTS

Best Season

Shawkey pitched exceptionally well for the Yankees in 1919, 1920, and 1922, winning 20 games, compiling an ERA below 3.00, and throwing at least 20 complete games each season. His 2.45 ERA in 1920 led all AL hurlers, and he tossed a career-high 22 complete games and 299 2/3 innings in 1922. Nevertheless, it would be difficult not to select 1916 as Shawkey's finest season. The right-hander finished second in the league to Walter Johnson with 24 wins; compiled a career-low 2.21 ERA; threw 21 complete games, 277 innings, and 4 shutouts; and led the American League with 8 saves. He also allowed just 204 hits in those 277 innings of work, establishing in the process easily the best hits:innings pitched ratio of his career.

Memorable Moments/Greatest Performances

Shawkey pitched the most historic game of his career on April 18, 1923, when he got the starting assignment for the first game ever played at Yankee Stadium—a contest he won by a score of 3–1. However, that was not the best game he ever pitched in a Yankee uniform. Shawkey threw two one-hitters for the Yankees, and he struck out 15 Philadelphia Athletics in 1919, establishing in the process a franchise record that stood for 59 years, until Ron Guidry fanned 18 batters in a 1978 contest. Shawkey also put together his finest stretch of pitching in 1919, hurling 31 1/3 consecutive scoreless innings at one point during the season en route to posting 10 straight victories. Perhaps the most memorable game that Shawkey pitched during that exceptional run was the 13-inning complete-game 2–1 victory he registered over Boston rookie (and future Yankee) Waite Hoyt.

NOTABLE ACHIEVEMENTS

- Four-time 20-game winner.
- Topped 16 victories three other times.

- Compiled ERA below 3.00 on six occasions.
- Completed at least 20 games four times.
- Threw more than 250 innings five times.
- Holds Yankee career record with seven 1–0 victories.
- Led AL pitchers in ERA once and saves twice.
- Five-time AL champion.
- Two-time world champion.

35

Tommy Henrich

Nicknamed "Old Reliable" by longtime Yankee announcer Mel Allen for his propensity for getting big hits in clutch situations, Tommy Henrich spent his entire 11-year career with the Yankees, helping them win eight pennants and seven world championships. Known for his steady defense and ability to perform well under pressure, Henrich joined Joe DiMaggio and Charlie Keller in forming one of the finest outfields in American League history. Although Henrich found himself being overshadowed by DiMaggio his entire time in New York, his teammates were keenly aware of the significant contributions that he made to the many championship ball clubs for which he played. Former Yankee teammate Bobby Brown stated, "Tommy was a terrific player. What made him so special was that he always played well in big games. It seemed like he never made any mistakes in the outfield. He was a true professional and an ultimate Yankee."

Originally signed by the Cleveland Indians in 1934, Thomas David Henrich spent three full years in Cleveland's farm system, excelling at every level. After batting .346 for the New Orleans Pelicans of the Southern Association in 1936, Henrich appeared ready to join the major-league club. However, the Indians instead sold his contract to the Milwaukee Brewers of the American Association, allegedly because they considered fellow minor-league outfielder Jeff Heath to be a better prospect. Believing that the Indians' primary motive was to conceal him in their farm system, Henrich and his father wrote to commissioner Kenesaw Mountain Landis, claiming that the franchise was denying the 24-year-old outfielder an opportunity to perform at the major-league level. Landis subsequently ruled in Henrich's favor, declaring him a free agent in April 1937. Henrich ultimately signed with the Yankees for a $25,000 bonus.

After debuting with the Yankees in May 1937, Henrich spent his first four years in New York vying for playing time in the outfield with young left fielder Charlie Keller and veteran right fielder George Selkirk, who replaced Babe Ruth as the team's starter at that position in 1935. Henrich appeared in more than 100 games just once between 1937 and 1940, hitting 22 homers, driving in 91 runs, scoring 109 others, and batting .270 in just under 500 official at bats in 1938. It was during the 1938 World Series, though, that Henrich provided an early glimpse into his ability to provide the team with big hits. Inserted into the number 3 spot in the Yankees batting order by manager Joe McCarthy, Henrich homered late in game 4 to help the Yankees complete their four-game sweep of the Chicago Cubs.

Having finally supplanted Selkirk as the team's starting right fielder by 1941, Henrich hit a career-high 31 home runs in helping the Yankees win their fifth world championship in six years. The 28-year-old outfielder also knocked in 85 runs, scored 106 times, and batted .277. After a somewhat less-productive 1942 campaign, Henrich missed the next three seasons while serving in the Coast Guard during World War II.

Henrich posted solid numbers when he returned to the team in 1946, hitting 19 homers, driving in 83 runs, and scoring 92 others. He followed that up with the first of what turned out to be his two most productive seasons. In 1947, Henrich hit 16 home runs, knocked in 98 runs, scored 109 others, batted .287, and led the AL with 13 triples en route to earning All-Star honors for the first of four straight times. The 35-year-old outfielder then hit 25 homers, batted .308, and led the league with 14 triples and 138 runs scored in 1948, earning in the process the first of two consecutive sixth-place finishes in the AL MVP voting. Henrich also drove in 100 runs, surpassing the 100-RBI mark for the only time in his career.

Henrich had another good year in 1949, hitting 24 homers, driving in 85 runs, scoring 90 others, and batting .287 while seeing a significant amount of playing time at first base. He transitioned into the role of part-time first baseman/pinch hitter the following year, which ended up being his last as an active player. Released by the Yankees at season's end, Henrich subsequently announced his retirement. He concluded his 11-year career with 183 home runs, 795 runs batted in, 901 runs scored, 1,297 hits, a .282 batting average, a .382 on-base percentage, and a .491 slugging percentage. Although none of those figures place Henrich among the franchise's all-time leaders, he served as an integral member of the championship Yankee ball clubs for which he performed. Yogi Berra said of his former teammate, "Tommy was a darn good ballplayer and teammate. He always took being a Yankee to heart. He won a lot of championships and did whatever he could to help us win."

Following his playing days, Henrich served as a member of Casey Stengel's coaching staff in 1951, before later taking on a similar role with the New York Giants and Detroit Tigers. He lived until the age of 96, passing away in 2009 after suffering a series of strokes. At the time of his death, he was the fifth-oldest living former major-league player and the oldest living Yankee.

CAREER HIGHLIGHTS

Best Season

Henrich had very good years in 1941 and 1947, hitting a career-high 31 homers and scoring 106 times in the first of those campaigns while knocking in 98 runs, scoring 109 others, and topping the junior circuit with 13 triples in the second. However, 1948 was clearly Henrich's finest season. In addition to hitting 25 home runs, batting .308, and compiling a .391 on-base percentage, he established career highs with 100 runs batted in, 181 hits, 42 doubles, 326 total bases, a .554 slugging percentage, and a league-leading 138 runs scored and 14 triples. Henrich placed among the AL leaders in eight offensive categories en route to earning a sixth-place finish in the league MVP balloting.

Memorable Moments/Greatest Performances

In his finest all-around season of 1948, Henrich tied a then AL record by hitting 4 grand slams. However, the outfielder gained far more notoriety over the course of his career for collecting a number of clutch hits during postseason play.

Facing the Dodgers in the 1947 World Series, Henrich drove in a pair of runs in the Yankees' 5–3 game 1 victory. He followed that up by homering during the team's 10–3 win in game 2. Henrich capped off his outstanding performance by driving in Phil Rizzuto with the deciding run of a 5–2 Yankee win in game 7.

Henrich proved to be an even bigger thorn in the side of the Dodgers when the Yankees faced them again in the Fall Classic two years later. He became the first player ever to hit a walk-off home run in World Series play when he ended game 1 with a leadoff homer against Don Newcombe in the bottom of the ninth inning. The blast gave the Yankees a 1–0 victory over their National League counterparts. Henrich also scored twice in the Yankees' series-clinching 10–6 game 5 win.

Nevertheless, Henrich is perhaps remembered best for the role he played in one of the most famous moments in World Series history. The outfielder stepped to the plate with two men out in the top of the ninth inning of game 4 of the 1941 Fall Classic. With the Dodgers clinging to a 4–3 lead over the Yankees, Brooklyn stood just one out away from evening the series at two games apiece. Facing Dodger relief pitcher Hugh Casey, Henrich swung at a full-count breaking ball for strike three. However, Dodger catcher Mickey Owen couldn't handle the sharp-breaking pitch, allowing the ball to elude him and Henrich, in turn, to reach first base. Joe DiMaggio followed with a single, and Charlie Keller drove in both base runners with a 2-run double. Joe Gordon later doubled home another 2 runs, giving the Yankees a 7–4 lead that they refused to relinquish. The victory gave the Yankees a 3–1 lead in the series, which they closed out the next day with a 3–1 victory. Henrich hit a solo home run during the series-clinching game 5 win.

NOTABLE ACHIEVEMENTS

- Hit more than 30 home runs once (31 in 1941).
- Knocked in 100 runs once (100 in 1948).
- Scored more than 100 runs four times.
- Batted over .300 three times.
- Compiled on-base percentage in excess of .400 three times.
- Posted slugging percentage in excess of .550 twice.
- Led AL in runs scored once and triples twice.
- 1949 *Sporting News* All-Star selection.
- Five-time AL All-Star.
- Eight-time AL champion.
- Seven-time world champion.

36

Rich Gossage

One of the pioneers of the closer role that has since become such an intricate part of our national pastime, Rich "Goose" Gossage struck fear into the hearts of opposing hitters. Gossage's mean-looking scowl, unorthodox delivery, and fastball that frequently approached 100 miles per hour made him easily the most intimidating relief pitcher of his time. Adding to the reliever's mound presence were his size and willingness to pitch inside to those who dared to step into the batter's box to face him. Hall of Famer Dave Winfield, who played with the 6'3", 220-pound Gossage in New York for three years, discussed the degree to which his former teammate instilled fear in opposing batters: "When you saw him work up into a frenzy and a foam in the bullpen—he'd come out sweatin' and snortin' and slinging that baseball—the manager's looking for someone, 'Where's my pinch-hitter?' and guys are drinking water, and they're going to the bathroom. They don't want any part of Goose."

The level of dominance that Gossage attained at the peak of his career made him, at least to some degree, the Mariano Rivera of his time. The fire-balling right-hander once went an entire season surrendering only 4 runs to the opposition, compiling in the process an ERA of 0.77 over the course of the campaign. And just as Rivera has relied primarily on only one pitch throughout most of his career, Gossage depended almost exclusively on his blazing fastball. Aside from the incredible consistency that Rivera has displayed through the years that sets him apart from all other relievers, the biggest difference between the two men is that Gossage frequently earned saves by entering games as early as the seventh inning.

Already a top-notch closer by the time he joined the Yankees in 1978, Richard Michael Gossage spent his first five major-league seasons with the Chicago White Sox after they selected him in the ninth round of the 1970 amateur draft. After working out of the Chicago bullpen his first four seasons, Gossage found himself being converted into a starter in 1976 by the pitching-starved White Sox, for whom he went just 9–17 in his only year as a member of the team's starting rotation. Subsequently dealt to the Pittsburgh Pirates for slugging outfielder Richie Zisk prior to the start of the 1977 campaign, Gossage returned to his more familiar role, saving 26 games, winning 11 others, compiling a brilliant 1.62 ERA, allowing only 78 hits in 133 innings of work, and striking out 151 batters for the Pirates. However, when Gossage became a free agent at the end of the year, he signed a six-year contract with the Yankees to become their new closer.

The first several weeks of the 1978 campaign did not go smoothly for New York's latest high-priced superstar. Gossage got off to a slow start, blowing several save opportunities during the season's first month. The reliever's early-season woes could be attributed in large part to the pressure that he felt from wanting to earn the trust of his new teammates and hometown fans. However, he also felt burdened by trying to replace as closer 1977 AL Cy Young Award winner Sparky Lyle, who Gossage relegated to setup duties in the Yankee bullpen. Furthermore, Gossage drew the ire of Billy Martin in spring training when he refused to comply with the Yankee manager's directive to hit an opposing player in the head with a pitch. The volatile Martin did not care much for outfielder Billy Sample, whom he managed in Texas. Gossage later revealed that Martin approached him during an exhibition game and told him to "drill that bleepin' Sample in the bleepin' head." Fearing he might kill Sample, Gossage declined to do so, thereby doing irreparable damage to his relationship with Martin.

Despite Martin's lack of fondness for Gossage, the Yankee manager found himself relying heavily on his ace reliever after he eventually righted himself. Gossage ended up having an outstanding year for the Yankees, finishing the campaign with a league-leading 27 saves, posting 10 victories of his own, compiling an ERA of 2.01, striking out 122 batters in 134 innings, and allowing just 87 hits en route to earning a spot on the AL All-Star Team and being named the AL Rolaids Reliever of the Year. Gossage also had an excellent postseason, helping the Yankees win their second straight world championship by saving their one-game playoff victory over the Boston Red Sox, picking up a save against Kansas City in the ALCS, and posting a victory and working six scoreless innings against the Dodgers in the World Series.

A clubhouse scuffle with teammate Cliff Johnson less than two weeks into the 1979 campaign resulted in an injured pitching hand for Gossage and a lengthy stint on the disabled list. Yet, he still managed to win five games and accumulate 18 saves. Back in top form in 1980, Gossage had one of his finest seasons, helping the Yankees compile a major-league best 103–59 record by going 6–2, with a 2.27 ERA and a league-leading 33 saves. He also allowed only 74 hits in 99 innings of work while amassing 103 strikeouts. Gossage's exceptional performance earned him a third-place finish in the league MVP voting. However, the ace reliever found his brilliant regular-season effort overshadowed by the 3-run home run he surrendered to George Brett in game 3 of the ALCS that all but eliminated the Yankees from the playoffs.

As good as Gossage was in 1980, he may have been even better the following year. The reliever was practically unhittable during 1981's split season, compiling a 0.77 ERA and a record of 3–2 with 20 saves while allowing only 22 hits in 47 innings of work. He was just as impressive in the postseason, saving all three wins versus the Brewers in the ALDS, picking up a save against the A's in the ALCS, and saving the Yankees' only two victories in the World Series against the Dodgers. During the postseason, Gossage allowed no runs and just 6 hits, while striking out 15 men, in 14 1/3 innings of work.

Goose had two more outstanding seasons for the Yankees before he decided to head for the West Coast when he became a free agent at the conclusion of the 1983 campaign. Gossage finished second in the American League with 30 saves in 1982, earning in the process his fourth and final All-Star nomination as a member of the Yankees. He followed that up with a record of 13–5, 22 saves, and a 2.27 ERA in his final season in pinstripes.

Seeking a more tranquil setting after spending six years pitching in a place that came to be known as the "Bronx Zoo" for the level of insanity that frequently pervaded Yankee Stadium at that time, Gossage chose to sign with the San Diego Padres. He spent four years in San Diego, helping the Padres capture their first National League pennant in 1984. From there, he moved on to the Chicago Cubs for one year, then on to the Giants, back to the Yankees briefly, and then on to Texas, Oakland, and Seattle before finally retiring at the end of the 1994 season. Gossage ended his career with 310 saves and a win total of 115, which places him third on the all-time list for relief pitchers, behind only Hoyt Wilhelm and Lindy McDaniel. Gossage's numbers as a Yankee include a record of 42–28, a 2.14 ERA, and 151 saves. His 2.14 ERA ranks as the best in team history, and his 151 saves place him third on the team's all-time list, behind only Mariano Rivera (603) and Dave Righetti (224).

When Gossage left the game, he did so with the admiration and respect of all those who played with and against him. Former Yankee teammate Ron Guidry confided, "I had guys tell me 'We would much prefer hitting off of you than hitting off of him, not because it's any easier, but you don't scare us as much.'"

Guidry also spoke of Gossage's mean streak: "Gossage would just as soon hit you upside the head as give you the time of day."

Jamie Quirk spoke of how intimidating it was to face Gossage on the mound: "I faced Goose many, many times and—very intimidating guy . . . very intimidating. But that's what he wanted. That's what got him the edge over the hitter."

Paul Molitor discussed how right-handed hitters in particular had a difficult time picking up the ball against Gossage: "He had that delivery where he hid, and you saw knees, and you saw elbows, and he hid the ball. Then, all of a sudden, out of nowhere, came this 98 mph fastball with movement."

Steve Balboni, who played with Gossage on the Yankees and faced him as a member of the Kansas City Royals, said, "He was the first guy that I know that was just overpowering. When he was on, he was almost unhittable."

The reluctance of the members of the Baseball Writers' Association of America to admit relief pitchers to the Baseball Hall of Fame kept Gossage out of Cooperstown for several years. However, he finally received the necessary 75% vote to gain induction in 2008, in his ninth year of eligibility.

YANKEE CAREER HIGHLIGHTS

Best Season

Although the Yankees fell short of reaching their ultimate goal of winning the World Series, Gossage had his most dominant season for them in 1981. The ace reliever went 3–2 with a 0.77 ERA, and he finished second in the league with 20 saves. Gossage allowed only 4 earned runs all year, struck out 48 batters in 46 2/3 innings of work, and permitted just 36 men to reach base (22 by hit and 14 by walk).

Memorable Moments/Greatest Performances

Gossage excelled for the Yankees during the latter stages of the 1978 campaign, with his most memorable effort coming on October 2, when he saved New York's one-game playoff victory over the arch-rival Boston Red Sox. Entering the tension-filled contest with one man out in the bottom of the seventh inning and the Yankees clinging to a 4–2 lead, Gossage struggled somewhat on the mound, allowing the Red Sox to score twice in the bottom of the eighth inning after Reggie Jackson increased the Yankee lead to three runs by homering in the top of the frame. Gossage subsequently allowed the tying run to reach third base with two men out in the bottom of the ninth, before he ended the affair by inducing Carl Yastrzemski to pop up to third baseman Graig Nettles for the final out. Gossage was also on the mound five days later when the Yankees clinched the pennant in the ALCS against the Kansas City Royals. Entering game 4 in the ninth inning with the Yankees holding a 2–1 lead, no one out, and a runner on at second base for Kansas City, Goose earned the save by striking out Clint Hurdle and retiring Darrell Porter and Pete LaCock on fly balls. Gossage also recorded the final out when the Yankees clinched their second straight world championship 10 days later against the Los Angeles Dodgers.

Gossage was even more impressive on September 3 of that year, when he completely dominated the Seattle Mariners. Replacing Sparky Lyle on the mound for the Yankees in the top of the ninth inning with runners on second and third and no one out, he preserved a 4–3 lead by striking out the next three batters on 11 pitches.

Yet, in spite of the dominance that Gossage often displayed during his six years in pinstripes, he is perhaps remembered best for his failures against Kansas City's George Brett. Facing Brett on October 10, 1980, with two men on base in the top of the seventh inning of game 3 of the ALCS, Gossage delivered a fastball that the Royals slugger deposited into Yankee Stadium's right-field upper deck. The blow turned the tide in the contest, putting the Royals in the lead and all but clinching the pennant for them. Brett reached Gossage again almost three years later during the regular season, blasting a go-ahead 2-run home run in the top of the ninth inning of a contest that subsequently became known as the "Pine Tar Game."

NOTABLE ACHIEVEMENTS

- Surpassed 30 saves twice.
- Topped 20 saves three other times.
- Surpassed 10 victories twice.
- Compiled ERA below 2.30 in 5 of 6 full seasons, including a mark of 0.77 in 1981.

- Led AL in saves twice.
- 1978 AL Rolaids Relief Man Award winner.
- Four-time AL All-Star.
- Two-time AL champion.
- 1978 world champion.

Charlie Keller

The third member of the Yankees' brilliant outfield of the 1940s, Charlie Keller might well have made it into the Hall of Fame had his career not been interrupted by World War II and abbreviated by a chronically bad back. Nicknamed "King Kong Keller" due to his exceptional physical strength and dark, bushy eyebrows, Keller had outstanding power at the plate, a keen batting eye, and solid base running and fielding skills. New York's starting left fielder for only six seasons, Keller led the team in home runs four times; slugging percentage, three times; runs scored, triples, and on-base percentage, twice each; and RBIs, hits, and doubles, once each.

An outstanding all-around athlete at the University of Maryland, from which he graduated in 1937, Charles Ernest Keller spent just two years in the Yankee farm system before earning a promotion to the big-league club prior to the start of the 1939 campaign. Keller began his professional career by winning *Sporting News* Minor League Player of the Year honors in 1937. In addition to leading the International League with a .353 batting average, 120 runs scored, 189 hits, and 14 triples, he hit 13 home runs and drove in 88 runs for the Newark Bears. In spite of Keller's exceptional performance, the Yankees elected to return him to Newark in 1938 since they had no openings in their starting outfield of Joe DiMaggio, Tommy Henrich, and George Selkirk. However, the organization knew that Keller's time had arrived when he batted .365, compiled a .569 slugging percentage, and topped the International League with 211 hits, 149 runs scored, 108 walks, and a .465 on-base percentage in 1938.

Upon his arrival in New York the following season, it did not take Keller long to establish himself as the team's starting leftfielder.

Teaming with DiMaggio and Henrich the next several years, Keller helped give the Yankees the best outfield in baseball. Yet, it took the powerfully built Keller some time to discover his power stroke. More of a gap-to-gap line-drive hitter when he first joined the Yankees, the left-handed-hitting Keller had to be coerced by team management to swing more for Yankee Stadium's short porch in right field. After batting .334, compiling a .447 on-base percentage, driving in 83 runs, scoring 87 others, and hitting 11 homers in 111 games and just under 400 official at bats as a rookie, the 23-year-old outfielder began to swing more for the fences in 1940. The results ended up being a lower batting average but an increase in home run production. Keller concluded his sophomore campaign with 21 homers, 93 RBIs, 102 runs scored, 15 triples, a .286 batting average, a league-leading 106 bases on balls, a .411 on-base percentage, and a .508 slugging percentage.

Keller followed that up with arguably his finest all-around season. Although the fabulous campaign turned in by Joe DiMaggio, who hit safely in a record 56 consecutive games over the course of the season, forced Keller to take a backseat to "The Yankee Clipper" in the eyes of the public, 1941 was a banner year for the leftfielder as well. Keller batted .298, scored 102 runs, and finished among the league leaders with 33 home runs, 122 runs batted in, 102 walks, a .416 on-base percentage, and a .580 slugging percentage. Keller earned his second of five All-Star selections and a fifth-place finish in the AL MVP voting. He punctuated his outstanding year by batting .389 and knocking in 5 runs during the Yankees' five-game victory over Brooklyn in the World Series.

Keller also performed extremely well for the Yankees in each of the next two seasons, combining for 57 home runs, 194 runs batted in, and 203 runs scored and helping New York capture two more pennants and another world championship. However, his playing career was temporarily put on hold when he spent all of 1944 and most of 1945 serving as a member of the US Merchant Marine during World War II.

After returning to the Yankees for the final six weeks of the 1945 campaign, Keller had his last big year for the club in 1946, hitting 30 homers, driving in 101 runs, scoring 98 others, and finishing second in the league with 113 bases on balls. A ruptured disk in his back severely limited Keller's playing time and offensive production in each of the next three seasons. Serving the team mostly as a part-time outfielder and pinch hitter, Keller combined to hit only 22 home runs and knock in just 96 runs from 1947 to 1949. Released by the Yankees at the conclusion of the 1949 campaign, Keller signed with the Detroit Tigers, with whom he spent the next two years serving almost exclusively as a pinch hitter. He returned to the Yankees in 1952, appearing in only two games before announcing his retirement at season's end. Keller concluded his 11 years in pinstripes with 184 home runs, 723 runs batted in, 712 runs scored, 1,053 hits, a .286 batting average, a .410 on-base percentage, and a .518 slugging percentage. He ranks fourth in team history in on-base percentage and eighth in slugging percentage.

CAREER HIGHLIGHTS

Best Season

Although Keller posted excellent offensive numbers in each of his six full seasons as a starter, the 1941, 1942, and 1946 campaigns were his three most productive years. In 1942, he hit 26 homers, drove in 108 runs, scored 106 others, batted .292, compiled a .417 on-base percentage, and posted a .513 slugging percentage. After returning to the Yankees from the merchant marine during the latter stages of the previous season, Keller hit 30 home runs in 1946, knocked in 101 runs, crossed the plate 98 times himself, batted .275, and finished with a .405 on-base percentage and a .533 slugging percentage. However, Keller compiled his best overall numbers in 1941, when he batted .298, scored 102 runs, posted a .416 on-base percentage, and established career highs with 33 home runs, 122 runs batted in, and a .580 slugging percentage. The slugging outfielder finished among the league leaders in eight offensive categories, including home runs (second) and RBIs (third). His .996 OPS also placed him third in the league rankings. Keller's outstanding performance earned him a spot on the AL All-Star Team and a fifth-place finish in the MVP balloting.

Memorable Moments/Greatest Performances

Keller had arguably his greatest individual game on July 28, 1940, when he hit 3 home runs during a 10–9 Yankee victory over the Chicago White Sox at Comiskey Park. He also accomplished the rare feat of hitting 2 consecutive pinch-hit home runs in 1948.

Nevertheless, Keller's most memorable performance took place during his rookie season of 1939, when he hit 2 home runs and knocked in 4 runs in game 3 of the World Series against the Cincinnati Reds. Keller's 2 homers made him the first rookie to go deep twice in one World Series game. The outfielder concluded the Fall Classic with 3 home runs, 6 runs batted in, 8 runs scored, a .438 batting average, a

.471 on-base percentage, and a 1.188 slugging percentage in leading the Yankees to a four-game sweep of Cincinnati.

NOTABLE ACHIEVEMENTS

- Hit more than 30 home runs three times.
- Knocked in more than 100 runs three times.
- Scored more than 100 runs three times.
- Batted over .300 twice.
- Compiled on-base percentage in excess of .400 seven times.
- Posted slugging percentage in excess of .550 on three occasions.
- Led AL in walks twice and on-base plus slugging once.
- Five-time AL All-Star.
- Six-time AL champion.
- Five-time world champion.

38

Bobby Murcer

One of the most popular players ever to wear a New York Yankees uniform, Bobby Murcer entered the major leagues with the immense pressure of trying to replace Mickey Mantle as the team's next true superstar. Although Murcer failed to reach the same level of greatness that his Yankee predecessor attained over the course of his career, he eventually developed into a perennial All-Star and the team's finest all-around player. The American League's 1972 leader in runs scored and total bases, Murcer actually had three tours of duty in New York, bridging the gap between two distinct generations of championship Yankees teams.

Born in Oklahoma City, Oklahoma, on May 20, 1946, Bobby Ray Murcer attended local Southeast High School, where he starred in baseball, football, and basketball. After signing a letter of intent to play for the Oklahoma Sooners, Murcer instead chose to sign an amateur free agent contract with the Yankees in June 1964. Murcer later recalled, "The Yankees offered me $10,000 less than the Dodgers did. I thought 'I'll just make it up in World Series money . . . no big deal.'"

Little did Murcer know at the time that the 1964 campaign would mark the end of the Yankee dynasty. After earning Carolina League MVP honors with New York's Greensboro affiliate in 1965, Murcer joined a Yankee team late in the year that found itself firmly entrenched in the American League's second division. Playing all his games at shortstop, the 19-year-old saw limited action down the stretch, appearing in only 11 contests, coming to the plate a total of just 37 times, batting .243, and hitting his first major-league home run. Murcer also joined the team briefly at the end of the 1966 season, batting just .174 in 69 at bats.

Murcer's first experience at the major-league level turned out to be a difficult one. Having grown up in Oklahoma, he seemed intimidated by the big city. Furthermore, he appeared to be a bit overwhelmed by the expectations that the team placed on him at the tender age of 19, when the organization began referring to him as "the next Mickey Mantle." In truth, Mantle and Murcer did share certain similarities. They were both from Oklahoma. They were both signed by the same scout, Tom Greenwade. And they both originally came up as 19-year-old shortstops. But that is where the similarities between the two men ended; although Murcer was a gifted athlete, he had neither the awesome power nor the blinding speed that Mantle possessed in his youth.

Called into the army at the end of the 1966 campaign, Murcer missed the next two seasons. However, his stint in the military turned out to be a blessing in disguise since he returned to the Yankees a new man in 1969. More mature both mentally and physically, Murcer seemed much better prepared to play major-league baseball. Reflecting on his military experience, Murcer said, "I think, all in all, it helped me—not only as a player, but also as a man—because, when I came back, I was much more ready to handle the rigors and the pressures of playing professional baseball, maturity-wise."

Still, Murcer had the unenviable task of trying to replace Mickey Mantle as the team's next great player. Adding to the pressures placed on Murcer by fans and the media were the high expectations that the team thrust on him when it assigned him the locker of the recently retired Mantle. Playing under close scrutiny, Murcer handled himself rather well his first two seasons. After struggling defensively at third base early in 1969, Murcer moved to center field, where he found a home. As he continued to learn his new position, Murcer put up solid offensive numbers, combining for 49 home runs, 160 runs batted in, and 177 runs scored in 1969 and 1970. Nevertheless, his batting averages of .259 and .251 disappointed Yankee fans, as did his strikeout totals of 103 and 100. Before long, Murcer found himself the occasional target of boos emanating from the stands in his home ballpark.

However, Murcer turned those boos into cheers in 1971, developing into one of the American League's finest all-around players over the course of the campaign. After constantly trying to take advantage of Yankee Stadium's short right-field porch by pulling the ball his first two seasons, the left-handed-swinging Murcer evolved into a more complete hitter. As former Chicago White Sox outfielder Carlos May said, "[Murcer] was tailor-made for that ballpark. He hung over the plate, and anything inside—lookout—home run."

Correspondingly, opposing pitchers tended to pitch Murcer out-side, causing him to frequently strike out or hit weak ground balls to the right side of the infield. Learning from his earlier mistakes, Murcer began hitting the ball more to left field in 1971, allowing him to be-come one of the junior circuit's elite batsmen.

Discussing Murcer's maturation as a hitter, former Yankee pitcher Al Downing stated, "After about 2 1/2 years the bell goes off and you say 'Why am I fighting myself? Just relax and do what I'm capable of doing.' I think that's what happened with Bobby. He settled in and became an outstanding ballplayer."

Murcer raised his batting average 80 points in 1971, finishing a close second to Tony Oliva in the American League batting race with a mark of .331. He also hit 25 home runs, drove in 94 runs, scored 94 others, and cut his strikeout total down to just 60. Murcer's .427 on-base percentage led the American League, and he finished among the leaders in slugging percentage, runs batted in, runs scored, and total bases. Murcer's strong throwing arm also enabled him to place near the top of the league rankings in outfield assists for the second of five consecutive times. Murcer's exceptional all-around performance earned him the first of four straight selections to the AL All-Star Team, a spot on the *Sporting News* All-Star squad, and a seventh-place finish in the league MVP voting.

Murcer had another outstanding season in 1972, batting .292 and establishing career highs in home runs (33), runs batted in (96), and runs scored (102). He led the American League in runs scored and total bases; he also placed among the leaders in five other offensive catego-ries. Murcer again earned *Sporting News* All-Star honors, won the only Gold Glove of his career for his outstanding defense in center field, and finished fifth in the league MVP voting.

After another fine season in 1973 in which he hit 22 homers, knocked in 95 runs, batted .304, finished ninth in the league MVP bal-loting, and earned his third straight *Sporting News* All-Star selection, Murcer's performance slipped somewhat in 1974. With the Yankees playing their home games in Shea Stadium while Yankee Stadium underwent major renovations, Murcer had a difficult time adjusting to the swirling winds and more distant right-field fence in Queens. Many balls he pulled to right field that would have been home runs in Yan-kee Stadium were caught on the warning track in Shea, enabling him to hit only 10 home runs all year. Murcer also scored just 69 runs and batted only .274. Yet, he still managed to lead the team with 88 runs batted in, do an excellent defensive job in right field after surrendering his prestigious spot in center to Elliott Maddox, and earn his fourth straight selection to the AL All-Star Team.

Concerned that Murcer appeared to be losing his power stroke, the Yankee front office made a move on October 22, 1974, that stunned Murcer and Yankee fans alike. General manager Gabe Paul informed the team's most popular player early that morning that he had been dealt to the San Francisco Giants for star outfielder Bobby Bonds. Distraught after hearing the news, Murcer swore to never forgive the Yankees, who he had always held close to his heart.

Murcer later recalled, "I was devastated by leaving the Yankees and the pinstripes, and I just didn't feel in my own mind that I belonged any other place but playing for the Yankees."

After recovering from the initial shock, Murcer ended up having a solid season for the Giants in 1975. Although playing in cold and windy Candlestick Park limited him to only 11 home runs, Murcer knocked in 91 runs, batted .298, struck out only 45 times in 526 at bats, walked 91 times, and earned a spot on the National League All-Star Team. After another productive season with the Giants in which he hit 23 homers and drove in 90 runs, Murcer was traded to the Cubs for two-time defending NL batting champion Bill Madlock.

Murcer posted good numbers in Chicago in 1977 and 1978, but the 32-year-old outfielder began to see his playing time diminish in 1979—a year in which he collected only 190 at bats during the first half of the season. Still longing for a return to New York, Murcer jumped at the opportunity that Chicago's GM presented to him when he mentioned that the Yankees had expressed interest in reacquiring the outfielder. Murcer returned to the team and the city he loved so dearly on June 26, after the Yankees obtained him for a minor-league pitcher and cash. Murcer's return to the organization turned out to be a stroke of fate, since it reunited him with former teammate and close friend Thurman Munson, who died tragically in a plane crash just six weeks later.

After rejoining the Yankees, Murcer briefly took over the starting center-field job from the recently departed Mickey Rivers, who had been traded to Texas for Oscar Gamble. He then moved to left field to make room for young outfield prospect Bobby Brown. Playing regularly the remainder of the season, Murcer hit 8 home runs, knocked in 33 runs, and batted .273 in 264 at bats. He received one of his greatest thrills two years later when he appeared in the World Series as a member of the team that originally signed him. Reflecting on his lone trip to the Fall Classic, Murcer said, "Being in a World Series in Yankee Stadium—that was a dream come true."

Murcer remained with the team another two years, serving mostly as a part-time designated hitter and pinch hitter. He retired early during the 1983 campaign to make room on the roster for a young prospect named Don Mattingly. Murcer was immediately given a job in the broadcast booth as an announcer, a position he held for more than 20 years.

Bobby Murcer never quite reached the level of greatness that many people predicted for him early in his career. Nevertheless, he was a very good player for quite a few seasons, and he was New York's best player throughout much of his first tenure with the team. In addition to earning four American League and three *Sporting News* All-Star selections, Murcer placed in the top 10 in the MVP voting three times. He finished in the league's top 5 in hits and total bases three times each; runs batted in, runs scored, batting average, slugging percentage, and bases on balls, two times each; and home runs and on-base percentage, once each. He also led all league outfielders in assists on two occasions. Murcer finished his career with 252 home runs, 1,043 runs batted in, 972 runs scored, 1,862 hits, and a .277 batting average. His Yankee numbers include 175 homers, 687 RBIs, 641 runs scored, 1,231 hits, and a .278 batting average.

Former Yankee teammate Roy White expressed the belief that Murcer would have posted significantly better numbers had he remained in New York his entire career. White suggested,

> If Bobby would have had a chance to play his whole career with the Yankees, he would have had some great numbers. He probably could have added close to another 150 home runs onto his home run total because he had a great swing for Yankee Stadium—a very compact, short stroke. Him getting traded and going to the other teams, I think it hurt his overall numbers. I think he could have been that much greater a player if he could have been with us. Plus, he was really upset about leaving New York. In his heart he was all Yankee.

While Murcer's departure from New York may have adversely affected the statistics he compiled over the course of his career, it did not diminish in the least his popularity with Yankee fans. Loved both as a player and as an announcer, Murcer remained in the Yankee television booth for 23 years, until he was diagnosed with a brain tumor on Christmas Eve 2006. He underwent surgery a few days later, after which he learned that the tumor was malignant. Murcer made his first postoperative appearance on fellow Yankee broadcaster Michael Kay's radio show on January 23, 2007. After being interviewed by Kay and taking telephone calls from listeners, Murcer ended the conversation by saying, "I want to thank you very much for giving me the forum to do this because I wanted you to know that, even though this looks bad, I'm doing great. I really am. I'm in a great place. God has given me peace and the overwhelming love has been insurmountable for me to even deal with. I can feel the fans. I can feel their thoughts and their prayers, and I wanted to tell them how much I love them."

Murcer returned to work in the Yankee television booth on May 1, 2007, and spent the remainder of the year announcing games for the team. In late February 2008, an MRI scan led Murcer's doctors to perform a biopsy, which happily revealed scar tissue instead of a recurrence of brain cancer. However, Murcer suffered a relapse some four months later and passed away on July 12. Murcer's death came only months after he released his autobiography, which ironically was entitled *Yankee for Life*.

YANKEE CAREER HIGHLIGHTS

Best Season

It is an awfully close call between Murcer's 1971 and 1972 campaigns. Although he also played very well in 1973, those were easily Murcer's two best years.

In 1972, Murcer batted .292, compiled a .361 on-base percentage, and established career highs with 33 home runs, 96 RBIs, and a league-leading 102 runs scored and 314 total bases. However, Murcer posted comparable offensive numbers the previous year, when he hit 25 homers, knocked in 94 runs, scored 94 others, and accumulated 287 total bases. He also finished a close second in the AL batting race with a mark of .331 and topped the circuit with a .427 on-base percentage. And even though Murcer hit 8 fewer home runs than he did in 1972, he finished with a slightly higher slugging percentage (.543 to .537). Perhaps the best argument that could be waged on behalf of 1971 was Murcer's league-leading .969 on-base plus slugging, which exceeded his 1972 mark of .898 by 71 points. Murcer was clearly among the American League's elite players both years. But I will place his 1971 performance ever so slightly ahead of the effort he turned in one year later.

Memorable Moments/Greatest Performances

During his time in New York, Murcer often demonstrated that he had a flair for the dramatic. He hit 3 home runs in a game twice as a member of the Yankees, accomplishing the feat for the first time during a doubleheader against the Cleveland Indians on June 24, 1970. After homering against Sam McDowell in his final at bat of the first contest, Murcer hit three consecutive homers in the nightcap, making him one of only four Yankee players in history to hit home runs in four straight at bats (Lou Gehrig, Johnny Blanchard, and Mickey Mantle were the others). Murcer again hit 3 home runs in one game on July 13, 1973, driving in all 5 runs during a 5–0 Yankee win over Kansas City at Yankee Stadium.

In August 1972, Murcer became the first Yankee to hit for the cycle since Mickey Mantle accomplished the feat 15 years earlier.

However, the most memorable game of Murcer's career (and arguably his greatest performance) took place on August 6, 1979, just four days after his close friend Thurman Munson died in a plane crash. Earlier that very same day, Murcer and Lou Piniella both delivered eulogies at their team captain's funeral. Included in Murcer's eulogy were the words "Someday the Yankees may have another captain . . . no greater honor could be bestowed on a man than to be a successor to this man." He added, "Thurman Munson, who wore the pinstripes, was number 15, but in living, loving, and legend, history will record my friend as Number 1."

Following the service, the Yankees seriously considered canceling that evening's game against the Baltimore Orioles. The team finally decided to go through with the nationally televised contest, though, after Murcer went to George Steinbrenner and told him of Diane Munson's request. Murcer had spent the previous evening at the Munson home, and the widow of the Yankees' fallen captain informed him that she wanted the team to play the next day because her husband would have wanted it that way. Piniella arrived at the ballpark that evening too distraught to play, but fellow eulogist Murcer felt differently. Even though he broke into tears while delivering his eulogy, Murcer told manager Billy Martin that, for some reason, he felt as if he needed to play that night.

With the Yankees trailing Baltimore 4–0 in the bottom of the seventh inning, Murcer hit a 3-run homer to right field to close the gap to 4–3. Then, coming up in the bottom of the ninth with runners on second and third, no one out, and the Yankees still trailing 4–3, Murcer continued his heroics by winning the game with a line-drive, two-run single to left field.

Looking back on the events of the evening, Murcer recalled, "It was a special night, and sometimes extraordinary things happen on special nights. Was it meant to be? Maybe it was . . . I don't know."

He then added, "I do know one thing, that after the game, the bat that I used that night I never did use again. In fact, I gave it to Diane [Munson]. This was special for me, special for Thurman, and whatever this bat produced needed to be in the Munson family, so I gave it to her."

NOTABLE ACHIEVEMENTS

- Hit more than 30 home runs once.
- Scored more than 100 runs once.
- Batted over .300 twice.
- Compiled on-base percentage in excess of .400 once.
- Led AL in runs scored, total bases, on-base percentage, and on-base plus slugging once each.
- One of only six Yankee players to hit 3 home runs in one game more than once.
- One of only four Yankee players to hit 4 consecutive home runs.
- Three-time *Sporting News* All-Star selection.
- Four-time AL All-Star.
- 1972 Gold Glove winner.
- 1981 AL champion.

Roy White

Steady and dependable, Roy White patrolled left field for the New York Yankees for more than a decade, first joining the team in 1965, at the beginning of the most unsuccessful period in franchise history. A solid switch hitter who possessed good speed and outstanding ball-hawking skills, White served as New York's starting leftfielder from 1968 to 1978, warding off challenges his last few seasons from a seemingly endless array of outfielders that the team acquired to eventually replace him. Often overlooked and underappreciated, White was New York's most consistent everyday player during the dark days of the late 1960s, before making key contributions to three pennant-winning teams and two world championship clubs his final few years.

Born in Los Angeles, California, on December 27, 1943, Roy Hilton White signed with the Yankees as an amateur free agent in 1961 after graduating from Compton's Centennial High School. He began his minor-league career the following year as an 18-year-old switch-hitting second baseman with the Greensboro Yankees in the Class B Carolina League. White showed great promise in his second full season in the minors, batting .309 as Greensboro's leadoff hitter and topping the circuit with 117 runs scored en route to earning a spot on the league's All-Star team. After spending the entire 1964 season and most of the following year in the minors, White finally joined the Yankees toward the tail end of the 1965 campaign. Upon his arrival, White was quickly converted into an outfielder by the major-league club.

After batting .333 over the final three weeks of the 1965 season, White got off to a fast start the following year. However, he eventually slumped badly, ending the campaign on the bench with a batting average of just .225. He then batted just .224 in 214 official plate appearances in 1967, while splitting his time between the outfield and third base.

White discussed the struggles he experienced during the early stages of his career, saying,

> I think it was switching positions . . . from being an infielder, to an outfielder, to an infielder, back to an outfielder. I think that affected my hitting. Actually, in 1966, I was leading the Yankees in hitting and in home runs about six weeks into the season. Then I got home run happy. I started thinking that it was easy. Then I got myself into a terrible slump and ended up being on the bench by June. I had seven home runs in May and, at the end of the season, I still had seven. I ended up hitting around .220 in a couple of hundred at bats. All of the position switching started around then, and I just had trouble finding a spot where I finally got comfortable.

White's fortunes finally began to change in 1968, after manager Ralph Houk informed him that he intended to use him strictly as an outfielder. White revealed, "In spring training of 1968, Ralph Houk said, 'You're just going to be an outfielder now. Let's not worry about going back into the infield. Just stay out there and learn how to play it to the best of your ability.' That was kind of a load off of my mind, knowing that I was going to be in the outfield and that I had nothing else to concentrate on."

After seeing some action in both right field and center field early in the year, White found a permanent home in left. "I think we were on a road trip," White recalled. "Then, when we came back from the road, Ralph called me into his office and said, 'I'm gonna play you in left. It's a big left field in Yankee Stadium and you'd be the ideal guy, with your speed, to cover the ground out there.' From that point on, I was in left field."

White's insertion into the everyday lineup enabled him to develop into New York's best all-around player. In addition to playing a stellar left field, he led the team in virtually every offensive category, topping his mates with 62 runs batted in, 89 runs scored, 20 stolen bases, 7 triples, and a .267 batting average. He also finished a close second to Mickey Mantle with 17 home runs. After batting in a number of different spots in the Yankee lineup during the early stages of the season, White eventually assumed the cleanup spot in the batting order. Reflecting on how he felt hitting immediately behind Mantle in the lineup, White revealed, "That was really amazing . . . pretty shocking actually. That was after another meeting with Ralph. He called me in and said, 'Roy, I'm gonna hit you number four. I just don't have anybody else. They're pitching around Mickey. He's not getting very many good pitches to hit, and you're the most reliable guy on the club, so I'm gonna hit him three and hit you four.'"

White continued to bat fourth in the Yankee order for the next half-dozen seasons, having his two best years while hitting cleanup. After leading the team in batting for the second consecutive time with a .290 batting average in 1969, he had his finest all-around season in 1970, establishing career highs in home runs (22), runs batted in (94), runs scored (109), base hits (180), and batting average (.296) while earning his second straight selection to the American League All-Star Team. White followed that up by hitting 19 home runs, driving in 84 runs, scoring 86 others, and batting .292 in 1971.

Even though White manned the cleanup spot in the Yankee batting order for a number of years, at only 5'10" and 170 pounds, he was far from a prototypical fourth-place hitter.

White was much better suited to hit either first or second in the lineup since doing so would have enabled him to better use his abilities to get on base, score runs, work the count, hit and run, steal bases, and do the little things to help his team win. He was an extremely patient hitter, finishing among the top ten players in the league in bases on balls seven times during his career and even leading the league with 99 walks in 1972. He also topped the circuit in runs scored once, placing among the league leaders in that particular category five other times as well and crossing the plate more than 100 times in two different seasons.

However, the Yankees simply did not have anyone else more capable than White of batting fourth throughout much of his career. White himself admitted, "I was pretty well miscast in the number four slot. I had to change my mentality, especially batting left-handed in Yankee Stadium, with the shorter porch in right. If it was a tie ballgame, or, if we were down by a run in the later innings, I had to look for a pitch that maybe I could try to pull and that I had a chance to hit out. That wasn't really the type of player that I was."

New York finally provided White with a better supporting cast his final few years with the team, enabling him to move to his more natural number 2 spot in the lineup. Hitting second for the pennant-winning Yankees in 1976, he batted .286, stole a career-high 31 bases, and led the American League with 104 runs scored.

Two years prior to that, though, White had to prove himself all over again when Bill Virdon took over as manager of the team. In a scenario that became all too familiar later in White's career, his abilities and overall contributions to the team were underestimated by Virdon, who seemed intent on limiting the veteran outfielder's playing time early in the season. Even though White did an outstanding defensive job for the Yankees the previous six seasons, leading all league left fielders in fielding percentage four straight times at one point and annually finishing among the leaders in range factor, he rarely played the outfield the first two months of the 1974 campaign, more often than not being used instead as a designated hitter or pinch hitter. Instead of playing White in his familiar spot in left field, manager Virdon preferred to use Elliott Maddox in center, Bobby Murcer in right, and Lou Piniella in left. Even on those rare occasions when White started in left, he frequently found himself being replaced in the late innings for defensive reasons. It took Virdon half a year to realize that he had made an error in judgment.

White later revealed, "In spring training of 1974, Virdon came in, and he had never seen me play before. I think I'm one of those guys you gotta see me play everyday or you probably couldn't appreciate some of the little things that I tried to do as a player. So, I think he formed an opinion of me right away, and he later called me into his office one day—and he even said it to the press—that he underestimated me as a ballplayer when he first got there and didn't realize that I was a good player until after he had seen me play everyday."

Still, even those more familiar with White as a player seemed to have a difficult time fully appreciating all the little things he did to help the team win. After leading the league in runs scored in 1976, he received slightly less playing time in 1977, and he saw his role diminish even further in 1978. Surrounded by more colorful and charismatic players such as Reggie Jackson, Thurman Munson, Mickey Rivers, and Lou Piniella, White often found his skills being taken for granted by the Yankee brass, which seemed intent on replacing him with someone else his last few years with the team. White himself later admitted, "It seemed like, for awhile, they were always trying to find somebody to replace me. I never was a big power guy and they may have just been looking for someone who had more power." As a result, players such as Gary Thomasson and Jay Johnstone, who had been platoon players throughout most of their careers, saw more action in left field for much of the 1978 season than White.

However, when Bob Lemon replaced Billy Martin as manager in July, he immediately inserted White into the starting lineup. After seeing extremely limited playing time under Martin and struggling in his part-time role, White became one of New York's hottest hitters over the season's final two months. Raising his batting average almost 70 points to .269 by season's end, White helped the Yankees overcome a deficit of 14 1/2 games to the Boston Red Sox and eventually capture the AL East title.

In spite of the success that White experienced during the latter stages of the 1978 campaign, he saw his playing time reduced again the following year. Appearing in just 81 games in 1979, White accumulated only 205 at bats and batted just .215. After becoming a free agent at the end of the year, he briefly toyed with the idea of signing with the California Angels. However, White eventually chose to go to Japan, where he spent the final three years of his playing career as a teammate of the legendary Sadaharu Oh on the Tokyo Giants. After retiring as an active player at the conclusion of the 1982 campaign, White returned to the states, where he eventually rejoined the Yankees as a coach during the mid-1980s. White spent three years on New York's coaching staff, before serving for a time as hitting instructor for the Oakland A's Triple-A affiliate. He returned to the Yankees as first base coach at the start of the 2004 season, spending two more years in pinstripes before being relieved of his duties at the conclusion of the 2005 campaign.

Over parts of 15 seasons with the Yankees, White hit 160 home runs, drove in 758 runs, scored 964 others, accumulated 1,803 hits, stole 233 bases, batted .271, and compiled a lifetime on-base percentage of .360. He ranks in the top 10 in franchise history in games played, at bats, base hits, runs scored, and stolen bases. Equally significant are the contributions he made to three consecutive pennant-winning teams and two world championship clubs during the latter stages of his career, when his quiet class and dignity made him one of the most respected men on the turbulent Yankee teams of the late-1970s.

CAREER HIGHLIGHTS

Best Season

White batted .286, scored a league-leading 104 runs, and stole a career-high 31 bases for the Yankees' 1976 AL championship ball club. He also had a very good year in 1971, when he hit 19 home runs, drove in 84 runs, scored 86 others, and batted .292. However, White had his finest all-around season in 1970, when he stole 24 bases, compiled a .387 on-base percentage, and established career highs with 22 home runs, 94 runs batted in, 109 runs scored, 180 hits, a .296 batting average, and a .473 slugging percentage. He finished among the league leaders in eight offensive categories, committed only 2 errors in the outfield all year, led all AL left fielders in fielding percentage and range factor, and earned a spot on the AL All-Star Team for the second straight year.

Memorable Moments/Greatest Performances

An outstanding clutch performer throughout his career, White came up with countless big hits for the Yankees during his time in pinstripes. He delivered arguably his two most memorable hits during the 1978 postseason.

With the Yankees leading the Royals 2–1 in that year's ALCS, White stepped up to the plate to face Kansas City ace Dennis Leonard with the score tied 1–1 with one man out in the bottom of the sixth inning of game 4. Batting left-handed against Leonard, White helped clinch the series for the Yankees by driving the right-hander's first pitch into the right-field stands. The blow gave the Yankees a 2–1 lead that Ron Guidry and Goose Gossage protected the rest of the way, putting New York into the World Series for the second straight year.

White subsequently excelled against Los Angeles in the Fall Classic. Although the left fielder delivered his biggest hit of the series when he homered against Dodger right-hander Don Sutton in the bottom of the first inning of New York's 5–1 game 3 victory, he performed exceptionally well throughout the six-game series. White batted .333, drove in 4 runs, and scored 9 others, the most significant of which came in the bottom of the 10th inning of game 4, when he crossed the plate with the winning run on a single by Lou Piniella.

NOTABLE ACHIEVEMENTS

- Hit more than 20 home runs once.
- Scored more than 100 runs twice.
- Surpassed 20 stolen bases four times, topping 30 thefts once.
- Led AL in runs scored and walks once each.
- Led AL left fielders in fielding percentage four times and range factor six times.
- Went entire 1971 season (145 games and 320 chances) without committing an error.
- Set AL record with 17 sacrifice flies in 1971.
- Homered from both sides of plate in same game five times during career.
- Two-time AL All-Star.
- Three-time AL champion.
- Two-time world champion.

Rickey Henderson

Widely regarded as the greatest leadoff hitter in baseball history, Rickey Henderson had already established himself as the most dynamic and exciting player in the game by the time that he joined the Yankees in 1985. Blessed with the speed of a sprinter and a body made of iron, Henderson had the ability to create a run all by himself with his legs or his powerful bat. No one else in the sport had the outfielder's ability to bring a crowd to its feet in such a variety of ways. Henderson thrilled fans everywhere with his daring base running, frequently turning a base on balls or a single into a run by stealing second base, advancing to third on an infield out, and scoring on a sacrifice fly. His muscular frame also enabled him to drive the opposing pitcher's offering more than 400 feet from home plate, well into the outfield stands. And Henderson's headfirst slides and patented "snatch catch" became his trademarks, exhibiting the passion and style with which he played the game.

Over the course of his 25-year playing career, Henderson ended up establishing all-time major-league records in stolen bases, runs scored, unintentional walks, and home runs leading off a game. He led his league in stolen bases a record 12 times, surpassing 100 thefts on three occasions. Henderson also topped his circuit in runs scored five times. Those are the figures that prompted Mitchell Page, Henderson's one-time Oakland A's teammate, to say, "But it wasn't until I saw Rickey that I understood what baseball was about. Rickey Henderson is a run, man. That's it. When you see Rickey Henderson, I don't care when, the score's already 1–0. If he's with you, that's great. If he's not, you won't like it."

Henderson was only with the Yankees for parts of five seasons, preventing him from finishing any higher than 40th in these rankings. Nevertheless, he accomplished enough during his 4 1/2 years in New York to earn a spot in our top 50. With 326 stolen bases in pinstripes, Henderson ranks second on the Yankees' all-time list in career steals. He also holds the top three single-season marks in club history. Henderson represented the Yankees on the AL All-Star Team four times; he also earned a top-5 finish in the league MVP voting while wearing the pinstripes. Yet, in spite of the success that Henderson experienced in a Yankee uniform, his time in New York ended in acrimony, with the enigmatic outfielder literally forcing the team to trade him away.

In desperate need of a center fielder and dynamic offensive presence at the top of their batting order, the Yankees sent five players (Tim Birtsas, Jay Howell, Stan Javier, Eric Plunk, and Jose Rijo) to the Oakland Athletics for Henderson on December 5, 1984. Only 25 years old at the time, Henderson had already spent six years with the A's after originally being selected by them in the fourth round of the 1976 amateur free agent draft. In 1980, his first full major-league season, Henderson batted .303, compiled a .420 on-base percentage, scored 111 runs, and stole a league-leading 100 bases, joining in the process Lou Brock (118) and Maury Wills (104) as the only players of the modern era to reach the century mark in steals in a single season.

After performing exceptionally well during the strike-shortened 1981 campaign, Henderson continued his string of seven consecutive seasons in which he led the American League in stolen bases, establishing a new major-league record by swiping 130 bags in 1982. He also scored 119 runs and walked a league-leading 116 times, enabling him to compile an impressive .398 on-base percentage, even though he batted just .267.

Henderson spent two more years in Oakland, posting batting averages of .292 and .293 while combining for 174 stolen bases and 218 runs scored. As his muscular frame continued to develop, he became more of a power hitter. Henderson established a new career high with 16 homers in 1984, a figure that he later surpassed on six occasions after growing into the powerful 5'10", 195-pound frame that eventually earned him the nickname "Man of Steal."

After being acquired by the Yankees at the conclusion of the 1984 campaign, Henderson initially seemed pleased with the idea of coming to New York. Yet, he bristled at the idea of moving from his more natural position of left field to center field, believing that the change in positions might prove harmful to his legs, which he considered to be his greatest asset. Henderson subsequently alienated much of the New

York media that greeted him when his plane landed at the airport, telling the assembled mass, "Don't need no press now, man."

In spite of the somewhat shaky start that Henderson got off to when he first arrived in New York, the outfielder ended up winning everyone over with his exceptional play and charismatic personality. After missing the season's first 15 games with a sprained ankle, Henderson went on to have one of his finest all-around seasons in 1985. He batted .314, compiled a .419 on-base percentage, established new career highs with 24 home runs and 72 runs batted in, and led the American League with 80 stolen bases and 146 runs scored. Henderson's 80 steals and 24 homers made him the first player in major-league history to surpass 80 stolen bases and 20 home runs in the same year (Cincinnati's Eric Davis later joined him). Meanwhile, his 146 runs scored represented the highest total compiled by any player since Ted Williams scored 150 times for Boston in 1950. Henderson's magnificent season earned him a spot on the *Sporting News* All-Star Team and a third-place finish in the league MVP voting, behind teammate Don Mattingly and Kansas City's George Brett.

Moreover, Henderson's broad smile and exciting style of play quickly made him a fan favorite at Yankee Stadium. He not only produced on the field but also provided entertainment with his flashy and innovative mannerisms that eventually earned him the nickname "Style Dog." Henderson became known for his snatch catch, which enabled him to turn a routine fly ball out into a form of entertainment. The outfielder typically swatted at the ball from over his head, before bringing his glove to his side in one swift motion after making the catch.

Although Henderson's batting average fell to .263 in 1986, he led the American League in runs scored (130) and stolen bases (87) for the second straight year while posting a career-best 28 home runs and 74 RBIs. A series of hamstring injuries limited Henderson to just 95 games the following year, bringing to an end his reign as stolen-base champ. Nevertheless, he performed well whenever he took the field, batting .291, hitting 17 homers, scoring 78 runs, and stealing 41 bases. Upset over failing to win the stolen-base title for the first time in eight years, the eccentric outfielder placed a telephone call to Seattle's Harold Reynolds, who ended up topping the circuit with 60 steals. Reynolds later revealed the contents of their brief conversation: "The phone rings. 'Henderson here.' I say, 'Hey, what's going on, Rickey?' I think he's calling to congratulate me, but he goes, 'Sixty stolen bases? You ought to be ashamed. Rickey would have 60 at the [All-Star] break.' And then click, he hung up."

Henderson's rather unusual telephone call to Reynolds really should not have come as much of a surprise to the Seattle second baseman. Noted for his self-absorption and tendency to refer to himself in the third person, Henderson was one of baseball's most unusual and enigmatic figures. He frequently spoke to himself on and off the field. Over the course of his career, Henderson developed a reputation for standing completely naked in front of a full-length mirror in the locker room for several minutes before each game, repeating to himself several times, "Rickey's the best." On one particular occasion, Henderson struck out in a game in Seattle. A former teammate revealed that he then heard Henderson say to himself as he passed him by, "Don't worry, Rickey, you're still the best." San Diego GM Kevin Towers disclosed that Henderson once left the following telephone message for him while looking for a job: "This is Rickey calling on behalf of Rickey. Rickey wants to play baseball."

Although people may have frequently found humor in Henderson's somewhat bizarre behavior, they had a difficult time finding fault with his performance on the field. After returning to New York's lineup fully healthy in 1988, he went on to bat .305, compile a .394 on-base percentage, score 118 runs, and lead the league with 93 stolen bases. However, Henderson's popularity with the fans of New York began to wane when he failed to live up to expectations in 1989. Immersed in the worst prolonged slump of his career, the outfielder batted just .247 during the season's first half, while stealing only 25 bases and scoring just 41 runs. Further alienating Henderson to Yankee fans was the lack of interest and hustle he frequently displayed on the field, even though the Yankees moved him back to his preferred position of left field earlier in the year. Henderson's lackadaisical and dispassionate play earned him a ticket out of New York, something he seemed to want since the team appeared headed in the wrong direction. Dealt back to Oakland, the defending AL West champs, Henderson reasserted himself as one of baseball's best players. He batted .294 over the season's final three months, hit 9 home runs, drove in 35 runs, scored 72 others, and stole 52 bases to lead the A's to their second straight division title. Henderson then performed magnificently during the postseason, batting .400, with 2 homers, 5 RBIs, and 8 runs scored against Toronto in the ALCS, before posting a .474 batting average during Oakland's four-game sweep of San Francisco in the World Series.

Henderson's departure served as one of the key factors that ushered in a dark period in Yankee history. After concluding the 1989 campaign with a record of only 74–87, the team failed to post more than 76 victories in any of the next three seasons. Meanwhile, Henderson captured AL MVP honors in 1990, when he led the A's to their third consecutive American League pennant. He later went on to establish himself as baseball's all-time stolen-base king, as well as the all-time leader in runs scored, unintentional walks, and leadoff home runs. Henderson won another world championship as a member of the Toronto Blue Jays in 1993, beginning a nomadic existence his final 10 seasons that included stops in San Diego, Anaheim, Seattle, Boston, Los Angeles, a return trip to New York as a member of the Mets, and two more stays in Oakland. He ended his major-league career at the conclusion of the 2003 campaign with 297 home runs, 1,115 runs batted in, 2,295 runs scored, 3,055 hits, 1,406 stolen bases, 2,190 walks, a .279 lifetime batting average, and a .401 on-base percentage. Henderson's Yankee numbers include 78 home runs, 255 RBIs, 513 runs scored, 663 hits, 326 stolen bases, 406 bases on balls, a .288 batting average, and a .395 on-base percentage. While the Yankees faltered terribly after Henderson left New York midway through the 1989 campaign, they won no fewer than 85 games in any of his four full years with the team, posting as many as 97 victories in 1985 and finishing second in the AL East on two occasions.

The impact that Henderson made on the Yankees during his relatively brief time in New York would tend to support the comments made by sportswriter Tom Verducci, who wrote, "Baseball is designed to be an egalitarian sort of game in which one player among the 18 is not supposed to dominate. . . . Yet in the past quarter century Henderson and Barry Bonds have come closest to dominating a baseball game the way Michael Jordan could a basketball game."

YANKEE CAREER HIGHLIGHTS

Best Season

Henderson had an outstanding year for the Yankees in 1988, when he batted .305, placed among the league leaders with 118 runs scored and a .394 on-base percentage, and topped the circuit with an all-time Yankee single-season record 93 stolen bases. However, Henderson had his best season in pinstripes three years earlier, earning a third-place finish in the 1985 AL MVP voting by hitting 24 homers, driving in 72 runs, batting .314, compiling a .419 on-base percentage, posting a .516 slugging percentage, and leading the league with 146 runs scored and 80 steals. Henderson's 146 runs scored in 143 games made him the first player since Jimmie Foxx in 1939 to amass more runs scored than games played. In addition to earning AL All-Star honors and a spot on the *Sporting News* All-Star Team, he won the Silver Slugger Award for one of three times in his career.

Memorable Moments/Greatest Performances

On June 26, 1985, Henderson tied a Yankee record by stealing four bases in one game, a feat he later matched on four occasions. Henderson also had a number of exceptional days at the plate for the Yankees, including a 5-for-5 effort against Baltimore during a 10–0 victory over the Orioles at Memorial Stadium on June 17, 1985. However, he may well have turned in his finest all-around performance against the Chicago White Sox at Comiskey Park on May 6, 1986. Henderson helped lead the Yankees to a 10–6 win over the White Sox by collecting 3 hits, including a home run, driving in 3 runs, scoring 3 others, and stealing 3 bases.

Henderson also reached a pair of milestones while wearing the pinstripes. He stole his 75th base of the 1985 campaign during a 10–2 Yankee win over Detroit on September 25, breaking in the process the club's single-season record previously set by Fritz Maisel in 1914. Some 3 1/2 years later, on April 9, 1989, Henderson stole the 800th base of his career, making him just the fourth player in major-league history to reach that plateau (Lou Brock, Billy Hamilton, and Ty Cobb were the first three).

NOTABLE ACHIEVEMENTS

- Hit more than 20 home runs twice.
- Batted over .300 twice.
- Scored more than 100 runs three times, surpassing the 130 mark twice.
- Surpassed 80 stolen bases three times.
- Compiled on-base percentage in excess of .400 twice.
- Led AL in stolen bases three times and runs scored twice.
- Won Silver Slugger Award in 1985.
- 1985 *Sporting News* All-Star selection.
- Four-time AL All-Star.

41

Sparky Lyle

The Yankees made one of the best trades in franchise history on March 22, 1972, when they dealt journeyman first baseman/third baseman Danny Cater to the Boston Red Sox for reliever Sparky Lyle. Cater, a solid line-drive hitter with very little power, ended up assuming a part-time role in Boston the next three years, totaling only 14 home runs and 83 runs batted in. Meanwhile, Lyle spent seven years in New York, establishing himself during that time as arguably the American League's premier closer. The left-handed reliever saved more games than any other pitcher during the 1970s, topping the junior circuit in saves twice while earning two top-10 finishes in the league MVP voting and becoming the first relief pitcher to win the AL Cy Young Award.

One of baseball's first true closers, Albert Walter Lyle differed from other outstanding relief pitchers that preceded him in that he was bred exclusively for work as a reliever. While previous standouts such as Hoyt Wilhelm, Joe Page, and Lindy McDaniel all served as starters at some point during the early stages of their respective careers, Lyle never started a single game in the major leagues. Lyle received his introduction to organized baseball while growing up in Reynoldsville, Pennsylvania, where he began playing American Legion ball for the DuBois team while attending Reynoldsville High School. Featuring a fastball, curveball, and changeup in his early years as a starting pitcher, Lyle once struck out 31 batters while working 14 innings in a state tournament game for DuBois. The left-handed hurler's success at the American Legion level eventually earned him a tryout with the Pittsburgh Pirates, who elected to sign the harder-throwing Bruce Dal Canton instead. Baltimore Orioles scout George Staller also expressed interest in Lyle, though, finally signing the 19-year-old pitcher to an amateur free agent contract on June 17, 1964.

Working as both a starter and a reliever in his first professional season, Lyle split the 1964 campaign between the Bluefield Orioles and the Fox Cities Foxes—Baltimore's Midwest League affiliate. Selected by the Boston Red Sox in the first-year draft on November 30, 1964, Lyle spent the next 2 1/2 years working his way up the Red Sox farm system. He picked up the slider, which eventually became his signature pitch, while at Pittsfield in 1966. Lyle later credited Ted Williams with introducing him to the pitch at spring training prior to the start of the season. Lyle recalled, "[Williams] told me it was the best pitch in baseball because it was the only pitch he couldn't hit even when he knew it was coming."

Called up by the Red Sox in the middle of the 1967 campaign, Lyle helped the team capture the American League pennant by saving 5 games during the season's second half while compiling an outstanding 2.28 ERA in his 27 relief appearances. He established himself as Boston's top reliever the following year, compiling a record of 6–1, saving 11 games, and posting a 2.74 ERA. Lyle saved 53 more games for the Red Sox over the next three seasons, before being acquired by the Yankees for Cater prior to the start of the 1972 campaign.

Lyle developed into arguably baseball's best relief pitcher in New York, leading the American League with 35 saves in 1972 while winning another nine games and pitching to a brilliant 1.92 ERA en route to earning a third-place finish in the league MVP voting. Lyle's 35 saves established a new American League record at the time. Although he pitched less effectively the following year, the left-handed reliever still managed to place among the league leaders with 27 saves. Lyle returned to top form in 1974, winning 9 games coming out of the bullpen, compiling a 1.66 ERA, and earning his second of three selections to the AL All-Star Team. After struggling somewhat in 1975, Lyle helped the Yankees capture the first of three straight American League pennants the following year by topping the junior circuit with 23 saves while posting an exceptional 2.26 ERA. Lyle pitched even more effectively in 1977, compiling a record of 13–5, along with 26 saves and an ERA of 2.17 en route to becoming the first relief pitcher ever to win the AL Cy Young Award.

In spite of Lyle's magnificent 1977 campaign, Yankee owner George Steinbrenner elected to pursue free agent closer Rich Gossage when he became available at the end of the year. Although popular opinion suggested that the addition of Gossage would likely give New York the most dynamic one-two bullpen combination in history, the arrival of the flame-throwing right-hander all but signaled the end of Lyle's time in New York. Assigned a far less prominent role in the Yankee bullpen, Lyle served primarily as Gossage's setup man, surrendering to the team's latest free agent acquisition the more prestigious role he held the previous six years. Lyle's diminished role in the bullpen prompted teammate Graig Nettles to quip during the 1978 campaign that the reliever went "from Cy Young to sayonara." Even though Lyle finished the season with a record of 9–3, he saved only 9 games while posting a somewhat atypical 3.47 ERA.

With Lyle no longer a major part of the team's future plans, the Yankees included the 34-year-old reliever in a huge 10-player deal with the Texas Rangers at the end of the year that netted them Dave Righetti. Lyle spent two years in Texas before moving on to Philadelphia and Chicago, never again achieving the same level of success he had in New York. He retired at the conclusion of the 1982 campaign with 238 career saves, which placed him second only to Rollie Fingers on the all-time list at the time. Lyle earned 141 of those saves as a member of the Yankees. He also compiled a 57–40 record during his time in New York, along with an outstanding 2.41 ERA, which places him third all-time among Yankee pitchers. His 141 saves also place him fourth on the team's all-time list, behind only Mariano Rivera (603), Dave Righetti (224), and Rich Gossage (151).

In addition to being one of the finest relief pitchers of his time, Lyle was one of the most charismatic. Shortly after he joined the Yankees in 1972, he established a ritual in his home ballpark of entering games to the tune of "Pomp and Circumstance." The reliever subsequently threw down his warm-up jacket upon reaching the infield and strode to the mound in a menacing manner, with a huge chaw of tobacco protruding from his jaw. Yankee fans loved Lyle's performance, which soon became akin to a theatrical event.

Possessing the perfect makeup for a top relief pitcher, Lyle remained unphased by even the most dire set of circumstances, exhibiting the swagger and self-confidence that all closers need, as well as the guts of a riverboat gambler. He also had a tremendous slider that completely neutralized right-handed hitters. While Lyle threw his best pitch with less velocity than teammate Ron Guidry, his slider broke down and in to right-handers just as sharply. In fact, Guidry developed the pitch that eventually made him an extremely successful hurler while working with Lyle in the Yankee bullpen early in 1977.

American League batters marveled at not only the movement that Lyle had on his signature pitch but also the level of success that he achieved despite lacking an overwhelming arsenal of pitches. Former outfielder Tom Grieve said of the reliever, "For a guy that really didn't have an exceptional fastball, he saved a lot of games with guts, determination, and a hard slider that he could throw to right-handed hitters."

Willie Randolph said of his former teammate, "I never faced Sparky, but I know he had to be hellacious. You knew the slider was coming, but you still could hardly hit it."

Randolph added, "He had ice water in his veins; he didn't care; he left it on the field and had a good time doing it."

YANKEE CAREER HIGHLIGHTS

Best Season

Lyle pitched exceptionally well for the Yankees in 1974, posting a record of 9–3, saving 15 games, and compiling a 1.66 ERA. He was even better in his Cy Young campaign of 1977, going 13–5, with a 2.17 ERA and 26 saves. A true workhorse for the Yankees all year long, Lyle led all AL pitchers with 72 relief appearances and 60 games finished en route to becoming the first AL reliever to win the Cy Young Award. He also worked a career-high 137 innings. Nevertheless, I elected to go with 1972 as Lyle's finest season. In his first year in pinstripes, Lyle finished 9–5, with a 1.92 ERA and a league-leading 35 saves, which established a new American League record at the time. The Yankees' new closer worked 108 innings, allowing opposing batters only 84 hits while striking out 75. Meanwhile, in his 137 innings of work in 1977, Lyle surrendered 131 hits to the opposition while striking out just 68 men. It was extremely difficult not to select 1977 since Lyle won the Cy Young Award and helped lead the Yankees to the world championship. But his overall numbers in 1972 were just a bit more impressive.

Memorable Moments/Greatest Performances

Lyle put out a number of fires during his seven seasons in pinstripes, coming to the rescue of many a starting pitcher. However, he made his most memorable pitching performance during the 1977 American League Championship Series. With the Yankees trailing Kansas City 2–1 and facing elimination in game 4, Lyle replaced faltering Yankee starter Ed Figueroa in just the bottom of the fourth inning. The eventual Cy Young Award winner worked the final 5 2/3 innings of the pivotal contest, allowing the Royals no runs on only 2 hits, to preserve New York's 6–4 victory. Lyle returned the next day to toss another 1 1/3 scoreless frames during the Yankees' 5–3 come-from-behind victory that propelled them into the World Series. The closer subsequently excelled against the Dodgers in the World Series as well, concluding the postseason with a record of 2–0 and an ERA of 0.96 in just over nine innings of work.

NOTABLE ACHIEVEMENTS

- Surpassed 30 saves once.
- Topped 20 saves three other times.
- Compiled ERA below 2.30 four times, including two marks below 2.00.
- Led AL in saves twice.
- 1977 AL Cy Young Award winner.
- Three-time AL All-Star.
- Three-time AL champion.
- Two-time world champion.

42

Allie Reynolds

Allie Reynolds did not start his first game for the Yankees until he reached his 30th birthday. Nevertheless, the native of Bethany, Oklahoma, spent eight successful years in New York, establishing himself during that time as one of the American League's premier pitchers and as one of the top hurlers in franchise history. The hard-throwing right-hander posted a winning record in each of his eight seasons in pinstripes, surpassing 16 victories six times and compiling a winning percentage in excess of .700 on three occasions. Often used by manager Casey Stengel to close out games as well, Reynolds saved a total of 41 games for the Yankees over the course of those eight seasons. Reynolds's tremendous versatility contributed significantly to six world championships for the Yankees, including five in succession from 1949 to 1953. The fact that Reynolds was even a member of those championship ball clubs can be attributed largely to Joe DiMaggio, on whom the right-hander made an extremely favorable impression during his time in Cleveland.

Nicknamed "Superchief" due to his part-Indian heritage, Allie Pierce Reynolds spent his early years in organized baseball playing for Oklahoma Agricultural and Mechanical College (now known as Oklahoma State University). Sporting an overpowering fastball, Reynolds signed with the Cleveland Indians in 1939, after which he spent the next three years working his way up the team's farm system before finally joining the major-league club late in 1942. The 26-year-old flamethrower became a regular member of Cleveland's starting rotation the following year, having his best season for the Indians in 1945, when he won 18 games and compiled a 3.20 ERA.

The Indians developed a surplus in pitching when players began returning to the major leagues from World War II in 1946, making them extremely attractive to the Yankees as a potential trading partner. With Joe Gordon having had a subpar year in New York, the Yankees offered the second baseman to the Indians, who in turn offered them a choice of pitchers. After consulting with Joe DiMaggio, who recommended that the Yankees take Reynolds, New York dealt Gordon to the Tribe for the hard-throwing right-hander on October 11, 1946.

Reynolds experienced immediate success in New York, compiling a record of 19–8 and an ERA of 3.20 in his first season in pinstripes. Although he surrendered a league-leading 23 home runs to opposing batters, he finished second in the circuit in wins, winning percentage (.704), and shutouts (4). Reynolds followed that up with four straight standout seasons in which he posted a combined record of 66–33. Joined by Vic Raschi and Eddie Lopat, Reynolds gave the Yankees a formidable "Big Three" at the top of their starting rotation that enabled them to win five consecutive world championships from 1949 to 1953. After winning 16 games in 1950 despite pitching with bone chips in his elbow, Reynolds hurled two no-hitters the following year, making him the first AL hurler to accomplish the feat. Reynolds also posted 17 victories and a league-leading 7 shutouts over the course of that 1951 campaign, en route to earning a third-place finish in the AL MVP balloting and winning the Hickok Belt as the top professional athlete of the year. Still, the best had yet to come.

Reynolds had the finest season of his career in 1952, when he finished 20–8, with a league-leading 2.06 ERA, 160 strikeouts, and 6 shutouts. He also placed third among AL hurlers with a career-high 24 complete games. Reynolds's exceptional performance earned him a second-place finish in the league MVP voting and his second consecutive selection to the *Sporting News* All-Star Team.

In spite of the success that Reynolds experienced as a starter, Yankee manager Casey Stengel frequently used him in relief during the latter stages of ball games. An outstanding all-around athlete, Reynolds had the ability to either start or relieve and to do either job extremely well. In fact, it may well have been Reynolds's tremendous versatility that has continued to keep him out of the Hall of Fame. Starting as many as 31 games only twice for the Yankees, Reynolds ended up compiling a lifetime record of 182–107, leaving him a bit short of the win total that he likely would have needed to gain admittance to Cooperstown. Reynolds acknowledged the impact that his part-time role as a reliever had on his Hall of Fame candidacy when he later suggested, "I knew that was going to happen. All the relief work I did was really a career-shortener. But, to me, teamwork was more important than some kind of honor."

After having his finest season in 1952, Reynolds assumed a more prominent role in the Yankee bullpen the following year, starting only 15 games, posting 13 victories, and finishing third in the league with 13 saves. He continued to function as a dual starter/reliever in 1954, winning another 13 games and saving 7 others. The 37-year-old hurler retired at the end of the year having compiled a record of 131–60 and an ERA of 3.30 in his eight seasons in pinstripes. His 131 victories place him 10th on the Yankees' all-time list. Reynolds also ranks ninth in winning percentage (.686) and fifth in shutouts (27).

With Reynolds in attendance on August 26, 1989, the Yankees dedicated a plaque in his honor, to hang in Monument Park at Yankee Stadium. The plaque calls Reynolds "one of the Yankees' greatest right-handed pitchers." Reynolds died a little over five years later, on the day after Christmas 1994 at the age of 77. In his honor, the Jim Thorpe Association established the Allie Reynolds Award, presented annually to "Oklahoma's outstanding high school senior, based on accomplishments, sports, civics, character and leadership."

YANKEE CAREER HIGHLIGHTS

Best Season

Reynolds pitched exceptionally well for the Yankees in 1947 and 1951. In the first of those years, he finished 19–8, with a 3.20 ERA, 17 complete games, 242 innings pitched, and 4 shutouts. Reynolds compiled a record of 17–8 in 1951, posted a 3.05 ERA, tossed 16 complete games and 221 innings, and led all AL hurlers with seven shutouts. His 2 no-hitters helped him win the Hickok Belt as the top professional athlete of the year. However, Reynolds had his finest season for the Yankees one year later, when he won 20 games for the only time in his career. In addition to compiling a record of 20–8, he threw a league-leading 6 shutouts, topped the circuit with 160 strikeouts, tossed 244 innings, and established career bests with 24 complete games and a league-leading 2.06 ERA.

Memorable Moments/Greatest Performances

An exceptional postseason performer throughout his career, Reynolds developed a reputation during his time in New York for excelling in big-game situations. He posted a lifetime record of 7–2, with a 2.79 ERA and 4 saves in World Series play, helping the Yankees win all six Fall Classics in which he appeared.

Reynolds recorded one of his most memorable performances against Brooklyn in game 1 of the 1949 World Series, out-dueling Dodger ace Don Newcombe by a score of 1–0. Reynolds shut out the Dodgers on just 2 hits, striking out 9, and earning the victory when Tommy Henrich led off the bottom of the ninth inning with a walk-off home run. He also got the save in game 4, pitching 3 1/3 hitless innings and striking out 5. For the series, Reynolds got a win and a save, pitched 12 1/3 scoreless innings, struck out 14 batters, and allowed only 2 hits.

Reynolds was at it again the following year, getting the best of Philadelphia ace Robin Roberts in game 2 of the Fall Classic. Reynolds defeated Roberts by a score of 2–1 in 10 innings when Joe DiMaggio homered off the Philadelphia right-hander in the top of the 10th. Reynolds also came out of the bullpen in game 4 to record the final out of the Yankees' four-game sweep.

Reynolds starred again in the 1952 Fall Classic, evening up the series against the Dodgers at two games apiece with a 4-hit shutout in game 4. He returned to the mound in relief in games 6 and 7, earning a save and a win, in helping the Yankees capture their fourth straight world championship. Reynolds concluded the series with a record of 2–1, a save, and an ERA of 1.77.

Still, Reynolds's crowning achievement has to be considered the 2 no-hitters he threw in 1951. After hurling a 1–0 no-no against Cleveland on July 12, he duplicated his earlier effort by blanking Boston 8–0 at Yankee Stadium on September 28. Adding to the drama in the second contest was the fact that Reynolds had to retire Ted Williams for the final out twice since Yogi Berra prolonged the Boston slugger's at bat by dropping the first of his two consecutive foul pops.

NOTABLE ACHIEVEMENTS

- Won 20 games once (1952).
- Topped 16 victories five other times.
- Compiled ERA below 3.00 once (2.06 in 1952).
- Tossed more than 20 complete games once (24 in 1952).
- Led AL pitchers in ERA and strikeouts once each and in shutouts twice.
- Threw 2 no-hitters.

- 1951 Hickok Belt winner.
- Two-time *Sporting News* All-Star selection.
- Five-time AL All-Star.
- Six-time AL champion.
- Six-time world champion.

Vic Raschi

His name synonymous with those of Allie Reynolds and Eddie Lopat—the other two members of the Yankees' "Big Three"—Vic Raschi anchored a starting rotation that helped lead New York to five consecutive world championships from 1949 to 1953. Known for his blazing fastball and tremendous determination, Raschi won 21 games for the Yankees three straight times, compiling an exceptional overall record of 120–50 during his eight years in pinstripes. The hard-throwing right-hander's .706 career winning percentage places him sixth in team history, and his 24 shutouts rank him in the club's all-time top 10. An outstanding big-game pitcher, Raschi posted a 5–3 record and a 2.24 ERA in World Series play, completing three of his eight starts, tossing a 2-hit shutout in one contest, and allowing just 1 run on 3 hits in another.

Victor John Angelo Raschi did not become a regular member of the Yankees' starting rotation until he was 29 years old. Born in West Springfield, Massachusetts, on March 28, 1919, Raschi was scouted by the Yankees as a teenager and originally signed a contract with the team at the tender age of 14 that guaranteed his college education. However, before Raschi earned his degree from the College of William and Mary, the Yankees persuaded him to drop out of school in 1941 to get some minor-league experience before he fulfilled his military obligations. After serving as a physical trainer for the Army Air Forces during World War II, Raschi spent time at New York's minor league affiliates in Portland and Newark before being called up to the Yankees late in 1946. Although the 27-year-old hurler won both his starts, the Yankees returned him to the minors for more seasoning at the end of the year. Raschi returned to the club the following year, though, earning a permanent spot in the starting rotation by winning seven of his nine decisions.

Raschi began his exceptional run in 1948, compiling a record of 19–8 and a 3.84 ERA and finishing among the league leaders with 18 complete games and 6 shutouts en route to earning AL All-Star honors for the first of four times. The "Springfield Rifle," as he came to be known, improved on his performance the following year, when he helped lead the Yankees to the first of their five consecutive world championships by posting 21 victories for the first of three straight times. Raschi concluded the campaign with a record of 21–10, a 3.34 ERA, and a career-high 21 complete games and 275 innings pitched. He followed that up with marks of 21–8 and 21–10 the next two years, earning a top-10 finish in the AL MVP voting both times. He also earned his only selection to the *Sporting News* All-Star Team in 1950.

The menacing scowl that Raschi wore on his dark, unshaven face contributed greatly to the success he experienced during his time in New York. However, even more important were his ability to throw his fastball by opposing batters, his outstanding arsenal of pitches, and his tremendous will and determination. Raschi never missed an assignment, even as the pain in his rapidly deteriorating knees continued to grow. And as Jim Turner, who served as Raschi's pitching coach in New York, later recalled, "He had good control for a power pitcher."

Although Raschi's string of 21-win seasons ended in 1952, he still managed to compile an outstanding 16–6 record and a career-low 2.78 ERA. The right-hander excelled against Brooklyn in that year's World Series, posting two of the Yankees' four victories, while compiling an ERA of 1.59, allowing the Dodgers only 12 hits in 17 innings of work, and striking out 18. In fact, from 1950 to 1952, Raschi posted a combined record of 4–1 in World Series play, along with a composite ERA of just under 1.00. He also surrendered just 26 hits in 36 total innings of work.

The Yankees won their fifth straight world championship in 1953, with Raschi serving as a primary contributor by going 13–6 with a 3.33 ERA. However, when the 34-year-old right-hander balked at the idea of taking a pay cut at season's end, the Yankees sold him to the St. Louis Cardinals for $85,000. Raschi spent a little over one year in St. Louis, compiling a record of 8–9 for the Cardinals, before finishing his career back in the American League with the Kansas City Athletics in 1955. He concluded his relatively brief 10-year career with a record of 132–66 and an ERA of 3.72. After his retirement, Raschi operated a liquor store until he passed away at the age of 69 in October 1988 after suffering a heart attack.

YANKEE CAREER HIGHLIGHTS

Best Season

Although Raschi earned his only selection to the *Sporting News* All-Star Team in 1950, when he finished 21–8 with a 4.00 ERA, he had better years in both 1949 and 1951. It could also be argued that he pitched more effectively in 1952, when he compiled a career-low 2.78 ERA. However, since Raschi won only 16 games that year, I will go with one of his other 21-win campaigns. Raschi posted identical 21–10 records in 1949 and 1951. He also compiled extremely similar ERAs (3.34 in 1949 vs. 3.27 in 1951). The best arguments that could be waged on behalf of 1951 were that he led the American League with a career-high 164 strikeouts (he struck out 124 batters in 1949) and allowed slightly fewer base runners per nine innings (1.3 vs. 1.4). Nevertheless, I elected to go with 1949 since he was a bit more of a workhorse that year. Raschi established career highs in starts (37), complete games (21), and innings pitched (275), pushing 1949 just barely ahead of 1951, when he made 34 starts, tossed 15 complete games, and threw 258 innings.

Memorable Moments/Greatest Performances

Raschi won a number of big games for the Yankees. Perhaps his finest effort came against Philadelphia in the first game of the 1950 World Series, when he shut out the Phillies 1–0 on just 2 hits, getting the best of NL MVP Jim Konstanty in the process. Raschi also posted two victories against the Dodgers in the 1952 Fall Classic, one of which was a complete-game 3-hit gem in game 2 that he won by a score of 7–1.

Raschi registered arguably the most important victory of his career on the final day of the 1949 regular season when he broke a first-place tie between New York and Boston with a complete-game 5–3 win at Yankee Stadium that gave the Yankees the pennant.

Yet, the game that perhaps made Raschi more proud than any other took place on August 4, 1953. In addition to allowing the Tigers just 2 hits over six scoreless innings during a 15–0 win at Yankee Stadium, Raschi collected 3 hits in 4 at bats and drove in 7 runs. His 7 RBIs set an American League single-game record for pitchers.

NOTABLE ACHIEVEMENTS

- Three-time 20-game winner.
- Won 19 games one other time.

- Compiled ERA below 3.00 once (2.78 in 1952).
- Tossed more than 20 complete games once (21 in 1949).
- Threw more than 250 innings three times.
- Led AL pitchers in winning percentage and strikeouts once each and in games started twice.
- 1950 *Sporting News* All-Star selection.
- Four-time AL All-Star.
- Six-time AL champion.
- Six-time world champion.

Robinson Cano

Named after the legendary Jackie Robinson, Robinson Cano has been one of baseball's premier second basemen since he first joined the Yankees early in 2005. A superb left-handed hitter with a smooth and almost flawless swing, Cano has batted over .300 in five of his seven full seasons while surpassing 25 home runs three times and topping 100 RBIs twice. His outstanding hitting has already earned him three Silver Sluggers. Meanwhile, Cano's soft hands and powerful throwing arm helped him capture Gold Glove honors in 2010, when he led all AL second sackers in putouts for the third of four times, assists for the second of three times, and fielding percentage with a mark of .996 that established a new Yankee record for players at the position. Cano's rare combination of skills for a second baseman have earned him the admiration and respect of Yankee teammates, past and present.

Yankee captain Derek Jeter said of his double-play partner, "He's really confident, both offensively and defensively." Former Yankee outfielder Johnny Damon once commented, "We know how good [Cano] is. We just hope one day he remembers us." Alex Rodriguez stated simply, "He's incredible." Meanwhile, former Yankee manager Joe Torre once gushed, "[Cano] reminds me of two people—a combination of Robbie Alomar and Rod Carew."

Although Robinson Cano spent most of his youth in his homeland of the Dominican Republic, he learned how to speak English during the three years he lived in New Jersey, where he spent the seventh, eighth, and ninth grades in the Newark school system. After moving back to the Dominican Republic with his family, Cano attended San Pedro de Marcoris High School, signing with the Yankees as an amateur free agent shortly after he graduated in 2001. Cano spent the next four years in the Yankees' farm system, establishing himself during that time as one of the organization's top minor-league prospects. In fact, the second baseman earned Yankees' Minor League Player of the Year honors in 2004, which he split between the Eastern League's Trenton Thunder and the Columbus Clippers—New York's Triple-A affiliate.

Having traded Alfonso Soriano to Texas for Alex Rodriguez prior to the start of the 2004 campaign, the Yankees elected to promote Cano to the big-league club in May 2005, when neither Tony Womack nor Miguel Cairo displayed an ability to hold down the starting job at second base. The 22-year-old Cano responded by hitting 14 homers, driving in 62 runs, scoring 78 others, and batting .297 en route to earning a second-place finish in the AL Rookie of the Year voting.

Despite missing a month of the following season with a strained hamstring, Cano had an outstanding sophomore campaign, finishing a close third in the AL batting race with a mark of .342. Particularly effective after returning from the disabled list on August 8, Cano led the league in batting average, doubles, and runs batted in over the final two months of the season. In addition to batting .342, he finished the year with 15 homers and 78 RBIs.

After another solid year in 2007 in which he batted .306 and established new career highs with 19 home runs, 97 runs batted in, 93 runs scored, and 189 hits, Cano suffered through a subpar 2008 campaign that saw his numbers experience a precipitous drop in every offensive category. Cano hit only 14 homers, drove in just 72 runs, scored only 70 others, and posted career lows in batting average (.271), on-base percentage (.305), and slugging percentage (.410). The young second baseman's mediocre performance not only disappointed Yankee fans and the team's front office but also brought into question his work ethic and level of intensity.

Stunned by the criticism he received during the subsequent off-season, Cano approached the 2009 campaign as if he had something to prove. A more dedicated and somewhat more serious Cano performed extremely well for the Yankees, helping them capture their first AL East title in three years by hitting 25 home runs, knocking in 85 runs, scoring 103 others, batting .320, and establishing career highs with 204 hits and 48 doubles. He followed that up with the two best seasons of his career, establishing himself in the process as the American League's premier second baseman. Cano hit 29 homers, drove in 109 runs, scored 103 others, collected 200 hits, and batted .319 in 2010 en route to earning a third-place finish in the league MVP voting. He posted extremely comparable numbers in 2011, concluding the campaign with 28 home runs, 118 runs batted in, 104 runs scored, 188 hits, and a .302 batting average.

Heading into 2012, Cano has hit 144 home runs, knocked in 621 runs, scored 613 others, collected 1,263 hits and 286 doubles, batted .308, compiled a .347 on-base percentage, and posted a .496 slugging percentage in his seven seasons in New York. The .308 batting average that Cano has compiled to this point in his career is the ninth-best in team history. Meanwhile, his 48 doubles in 2009 represent the fourth-highest single-season total in franchise history. Considering that Cano is only 29 years old as of this writing, he figures to move up significantly in these rankings before his career ends.

CAREER HIGHLIGHTS

Best Season

Although Cano batted a career-high .342 and compiled an on-base plus slugging of .890 in 2006, he had a better all-around year in 2009. Despite posting a slightly lower batting average (.320) and on-base plus slugging (.871), Cano established new career highs with 25 home runs, 103 runs scored, 204 hits, and 48 doubles. Nevertheless, the 2010 and 2011 seasons were clearly the two best Cano has yet to experience. In the first of those campaigns, he hit 29 homers, drove in 109 runs, scored 103 others, collected 200 hits and 41 doubles, batted .319, and compiled a career-high .381 on-base percentage and .534 slugging percentage (for an on-base plus slugging of .914) en route to earning a third-place finish in the AL MVP balloting. Cano nearly matched those numbers in 2011, hitting 28 home runs, knocking in 118 runs, scoring 104 times, accumulating 188 hits and 46 doubles, batting .302, and posting an on-base percentage of .349 and a slugging percentage of .533 (for an on-base plus slugging of .882). Cano earned a Silver Slugger and AL All-Star honors each year, establishing himself in the process as the Yankees' best all-around player. It is a very close call, and either of those campaigns would make a good choice. In the end, I will elect to go with Cano's 2010 performance due to the defensive excellence he displayed over the course of the season. Although Cano also did an exceptional job in the field in 2011, committing only 10 errors and compiling a .987 fielding percentage, his 3 miscues and extraordinary fielding mark of .996 in 2010 both set new records for Yankee second basemen.

Memorable Moments/Greatest Performances

Cano gave an early indication of his hitting prowess by posting back-to-back 5-RBI games as a rookie in 2005. He subsequently began his postseason career in grand fashion by driving in 3 runs with a bases-clearing double off Cy Young Award winner Bartolo Colon in his first at bat against the Angels in the ALDS. Cano concluded the five-game series with 5 RBIs and a .263 batting average.

Yet, Cano's 2005 postseason performance paled by comparison to the efforts he turned in against Texas in the 2010 ALCS and Detroit in the 2011 ALDS. Although the Yankees ended up losing both those series, Cano proved to be a thorn in the side of the Texas and Detroit pitching staffs.

Against Texas in 2010, Cano helped the Yankees overcome a 5–0 deficit in game 1 by leading off the top of the seventh inning with a home run off C. J. Wilson. He subsequently tied the contest in the following frame with a single to center off left-handed relief specialist Derek Holland. Cano continued to torment the Rangers in games 2 and 4, homering in a losing effort in each of those contests. He homered again during a 6–2 Yankee victory in game 5, before the Rangers eliminated New York from the postseason tournament with a 6–1 win in game 6. Cano concluded the series with 4 home runs, 5 runs batted in, 5 runs scored, a .348 batting average, and a .913 slugging percentage.

Cano was equally impressive against Detroit in the 2011 ALDS, finishing the five-game series with 2 homers, 9 RBIs, and a .318 batting average. He put on a memorable performance in the Yankees' 8–1 game 1 victory, sandwiching a sixth-inning grand slam between two run-scoring doubles en route to knocking in six of New York's eight runs.

NOTABLE ACHIEVEMENTS

- Has hit more than 25 home runs three times.
- Has driven in more than 100 runs twice.
- Has scored more than 100 runs three times.
- Has batted over .300 five times, topping the .320 mark twice.
- Has surpassed 200 hits twice.
- Has topped 40 doubles five times.
- Has compiled a slugging percentage in excess of .500 four times.
- Led AL second basemen in putouts four times; assists, three times; fielding percentage, once.

- Holds Yankee single-season records for highest fielding percentage (.996) and fewest errors committed by a second baseman (3, set in 2010).
- Third in 2010 AL MVP voting.
- 2010 Gold Glove winner.
- Three-time Silver Slugger winner.
- Three-time *Sporting News* All-Star selection.
- Three-time AL All-Star.
- 2009 AL champion.
- 2009 world champion.

45

Tino Martinez

Seattle Mariner first baseman Tino Martinez made an extremely favorable impression on the Yankees during the 1995 American League Division Series played between the two clubs. In fact, Martinez's homer, 5 RBIs, and .409 batting average so impressed Yankee management that the team ended up trading for him during the subsequent off-season. With Don Mattingly's career drawing to a close as a result of back problems, the Yankees traded top prospects Russ Davis and Sterling Hitchcock to the Mariners on December 7, 1995, for Martinez and relief pitchers Jeff Nelson and Jim Mecir. Although Mecir contributed little to the Yankees over the course of the next two seasons, Nelson and Martinez ended up making huge contributions to a ball club that captured four of the next five world championships. Nelson developed into a mainstay of the Yankee bullpen, serving as an outstanding right-handed setup man first for John Wetteland and, later, Mariano Rivera. Meanwhile, Martinez provided the Yankees with exceptional production in the middle of their batting order, excellent defense at first base, and quiet leadership in the locker room that made him one of the cornerstones of the team's dynasty of the late 1990s.

Originally selected by the Seattle Mariners with the 14th overall pick of the 1988 amateur draft, Constantino Martinez spent five rather pedestrian seasons in Seattle after first joining the team in 1990. He finally experienced his breakout season at age 27 in 1995, hitting 31 home runs, driving in 111 runs, and batting .293 for a Mariners team that won its first AL West title. Although Martinez subsequently batted just .136 against Cleveland in Seattle's six-game ALCS loss to the Indians, his career received a huge boost some two months later when the Mariners made him the centerpiece of their five-player deal with the Yankees.

Martinez's early days in New York turned out to be extremely trying ones. Replacing the iconic Don Mattingly at first base proved to be a difficult task, particularly when one considers the unique relationship that the beloved Yankee captain shared with the fans of New York. Off to a slow start, Martinez frequently heard boos emanating from the stands at his home ballpark during the season's first month. He eventually righted himself, though, winning over the fans by hitting 25 home runs, batting .292, and knocking in a team-leading 117 runs in helping the Yankees capture their first World Series title in 18 years. The left-handed hitting slugger improved on those numbers considerably in 1997, earning his second selection to the AL All-Star Team, a spot on the *Sporting News* All-Star squad, and a second-place finish in the AL MVP voting by batting .296 and placing second in the circuit with 44 home runs and 141 runs batted in.

The Yankees won their first of three straight world championships the following year, with Martinez contributing a team-leading 28 homers and 123 runs batted in. After struggling throughout his earlier postseason career with the Yankees, Martinez batted .385 during New York's four-game sweep of San Diego in the 1998 World Series. He delivered arguably the biggest blow of that year's Fall Classic when he capped a 7-run rally by the Yankees in the bottom of the seventh inning of game 1 by hitting a grand slam that provided the Yankees with the winning margin in a 9–6 victory.

After Martinez again compiled outstanding numbers for the Yankees in 1999 (28 home runs, 105 RBIs, and 95 runs scored), his offensive productivity experienced a precipitous drop the following year. The first baseman hit only 16 homers, drove in just 91 runs, and scored only 69 others in 2000. Nevertheless, Martinez ended up having his finest postseason in pinstripes, helping the Yankees capture their third consecutive world championship by excelling in every round of the postseason tournament. After batting .421 and knocking in 4 runs against Oakland in the ALDS, he homered once and batted .320 against Seattle in the ALCS. Martinez then collected 8 hits en route to posting a batting average of .364 against the Mets in the World Series.

Martinez returned to top form in 2001, leading the club with 34 home runs and 113 runs batted in. But with the first baseman turning 34 during the subsequent off-season and Oakland slugger Jason Giambi representing the prize of the free agent class, the Yankees elected not to try to re-sign Martinez when he too became available to the highest bidder. Martinez ended up signing with the St. Louis Cardinals, with whom he spent the next two years. When Martinez's contract with the

Cardinals expired, he signed a one-year deal to play for his hometown Tampa Bay Devil Rays.

Although Martinez failed to compile the type of offensive numbers with either the Cardinals or Devil Rays that he typically posted for the Yankees, New York severely missed his quiet leadership. While Martinez was not nearly as demonstrative as Paul O'Neill on the field, he rivaled his teammate in terms of intensity. That fact became quite evident for all to see when Martinez charged the mound after being hit in the upper back by an Armando Benitez fastball during a 9–5 Yankee victory over the Orioles at Yankee Stadium on May 19, 1998. The incident precipitated a bench-clearing brawl between the two teams that clearly revealed the sense of unity and level of intensity that existed on New York's record-setting ball club.

After three years away from New York, Martinez returned to the Yankees in 2005, presumably to serve as a backup for Giambi at first base. However, injuries to Giambi forced Martinez into the Yankees' starting lineup for a period, with the 37-year-old veteran responding by hitting 17 homers in just over 300 official at bats. Nevertheless, the Yankees declined their $3 million option on Martinez at season's end, once again making him a free agent. Martinez subsequently chose to announce his retirement, ending his 16-year playing career with 339 home runs, 1,271 runs batted in, 1,008 runs scored, 1,925 hits, a .271 batting average, and a .344 on-base percentage. His Yankee numbers over seven seasons included 192 home runs, 739 RBIs, 566 runs scored, 1,039 hits, a .276 batting average, and a .347 on-base percentage. Martinez played for six division-winning, five pennant-winning, and four world championship ball clubs in New York.

YANKEE CAREER HIGHLIGHTS

Best Season

Although Martinez had several extremely productive years for the Yankees, the 1997 campaign was clearly his best. In addition to finishing second in the American League with 44 home runs and 141 runs batted in, Martinez placed among the leaders with 343 total bases and a .577 slugging percentage. He established career highs in all four categories and posted career bests in runs scored (96), hits (176), batting average (.296), and on-base percentage (.371). Martinez earned a spot on the AL All-Star Team, his lone selection to the *Sporting News* All-Star squad, and his only top-10 finish in the AL MVP voting (he placed second in the balloting).

Memorable Moments/Greatest Performances

Martinez hit two memorable home runs for the Yankees in World Series play. He delivered the first against San Diego's Mark Langston in the bottom of the seventh inning of game 1 of the 1998 Fall Classic. After the Yankees tied the score at 5–5 on a Chuck Knoblauch 3-run homer earlier in the frame, Martinez stepped to the plate to face Langston with the bases loaded. The Yankee first baseman eventually worked the count to 3–2, taking a very close call for ball three that could just as easily have been called a strike. Martinez drove the San Diego left-hander's next offering into the upper deck in right field, giving the Yankees a 9–5 lead that they nursed the rest of the way.

Martinez delivered one of the most stunning home runs in World Series history three years later in Game 4 of the 2001 Fall Classic against the Arizona Diamondbacks.

Facing Arizona closer Byung-Hyun Kim with two men out in the bottom of the ninth inning and the Yankees trailing the Diamondbacks by 2 runs, Martinez hit a game-tying 2-run homer over the right-center-field wall that helped propel New York to an extra-inning victory. Teammate Scott Brosius amazingly duplicated Martinez's feat the very next night, leading to another Yankee win in extra innings. However, the Diamondbacks took the final two games in Arizona, claiming in the process their first world championship.

Martinez also experienced a memorable moment in Yankee Stadium when he returned to the Bronx as a member of the Cardinals. Facing the Yankees for the first time in interleague play, Martinez found himself being given a standing ovation by Yankee fans, who greatly appreciated the many contributions he made to their four previous world championship ball clubs. An emotional Martinez subsequently went on to hit 2 home runs in the game off former teammate Andy Pettitte, after which he received two more thunderous ovations.

Not yet through providing thrills to the fans of New York, Martinez embarked on an exceptional run shortly after he rejoined the Yankees in 2005, hitting a home run in five straight games from May 7 to May 11. Held homerless on May 12, Martinez hit 3 more homers in the next two games, giving him a total of 8 long balls over the course of eight games—the hottest stretch of his career.

NOTABLE ACHIEVEMENTS

- Surpassed 30 home runs twice, topping the 40-homer mark once.
- Knocked in more than 100 runs five times, topping 120 RBIs twice.

- Compiled slugging percentage in excess of .500 three times.
- Led AL first basemen in assists once (1999).
- 1997 *Sporting News* All-Star selection.
- 1997 AL All-Star.
- 1997 Silver Slugger winner.
- Five-time AL champion.
- Four-time world champion.

Willie Randolph

The Yankees took a major step toward returning to prominence in the American League on December 11, 1975, when they traded pitcher George "Doc" Medich to the Pittsburgh Pirates for a package of three players that included second baseman Willie Randolph. Labeled a "can't miss" prospect by those familiar with the Pittsburgh organization, the 21-year-old Randolph immediately became the Yankees' starting second baseman—a role he filled for the next 13 seasons. During that time, Randolph remained a pillar of strength in the Yankee infield, serving as a stabilizing influence on a tumultuous team, both on the field and in the clubhouse. A five-time AL All-Star, Randolph helped the Yankees win five AL East titles, four American League pennants, and two world championships, even as the team went through a total of 32 different shortstops and 13 managerial changes. He did so by earning the respect of teammates and opponents alike with his mental toughness, quiet leadership, and consistency at the bat and in the field.

Born in Holy Hill, South Carolina, on July 6, 1954, William Larry Randolph Jr. grew impervious to the sort of pressure he eventually would face as a professional athlete while growing up in the rough-and-tumble section of Brooklyn known as Brownsville. Randolph's friend Mel Vitter later told Lee Jenkins of the *New York Times*, "Any kid coming out of that neighborhood has a toughness most kids don't, brings an energy most kids don't, and has a drive most people don't. . . . Willie was never blessed with huge physical ability. He was never the strongest or the fastest. He made himself with his attitude."

Randolph's attitude helped him advance rapidly through the Pittsburgh farm system after the team selected him in the seventh round of the 1972 amateur draft. However, with Rennie Stennett firmly entrenched at second base for the Pirates at the major-league level, Pittsburgh's front office elected to include Randolph in its swap with the Yankees after the young second baseman appeared in only 30 games with the club in 1975. Upon his arrival in New York the following year, Randolph fit in perfectly with new Yankee manager Billy Martin's aggressive style of play. Blessed with good running speed, excellent quickness, and superior instincts, Randolph ran the bases extremely well. He also did a solid job in the field and at the bat, using his patience at the plate and keen batting eye to gradually evolve into an exceptional second-place hitter in the Yankee batting order. After batting .267, scoring 59 runs, and stealing 37 bases hitting primarily out of the number 8 spot in the lineup as a rookie, Randolph ascended to the top of the batting order shortly thereafter, spending the remainder of his career manning the leadoff or number 2 spot in the lineup.

Randolph posted batting averages of .274 and .279 for New York's world championship ball clubs of 1977 and 1978, scoring a total of 178 runs over the course of those two campaigns while also stealing a total of 49 bases. Equally important, he remained one of the calming influences in a Yankee clubhouse often fraught with inner turmoil. Although never graced with an outgoing personality, Randolph served as a key motivator and cornerstone of the Yankee championship teams. Former Yankee catcher Fran Healy recalled of his one-time teammate, "He was quiet. . . . Very quiet. You could see there was more there, though. This was when all sorts of crazy stuff was going on there— with Reggie [Jackson], with Thurman Munson. But Willie, with all the turmoil in those years, he was the professional."

Lou Piniella, another member of those championship ball clubs in New York, said, "[Randolph] wasn't at all affected by it—he stayed out of it. He was quiet, he stayed to himself more than anything else— he went out and played, and played hard, and played to win. No, he wasn't affected by the atmosphere we had there at times."

After another solid performance in 1979, Randolph had one of his finest offensive seasons the following year, when he helped the Yankees compile a major-league best 103–59 record by scoring 99 runs, stealing 30 bases, batting .294, and walking a league-leading 119 times. The second baseman's .427 on-base percentage placed him second in the AL rankings. Kansas City subsequently swept the Yankees in the 1980 ALCS, but Randolph was one of the few bright spots for New York, collecting 5 hits in 13 official trips to the plate, for a .385 batting average.

Randolph continued to serve the Yankees well for the next five years, earning the honor of being named co-captain of the team early in 1986, along with Ron Guidry. Randolph had another outstanding season at the plate in 1987, driving in a career-high 67 runs, scoring 96 others, batting .305, and compiling a .411 on-base percentage en route to earning All-Star honors for the last of five times as a member of the Yankees. He remained in New York one more year, before the team elected to pursue free agent second baseman Steve Sax during the subsequent off-season. Randolph ended up signing his own free agent deal with the Dodgers, spending the next year and a half in Los Angeles, before moving on to Oakland, Milwaukee, and finally back to New York, where he concluded his playing career as a member of the Mets in 1992. Randolph retired from the game with 1,239 runs scored, 2,210 hits, 271 stolen bases, a career batting average of .276, and a .373 on-base percentage. He scored 1,027 runs as a member of the Yankees, collected 1,731 hits, stole 251 bases, batted .275, and compiled a .374 on-base percentage. Randolph ranks third in team history in stolen bases, and he is among the club's all-time leaders in runs scored and bases on balls (1,005). He played more games at second base (1,688) than anyone else in team history.

Upon retiring as a player, Randolph joined the Yankees as a coach for 11 years, after which he became manager of the Mets from 2005 to June 2008. He currently serves the Baltimore Orioles as third base coach.

Former Yankees teammate and manager Lou Piniella said of Randolph, "He was a heck of a ballplayer. He could run, he could field, he could steal bases, could hit for average, could get some big hits for you. He was just a little injury prone. Outside of that, Willie would man the second spot in your lineup, would swing a .300 bat for you, and play a heck of a defensive second base for you."

Piniella added, "With the changes that we had in the shortstop position, he and [Graig] Nettles were the glue of our infield. He was just a tremendous player and a tremendous competitor and another good person. We had a lot of good people over there on that ballclub."

YANKEE CAREER HIGHLIGHTS

Best Season

Randolph had his two finest seasons for the Yankees in 1980 and 1987. In the first of those years, he batted .294, compiled a career-best .427

on-base percentage, posted a .407 slugging percentage, stole 30 bases, scored 99 runs, and led the AL with 119 bases on balls. Although Randolph stole only 11 bases in 1987, he compiled comparable numbers in most other offensive categories, batting .305, posting on-base and slugging percentages of .411 and .414, respectively, and scoring 96 times. He was somewhat more productive in 1987, though, driving in a career-high 67 runs (he knocked in only 46 runs in 1980). In the end, I decided to go with 1980 for the simple reason that Randolph appeared in many more games. Injuries limited him to only 120 contests and 543 total plate appearances in 1987. Meanwhile, Randolph took the field for 138 games in 1980, accumulating 642 total plate appearances. Those 18 extra games and 100 more plate appearances made the second baseman more of a factor over the course of the regular season, helping the Yankees post the best record in all of baseball. Meanwhile, they finished fourth in the AL East in 1987, a full nine games behind the first-place Detroit Tigers.

Memorable Moments/Greatest Performances

Randolph never hit more than seven home runs in a season, leaving the yard a total of only 48 times in his 13 years with the Yankees. Still, several of his homers were big ones. On June 14, 1984, the Yankees overcame a ninth-inning 11–7 deficit to arch-rival Boston at Fenway Park to eventually defeat the Red Sox 12–11 in 10 innings. After Don Mattingly tied the score at 11 with a 2-out, 3-run homer in the top of the ninth, Randolph won the game with a solo blast the following frame.

Almost 15 months later, on September 5, 1985, the Yankees closed to within 2 1/2 games of first-place Toronto in the AL East with a 7–3 victory over the Oakland A's at Yankee Stadium. Randolph put on an unusual power display during the contest, hitting two home runs for the only time in his career en route to going 4 for 4 on the afternoon.

Randolph had another big day in the Yankees' 1987 home opener, going 4 for 5, with 5 runs batted in, 2 runs scored, and a stolen base during New York's 11–3 win over the Cleveland Indians.

However, Randolph may well have played his most memorable game against the Los Angeles Dodgers in the opening contest of the 1977 World Series. After tying the score at 2–2 with a solo homer in the bottom of the sixth inning, the Yankee second baseman led off the bottom of the 12th with a double to left field that put him at second with the potential winning run in a 3–3 tie. After the Dodgers walked Thurman Munson intentionally, Paul Blair delivered a ground ball single through the shortstop hole that brought Randolph home with the run that gave the Yankees a 4–3 victory and a 1–0 series lead.

NOTABLE ACHIEVEMENTS

- Batted over .300 once (.305 in 1987).
- Compiled on-base percentage in excess of .400 twice.
- Surpassed 30 stolen bases four times.
- Led AL in walks once (119 in 1980).
- Led AL second basemen in putouts and assists once each.
- Three-time *Sporting News* All-Star selection.
- Five-time AL All-Star.
- 1980 Silver Slugger winner.
- Four-time AL champion.
- Two-time world champion.

47

Bill Skowron

A muscular right-handed batter with tremendous power to the opposite field, Bill "Moose" Skowron spent nine productive years in New York, providing protection in the middle of the Yankee batting order to sluggers such as Mickey Mantle, Yogi Berra, and Roger Maris. After spending his first two seasons platooning at first base with the lefty-swinging Joe Collins, Skowron became the Yankees' regular first sacker in 1956. He subsequently went on to surpass 20 home runs in four of the next seven seasons while compiling a batting average in excess of .300 three times and knocking in more than 90 runs on two occasions. The Yankees won seven pennants and four world championships in Skowron's nine full years with them, with the powerful first baseman proving to be a huge contributor to the success that the team experienced during that time.

Originally signed by the Yankees in 1950 as a 19-year-old amateur free agent off the campus of Purdue University, William Joseph Skowron spent parts of four seasons working his way up through the team's farm system. The Yankees began to seriously entertain thoughts of promoting the 5'11", 200-pound first baseman to the major-league club when he captured Minor League Player of the Year honors in 1952 while playing for the Kansas City Blues in the American Association. After one more year of seasoning, Skowron arrived in New York for the first time in 1954. Splitting time at first base with veteran Joe Collins, the 23-year-old Skowron batted .340 and drove in 41 runs in only 215 official at bats. Skowron continued to excel in a part-time role the following year, batting .319 and knocking in 61 runs, in just under 300 official plate appearances.

Although the left-handed hitting Collins remained on the Yankees' roster for another two years, Skowron relegated him to a spot on the New York bench in 1956. Appearing in all but 20 of New York's 154 games, Skowron experienced his breakout season, hitting 23 home runs, driving in 90 runs, and batting .308. He followed that up with another solid performance in 1957, hitting 17 homers, knocking in 88 runs, and batting .304.

Although the home run totals that Skowron compiled for the Yankees during his first two full seasons would seem to indicate that he possessed only moderate power at the plate, nothing could be further from the truth. Skowron had the ability to drive the ball well over 400 feet—farther than perhaps anyone else on the team, with the exception of Mickey Mantle. Only Yankee Stadium's vast expanse in left and left-center fields prevented the right-handed hitting Skowron from posting significantly better power numbers. As a result, the first baseman learned how to take advantage of the ballpark's short porch in right field, using his tremendous strength to drive balls over the right field wall with great regularity.

After experiencing something of an off year in 1958, Skowron began the 1959 campaign with a flurry. Seemingly well on his way to having the most productive season of his young career, Skowron hit 15 homers, knocked in 59 runs, and batted .298 through early July. However, his season ended abruptly when he fractured his wrist in a collision at first base.

Fully recovered by the start of the 1960 campaign, Skowron returned to the Yankee lineup to bat .309 and establish new career highs with 26 home runs and 91 runs batted in. He compiled outstanding numbers again during New York's magical 1961 season, finishing third on the team with 28 homers and 89 RBIs. Skowron spent one more year in New York, hitting 23 home runs and driving in 80 runs for the Yankees' 1962 world championship ball club, before the team elected to part ways with him to make room at first base for promising young slugger Joe Pepitone. On November 26, 1962, the Yankees traded Skowron to the Los Angeles Dodgers for pitcher Stan Williams—a hard-throwing right-hander with a nasty disposition. Skowron spent one year in Los Angeles, coming back to haunt the Yankees in the 1963 World Series by homering once, driving in 3 runs, and batting .385 during the Dodgers' four-game sweep of his former team. Skowron returned to the American League the following year, splitting his final four seasons between the Washington Senators, Chicago White Sox, and California Angels. He retired at the conclusion of the 1967 campaign having hit 211 home runs, driven in 888 runs, and batted .282 over 14 major-league seasons. Skowron hit 165 homers, knocked in 672 runs, and batted .294 in his nine years in New York. He earned AL All-Star honors five times, one *Sporting News* All-Star selection, and one top-10 finish in the AL MVP voting as a member of the Yankees.

YANKEE CAREER HIGHLIGHTS

Best Season

Skowron performed very well for the Yankees in 1956 and 1961. In the first of those years, he hit 23 homers, drove in 90 runs, batted .308, compiled a .382 on-base percentage, and posted a .528 slugging percentage. Although Skowron knocked in 89 runs and hit a career-high 28 homers in the second of those campaigns, his overall numbers were not quite as good as the figures he posted in 1956 (he batted just .267 and compiled on-base and slugging percentages of .318 and .472, respectively). However, the marks that Skowron posted in 1960 compare favorably to the figures he compiled in any other year. The first baseman hit 26 home runs, batted .309, finished with a .353 on-base percentage and a .528 slugging percentage, and established career highs with 91 runs batted in, 166 hits, and 34 doubles. He also earned his only selection to the *Sporting News* All-Star Team and a ninth-place finish in the AL MVP voting, cracking the top 10 in the balloting for the only time in his career. The 1960 campaign would have to be considered Skowron's finest all-around season.

Memorable Moments/Greatest Performances

Skowron hit one of his most memorable home runs against the Washington Senators on April 22, 1959, when his 14th-inning blast established a new American League record for the longest game to end 1–0 on a home run.

However, the slugging first baseman achieved far more notoriety for the success he experienced during the 1958 World Series. After making the final out against the Braves in the previous year's Fall Classic, Skowron gained a measure of revenge against them in 1958. Trailing Milwaukee 3–1 after the first four contests, the Yankees closed the gap to 3–2 with a 7–0 victory in game 5. They then evened the series at three games apiece with a 10 inning 4–3 win in game 6 that saw Skowron drive in what turned out to be the game-winning run with an RBI single in the top of the 10th. Skowron continued his heroics in game 7, hitting a 3-run homer in the eighth inning that helped lead the Yankees to a 6–2 victory and their 18th world championship. Skowron concluded the series with 2 home runs and 7 runs batted in. A solid clutch performer throughout his career, Skowron hit .283, with 7 home runs and 26 RBIs in 35 World Series games as a member of the Yankees.

NOTABLE ACHIEVEMENTS

- Hit more than 20 home runs four times.
- Batted over .300 five times.
- Compiled slugging percentage in excess of .500 five times.
- Led AL first basemen in putouts and assists once each.
- 1960 *Sporting News* All-Star selection.
- Five-time AL All-Star.
- Seven-time AL champion.
- Four-time world champion.

48

Hideki Matsui

Already a legend in the Far East, where he rivaled Ichiro Suzuki as Japanese baseball's greatest superstar, Hideki Matsui quickly made a name for himself in the United States after he signed a three-year deal to play left field for the Yankees, beginning in 2003. Nicknamed "Godzilla" in his homeland for his prodigious home run–hitting feats, Matsui never reached the same level of dominance in the majors. Nevertheless, he established himself as one of the American League's premier outfielders and most consistent RBI men, earning the respect of teammates and opponents alike with his ability to perform well under pressure, strong work ethic, and outstanding level of professionalism. Yankees captain Derek Jeter stated on one occasion, "Matsui is one of my favorite players. He's one of my favorite teammates. He comes ready to play every day. He's a professional hitter. All he wants to do is win." Meanwhile, Yankees general manger Brian Cashman noted, "When we need a run, [Matsui] finds a way to drive it in."

Matsui drove in more than 100 runs in four of his seven seasons in the Bronx, helping the Yankees win three division titles, two American League pennants, and one world championship. He also hit more than 20 home runs four times, scored more than 100 runs three times, and batted over .300 twice. Moreover, Matsui continued to place his team before himself the entire time he remained in New York, preferring not to use his Japanese celebrity to draw any more attention to himself than was absolutely necessary.

Born in Ishikawa, Japan, on June 12, 1974, Hideki Matsui spent the first 10 years of his professional career playing for the Yomiuri Giants of Japan's Nippon Central League. A three-time winner of the Central League Most Valuable Player Award, Matsui gained widespread acclaim as Japanese baseball's top slugger while leading his team to three Japan Series titles. He also made nine consecutive All-Star teams and led the league in home runs and RBIs three times each.

After hitting a career-high 50 home runs for the Giants in 2002, Matsui signed a three-year deal to play for the Yankees on December 19, 2002. Arriving in the United States amid great fanfare, the 28-year-old outfielder seemed relatively unaffected by all the pageantry that surrounded him, preferring instead to focus strictly on baseball. Displaying the level of concentration that he retained throughout his career, as well as the flair for the dramatic he often exhibited, Matsui led the Yankees to victory in their home opener by becoming the first player in team history to hit a grand slam in his first game at Yankee Stadium. The left-handed-hitting slugger went on to earn AL All-Star honors and a second-place finish in the Rookie of the Year voting by hitting 16 homers, driving in 106 runs, and batting .287.

Matsui followed that up with an outstanding sophomore campaign during which he hit 31 home runs, knocked in 108 runs, scored 109 others, and batted .298. The Yankees captured the AL East title and appeared to be well on their way toward advancing to the World Series for the second straight year when they grabbed a 3–0 lead against Boston in the ALCS. However, their bats cooled and their pitchers faltered, leading to a historic collapse that resulted in a stunning comeback by the Red Sox. Yet, even as the rest of the team buckled around him, Matsui remained the one constant, going a respectable 5 for 19 over the final four contests. He concluded the series with 2 homers, 10 RBIs, and a .412 batting average.

Matsui had another fine year in 2005, hitting 23 homers, scoring 108 runs, and establishing career highs with 116 runs batted in, 192 hits, and a .305 batting average. But the outfielder hit a roadblock in early May 2006, when he fractured his left wrist while attempting to make a sliding catch in the first inning of a contest against the Boston Red Sox. The injury required immediate surgery, forcing Matsui to miss the next four months and bringing to an end the consecutive-games-played streak of 518 that he previously put together during his time in New York. In fact, Matsui also played in 1,250 straight games for the Giants, giving him a professional baseball streak of 1,768 games.

Returning to the Yankees fully healthy in 2007, Matsui had another productive year, hitting 25 home runs, driving in 103 runs, scoring 100 others, and batting .285. However, knee problems and advancing age began to take their toll on the 34-year-old outfielder the following year, limiting him to only 93 games, 9 homers, and 45 RBIs.

Serving the Yankees almost exclusively as a designated hitter in 2009, Matsui posted solid numbers in his final season in pinstripes, hitting 28 home runs, knocking in 90 runs, and batting .274. He subsequently led the Yankees to victory over the Philadelphia Phillies in the World Series by batting .615, with 3 home runs and 8 runs batted in. Matsui's extraordinary performance earned him World Series MVP honors, even though he started just three of the six contests.

In spite of Matsui's heroics during the Fall Classic, the Yankees expressed little interest in re-signing him when he became available as a free agent at season's end. Telling the *Yomiuri Shimbun* that he "loved the Yankees the best" but that he no longer felt valued after his agent called to negotiate with the club and "the Yankees had nothing prepared [in terms of contract terms]," Matsui subsequently elected to sign a one-year deal with the Los Angeles Angels of Anaheim on December 16, 2009. Serving primarily as a designated hitter, Matsui spent one year in Anaheim before he moved on to Oakland in 2011. As of this writing, he has compiled 173 home runs, 753 RBIs, 649 runs scored, 1,239 hits, and a .285 batting average over the course of his major-league career. Matsui hit 140 homers, knocked in 597 runs, scored 536 others, collected 977 hits, and batted .292 during his seven years with the Yankees.

YANKEE CAREER HIGHLIGHTS

Best Season

It was an extremely close call between Matsui's 2004 and 2005 campaigns. In the first of those years, he hit a career-high 31 homers, drove in 108 runs, scored 109 others, collected 174 hits, batted .298, compiled a .390 on-base percentage, and posted a .522 slugging percentage. The following season, Matsui hit 23 home runs; scored 108 runs; established career highs with 116 runs batted in, 192 hits, 45 doubles, and a .305 batting average; and compiled a .367 on-base percentage and a .496 slugging percentage. It was really a toss-up, but I finally elected to go with 2004 due to the greater level of consistency that Matsui displayed over the course of the season. He batted .294 during the first half of 2004 while posting a mark of .302 during the season's second half. Matsui also posted a mark below .278 only in June, surpassing that figure in each of the other five months. Meanwhile, the outfielder's performance tended to be far more erratic in 2005. After compiling batting averages of .250 and .271 in April and May, respectively, he batted .398 in June and .317 in July, before slumping to .254 in August and raising his average back up to .348 in September.

Memorable Moments/Greatest Performances

As I alluded to earlier, Matsui often demonstrated a flair for the dramatic during his seven seasons in pinstripes. He first displayed his penchant for getting big hits when the spotlight shone on him in his very first game at Yankee Stadium, when he highlighted New York's 2003 home opener by hitting a grand slam.

Matsui struck again on September 12, 2006, when, exactly four months after undergoing surgery on his injured wrist, he returned to the Yankee lineup by going 4 for 4, with a walk and 2 runs scored against the Tampa Bay Devil Rays.

On June 12, 2008, Matsui celebrated his 34th birthday by hitting a grand slam against the Oakland A's during a 4–1 Yankee victory. He celebrated his 35th birthday the following year by hitting a 3-run home run during a 9–8 win over the Mets.

Matsui actually hit a number of big home runs for the Yankees during that 2009 campaign. On July 20, he hit a game-winning homer in the bottom of the ninth inning that put the Yankees in first place for good. A month later, on August 21, he hit 2 home runs and drove in a career-high 7 runs during a 20–11 win over the Boston Red Sox at Fenway Park. In doing so, he became the first Yankee to knock in 7 runs in a game at Fenway since Lou Gehrig accomplished the feat in 1930. Two games later, Matsui concluded the most torrid stretch of his career by hitting 2 home runs for the third time in just seven games.

Still, the defining moment of Matsui's career would have to be considered his performance in the 2009 World Series. After leading the Yankees to a 3–1 victory in game 2 by hitting a home run off Philadelphia starter Pedro Martinez in the bottom of the sixth inning, Matsui found himself sitting on the Yankee bench when the series shifted to Philadelphia for the next three contests. With the designated hitter not in effect in the National League ballpark, Matsui hit a pinch-hit homer during New York's 8–5 game 3 win. After the Yankees and Phillies split the next two games, Matsui put on a memorable performance in the series finale.

With the Fall Classic having shifted back to Yankee Stadium for game 6, Matsui returned to New York's starting lineup as the designated hitter. He subsequently defeated the Phillies almost single-handedly, collecting 3 hits and driving in 6 runs during a 7–3 Yankee victory that gave the team its 27th world championship. Matsui concluded the series with 8 hits in 13 official at bats, for a batting average of .615. He hit 3 homers and knocked in 8 runs, tying Bobby Richardson's single-game World Series record (game 3 of the 1960 World Series) with 6 RBIs in game 6. Matsui joined Yankee legends Babe Ruth and Lou Gehrig as the only players in Major League history to hit at least 3 home runs and compile a batting average in excess of .500 in the same World Series.

NOTABLE ACHIEVEMENTS

- Hit more than 30 home runs once.
- Knocked in more than 100 runs four times.
- Scored more than 100 runs three times.
- Batted over .300 twice.
- Compiled slugging percentage in excess of .500 twice.
- First Japanese player to homer in World Series (game 2 of 2003 series).
- 2009 World Series MVP.
- Two-time AL All-Star.
- Two-time AL champion.
- 2009 world champion.

Mike Mussina

One of the best free agent pitchers ever signed by the Yankees, Mike Mussina helped stabilize New York's starting rotation for nearly a decade. After posting at least 15 wins for the Baltimore Orioles six times between 1992 and 2000, Mussina surpassed 15 victories another five times for the Yankees from 2001 to 2008, continuing in the process his American League record string of 17 consecutive seasons with no fewer than 11 wins. A cerebral and extremely well-focused individual, Mussina continued to excel on the mound long after his once-blazing fastball left him, displaying the intelligence and poise that helped make him one of baseball's biggest winners over the course of his 18-year major-league career. A hybrid of a control and power pitcher in his prime, the right-hander had the ability to either throw a mid-90s fastball past an opposing hitter or drop his patented knuckle-curveball on the outside corner against a bewildered batsman. With a fluid delivery and a slender, compact build, Mussina exemplified poise and athleticism on the mound. Meanwhile, he carried himself with an intellectual loner's reserve off the field, always remaining polite but often appearing moody and somewhat unapproachable to others. Former Baltimore Orioles pitching coach Ray Miller attempted to explain the approach that Mussina took with him to the mound, claiming that his one-time protégé's focus was the thing that truly set him apart: "We all have the ability to concentrate on our job. But to concentrate every second of every minute for three and a half hours—I mean, one lapse and you get burnt. Only the exceptional ones can do that. Mike has a kind of tunnel vision when he pitches. He gets locked into that kind of zone."

Mussina's extremely high concentration level enabled him to become a big winner almost as soon as he arrived in the major leagues.

After being selected by the Baltimore Orioles in the first round of the 1990 amateur draft with the 20th overall pick, Mussina spent just one year in the minors before earning his first call-up to the big-league club in August 1991. Joining Baltimore's starting rotation the following year, the 23-year-old Stanford University graduate earned AL All-Star honors for the first of five times as an Oriole by compiling an exceptional 18–5 record that enabled him to lead the league with a .783 winning percentage. He also finished third among AL pitchers with a 2.54 ERA en route to earning a fourth-place finish in the Cy Young voting. Mussina remained in Baltimore eight more years, winning at least 18 games three more times and earning four more top-5 finishes in the Cy Young balloting. He had two of his finest seasons for the Birds in 1994 and 1995, posting records of 16–5 and 19–9, respectively, along with ERAs of 3.06 and 3.29. Mussina also won four consecutive Gold Gloves as a member of the team, copping the honor each year from 1996 to 1999.

However, frustrated by the imprudent spending of Orioles owner Peter Angelos and the direction in which the team appeared to be headed, Mussina elected to leave Baltimore when he became a free agent at the conclusion of the 2000 campaign. The 32-year-old right-hander signed a six-year $88.5-million contract with the Yankees on November 30, 2000. Mussina later cited a recruitment call from New York manager Joe Torre as a major factor in his decision to sign with the club; it came just days after the Yankee skipper led the Bronx Bombers to their third straight World Series title.

Mussina pitched extremely well his first three years in New York, compiling records of 17–11, 18–10, and 17–8. He finished among the league leaders in wins and strikeouts each year, and his 3.15 ERA in 2001 placed him second in the league rankings. Yet, the Yankees failed to win the world championship in any of those years, losing the World Series in 2001 and 2003 and being eliminated in the first round of the postseason tournament in 2002. Adding to the frustration that Mussina undoubtedly felt was the fact that Yankee fans often seemed to take him for granted. With the homegrown Andy Pettitte, more colorful Roger Clemens, and popular David Wells also members of the team's starting rotation during that time, Mussina went almost unnoticed, never truly establishing himself as either a fan favorite or a staff ace.

Mussina continued to post solid win totals for the Yankees from 2004 to 2007, even as the velocity on his fastball diminished further. Developing more and more into an off-speed pitcher over the course of those four seasons, Mussina compiled a total of 51 victories for the club, even though he surrendered more runs and hits to the opposition per nine innings than at virtually any other point during his career.

Still, the crafty veteran had one more big year left in his aging right arm. Reinventing himself in 2008 by altering his approach somewhat and mixing up his pitches extraordinarily well, Mussina posted a record of 20–9 for the Yankees. His 20 victories at 39 years of age made him the oldest first-time 20-game winner in major-league history. He also compiled a 3.37 ERA en route to earning a sixth-place finish in the AL Cy Young voting. Nevertheless, Mussina surprisingly chose to announce his retirement shortly after the season ended, becoming the first pitcher since Sandy Koufax in 1966 to leave the game after winning at least 20 games the previous season. Mussina retired with a career record of 270–153, for an outstanding .638 winning percentage. He also compiled an ERA of 3.68 over 18 major-league seasons. In his eight years in New York, Mussina posted a record of 123–72 and an ERA of 3.88. His 1,278 strikeouts as a member of the Yankees place him sixth in team history. Despite winning 20 games just once, Mussina won at least 17 games on eight occasions—four times while pitching for the Yankees. Although the Yankees failed to win a world championship during Mussina's time with the club, they won six division titles and two American League pennants.

YANKEE CAREER HIGHLIGHTS

Best Season

Even though Mussina's 20 victories at 39 years of age in 2008 represented a truly extraordinary feat, he pitched more effectively for the Yankees his first three years with them, allowing fewer hits per innings pitched and striking out more batters. Mussina's first season in New York was probably his best. In addition to finishing 17–11 with a 3.15 ERA in 2001, the right-hander struck out 214 batters—the second-highest total of his career (he compiled 218 strikeouts for the Orioles in 1997). Mussina finished second in the league in ERA and strikeouts; he also placed among the leaders in wins, shutouts (3), complete games (4), and innings pitched (229).

Memorable Moments/Greatest Performances

Certainly, Mussina's 6–2 victory over the Boston Red Sox at Fenway Park on September 28, 2008, represented a landmark win for the 39-year-old right-hander since it made him the oldest first-time 20-game winner in Major League Baseball history. However, Mussina pitched most of his finest games for the Yankees much earlier in his career. In fact, he pitched arguably his two best games in pinstripes in his very first year in New York.

On May 24, 2001, Mussina locked up with Pedro Martinez in a classic pitcher's duel at Yankee Stadium that the Yankee right-hander won by a score of 2–1. Mussina allowed the Red Sox just 1 run on 6 hits over eight innings, striking out 12 Boston batters, before turning the ball over to Mariano Rivera, who worked a perfect ninth.

Later that year, on September 2, in a nationally televised Sunday night contest played at Fenway Park, Mussina pitched his most dominant game as a Yankee. Facing Boston starter David Cone, who allowed his former Yankee teammates only one unearned run over 8 1/3 innings, Mussina took a perfect game into the bottom of the ninth inning. After retiring the first two batters he faced, Mussina got two strikes on Red Sox pinch hitter Carl Everett. However, Everett subsequently broke up the right-hander's bid for perfection by hitting a soft line-drive single into left-center field. Mussina had to settle for a 1–0 one-hitter in which he struck out 13 Red Sox batters.

Still, Mussina turned in his two most significant efforts in postseason play. With the Yankees trailing the Oakland A's 2–0 in the 2001 American League Division Series, Mussina took the mound for the third contest. Aided by Derek Jeter's famous "flip" to Jorge Posada at home plate, Mussina worked seven scoreless innings, allowing the A's just 4 hits en route to getting the Yankees back into the series with a 1–0 victory. New York subsequently won the next two games as well, becoming in the process the first team to win a division series after losing the first two games at home.

Mussina turned in another heroic performance in game 7 of the 2003 ALCS. With the Yankees trailing Boston 4–0, Mussina made the first relief appearance of his career, coming in for a struggling Roger Clemens with no one out in the top of the fourth inning and with runners on first and third. Mussina proceeded to strike out Jason Varitek, before inducing Johnny Damon to ground into a double play. He subsequently worked another two scoreless frames, keeping the Yankees within striking distance in a game they eventually came back to win 6–5 on Aaron Boone's 11th-inning homer.

NOTABLE ACHIEVEMENTS

- Won 20 games in 2008.
- Won at least 15 games four other times for Yankees.

- Oldest pitcher in major-league history (39) to win 20 games for first time.
- Struck out more than 200 batters once.
- Won 3 Gold Gloves with Yankees (7 in total).
- Two-time AL champion.

Dave Righetti

The first pitcher in baseball history to throw a no-hitter and lead his league in saves during his career (Dennis Eckersley later duplicated the feat), Dave Righetti spent the better part of 10 seasons in a Yankee uniform, first arriving in the Bronx late in 1979 as a hard-throwing left-handed starter and leaving New York at the conclusion of the 1990 campaign as the club's all-time saves leader. After spending his first three years in pinstripes as a member of the Yankees' starting rotation, Righetti replaced Rich "Goose" Gossage as the team's closer in 1984, remaining in that role through 1990, when he left New York to sign as a free agent with the San Francisco Giants. In his seven seasons as a full-time reliever with the Yankees, Righetti compiled a total of 224 saves, which stood as the Yankee team record until Mariano Rivera eclipsed it in 2002. Righetti established a new major-league mark by amassing 46 saves for the Yankees in 1986. Although Chicago closer Bobby Thigpen set a new record just four years later by saving 57 games for the White Sox, Righetti's 46 saves remain the third-highest total ever posted by a Yankee reliever. The southpaw amassed more than 30 saves for the Yankees four times and won two AL Reliever of the Year Awards, doing so after he earlier captured AL Rookie of the Year honors and tossed a no-hitter against Boston as a starting pitcher.

Originally selected by the Texas Rangers with the 10th overall pick of the 1977 amateur draft, David Allan Righetti first garnered national attention on July 16, 1978, when he set a Texas League record by striking out 21 Midland Cubs batters while pitching for the Tulsa Drillers. Taking note of Righetti's extraordinary performance, the Yankees acquired the 19-year-old left-hander's services some four months later when they completed a 10-player trade with the Rangers that sent Sparky Lyle and four others to Texas.

After spending virtually all of the next two seasons in the minor leagues, Righetti earned a permanent call-up to the Yankees early in 1981, posting a record of 8–4 and a league-leading 2.05 ERA the rest of that strike-shortened campaign en route to earning AL Rookie of the Year honors. Righetti subsequently pitched well for New York during the American League playoffs, winning two games against Milwaukee in the ALDS and another against Oakland in the ALCS while allowing just 1 earned run and 12 hits in 15 total innings of work. However, he faltered against Los Angeles in the World Series, surrendering 3 runs on 5 hits to the Dodgers in just two innings of work in his lone start.

Righetti remained an effective member of New York's starting rotation in 1982 and 1983, compiling a combined record of 25–18 over the course of those two years while posting ERAs of 3.79 and 3.44. But the Yankees moved the 25-year-old southpaw to the bullpen when Rich Gossage departed for San Diego at the conclusion of the 1983 campaign. Although Righetti initially accepted his new role in the Yankee bullpen somewhat reluctantly, he eventually learned to embrace it. Making an extremely successful transition into being a full-time closer, Righetti saved a total of 60 games for the Yankees in 1984 and 1985. He also won another 17 games while compiling ERAs of 2.34 and 2.78. Righetti evolved into arguably the American League's top closer in 1986, finishing the campaign with 8 victories, a 2.45 ERA, and 46 saves. Particularly dominant during the season's second half, Righetti converted on 29 of his final 30 save opportunities, including both ends of a season-ending doubleheader against the Red Sox. The effort against Boston enabled Righetti to surpass Dan Quisenberry and Bruce Sutter, both of whom previously saved 45 games, as Major League Baseball's all-time single-season saves leader. Righetti's extraordinary performance earned him a fourth-place finish in the AL Cy Young voting. He also finished 10th in the league MVP balloting.

Although Righetti never again reached such heights, he remained an effective closer for the Yankees for another four years, averaging 29 saves a season for them through 1990. After becoming a free agent at the end of 1990, he elected to sign with the San Francisco Giants, with whom he spent the next three years. Having lost much of his effectiveness, Righetti left San Francisco after 1993, moving on to Oakland, Toronto, and Chicago, where he ended his career in 1995 as a part-time starter for the White Sox. Righetti retired from the game with a career record of 82–79, a 3.46 ERA, and a total of 252 saves. In addition to saving 224 games as a member of the Yankees, Righetti compiled a record of 74–61 and a 3.11 ERA while with the team.

YANKEE CAREER HIGHLIGHTS

Best Season

Righetti pitched extremely well in his first season in pinstripes, earning 1981 AL Rookie of the Year honors by going 8–4 with a league-leading 2.05 ERA as a starter. He also allowed a total of only 113 men to reach base (75 hits and 38 walks) in 105 innings of work. Nevertheless, Righetti experienced his greatest success in 1986, when he established a new major-league record by saving 46 games for the Yankees. In addition to leading the majors in saves, Righetti posted eight victories, compiled an outstanding 2.45 ERA, and struck out 83 batters in 107 innings of work while surrendering only 88 hits to the opposition. His exceptional performance earned him a spot on the AL All-Star Team and the AL Rolaids Relief Award for the first of two straight times.

Memorable Moments/Greatest Performances

Righetti's two saves against Boston on October 4, 1986, enabled him to establish a new single-season major-league mark that he held for the next four years. There is little doubt, though, that the most memorable moment of Righetti's career took place on July 4, 1983, when he became the first Yankee hurler to throw a no-hitter since Don Larsen tossed his perfect game against Brooklyn in the 1956 World Series. Righetti concluded his 4–0 no-no with a strikeout of American League batting champion Wade Boggs, who waved at a two-strike breaking ball. Righetti reminisced about the game 25 years later: "My biggest worry, because I had a tendency to fall toward third base, was [Boggs] tapping a ball between me and Mattingly, and me trying to get to first base. . . . I threw a lot of fastballs during the at bat, but the last slider I ended up throwing, he happened to miss it. Thank goodness."

NOTABLE ACHIEVEMENTS

- Saved more than 30 games four times, topping 40 mark once.
- Surpassed 20 saves three other times.

- Compiled ERA below 3.00 four times, including three marks below 2.50.
- Threw more than 200 innings once (1983).
- Led AL in saves and ERA once each.
- 1981 AL Rookie of the Year.
- Threw no-hitter versus Boston on July 4, 1983.
- Two-time AL All-Star.
- Two-time AL Reliever of the Year Award winner (1986 and 1987).
- Two-time AL Rolaids Relief Award winner (1986 and 1987).
- 1981 AL champion.

Summary and Honorable Mentions: The Next 50

With the 50 greatest players in New York Yankees history now identified, the time has come to select the best of the best. Solely on the basis of the rankings contained in this book, the members of the Yankees' all-time team are listed below. The squad includes the top player at each position, along with a pitching staff that features a five-man starting rotation, a closer, and a setup man. Our starting lineup also includes a designated hitter. Just for fun, let's name a second team as well.

FIRST TEAM

Starting Lineup

Mickey Mantle LF
Derek Jeter SS
Babe Ruth RF
Lou Gehrig 1B
Joe DiMaggio CF
Alex Rodriguez 3B
Yogi Berra DH
Joe Gordon 2B
Bill Dickey C

Pitching Staff

Whitey Ford SP
Red Ruffing SP
Lefty Gomez SP
Ron Guidry SP
Jack Chesbro SP
Mariano Rivera CL
Rich Gossage SU

SECOND TEAM

Starting Lineup

Earle Combs CF
Bernie Williams LF
Don Mattingly 1B
Dave Winfield RF
Paul O'Neill DH
Tony Lazzeri 2B
Thurman Munson C
Graig Nettles 3B
Phil Rizzuto SS

PITCHING STAFF

Herb Pennock SP
Waite Hoyt SP
Mel Stottlemyre SP
Andy Pettitte SP
Bob Shawkey SP
Sparky Lyle CL
Dave Righetti SU

Although I limited my rankings to the top 50 players in Yankees history, many other fine players have donned the pinstripes over the years, some of whom narrowly missed the final cut. The following is a list of those players deserving of an honorable mention. These are the men whom I deemed worthy of being slotted into positions 51 to 100 in the overall rankings. The statistics they compiled during their time in New York and their most notable achievements as Yankees are also included.

51—RED ROLFE (3B, 1934–1942)

Yankee Numbers

69 HR, 497 RBIs, 942 runs scored, 1,394 hits, .289 AVG, .360 OBP, .413 SLG PCT

Notable Achievements

- Batted over .300 four times.
- Scored more than 100 runs seven times.
- Collected more than 200 hits once (213 in 1939).
- Led AL in runs scored, hits, doubles, and triples once each.
- Three-time *Sporting News* All-Star selection.
- Four-time AL All-Star.
- Six-time AL champion.
- Five-time world champion.

52—WALLY PIPP (1B, 1915–1925)

Yankee Numbers

80 HR, 826 RBIs, 820 runs scored, 1,577 hits, .282 AVG, .343 OBP, .414 SLG PCT

Notable Achievements

- Batted over .300 three times.
- Knocked in more than 100 runs twice.
- Scored more than 100 runs once.
- Collected at least 10 triples seven times.
- Led AL in home runs twice and triples once.
- Fourth in franchise history with 121 triples.
- Three-time AL champion.
- 1923 world champion.

53—SPUD CHANDLER (P, 1937–1947)

Yankee Numbers

Record: 109–43, .717 WIN PCT, 2.84 ERA, 109 CG, 26 shutouts

Notable Achievements

- Two-time 20-game winner.
- Compiled ERA below 3.00 six times.
- Threw 20 complete games twice.
- Threw more than 250 innings twice.
- Led AL in wins, WIN PCT, CG, and shutouts once each.
- 1.64 ERA in 1943 is lowest single-season mark in team history.
- Ranks among all-time Yankee leaders in WIN PCT, complete games, and shutouts.
- 1943 AL MVP.
- 1943 *Sporting News* All-Star selection.
- Four-time AL All-Star.
- Seven-time AL champion.
- Six-time world champion.

54—EDDIE LOPAT (P, 1948–1955)

Yankee Numbers

Record: 113–59, .657 WIN PCT, 3.19 ERA, 91 CG, 20 shutouts

Notable Achievements

- Won 21 games in 1951.
- Surpassed 15 victories four other times.
- Compiled ERA below 3.00 three times.
- Threw 20 complete games once.
- Threw more than 200 innings four times.
- Led AL in WIN PCT and ERA once each.
- 1951 AL All-Star.
- Five-time AL champion.
- Five-time world champion.

55—BEN CHAPMAN (OF, 1930–1936)

Yankee Numbers

60 HR, 589 RBIs, 626 runs scored, 1,079 hits, 184 SB, .305 AVG, .379 OBP, .451 SLG PCT

Notable Achievements

- Batted over .300 four times.
- Knocked in more than 100 runs twice.
- Scored more than 100 runs four times.
- Collected at least 10 triples four times.
- Stole more than 20 bases four times, including AL-leading 61 in 1931.
- Led AL in steals three times and triples once.
- Tied for sixth in franchise history with 184 stolen bases.
- Hit 3 home runs in one game in 1932.
- Four-time AL All-Star.
- 1932 AL champion.
- 1932 world champion.

56—HANK BAUER (OF, 1948–1959)

Yankee Numbers

158 HR, 654 RBIs, 792 runs scored, 1,326 hits, .277 AVG, .347 OBP, .444 SLG PCT

Notable Achievements

- Batted over .300 twice.
- Hit more than 20 home runs twice.
- Led AL with 9 triples in 1957.
- Three-time AL All-Star.
- Nine-time AL champion.
- Seven-time world champion.

57—HAL CHASE (1B, 1905–1913)

Yankee Numbers

20 HR, 494 RBIs, 551 runs scored, 1,182 hits, 248 SB, .284 AVG, .311 OBP, .362 SLG PCT

Notable Achievements

- Batted over .300 twice.
- Stole more than 30 bases four times, topping 40 mark once.
- Fourth in franchise history with 248 stolen bases.

58—FRANK CROSETTI (SS, 1932–1948)

Yankee Numbers

98 HR, 649 RBIs, 1,006 runs scored, 1,541 hits, .245 AVG, .341 OBP, .354 SLG PCT

Notable Achievements

- Scored more than 100 runs four times.
- Led AL with 27 stolen bases in 1938.
- Two-time AL All-Star.
- Eight-time AL champion.
- Seven-time world champion.

59—GIL MCDOUGALD (3B, SS, 2B, 1951–1960)

Yankee Numbers

112 HR, 576 RBIs, 697 runs scored, 1,291 hits, .276 AVG, .356 OBP, .410 SLG PCT

Notable Achievements

- Batted over .300 twice.
- Compiled on-base percentage in excess of .400 once.
- Led AL with 9 triples in 1957.
- Led all AL second basemen in fielding percentage twice.
- Led all AL shortstops in fielding percentage once.
- 1951 AL Rookie of the Year.
- Five-time AL All-Star.
- Eight-time AL champion.
- Five-time world champion.

60—LOU PINIELLA (OF, DH, 1974–1984)

Yankee Numbers

57 HR, 417 RBIs, 392 runs scored, 971 hits, .295 AVG, .338 OBP, .413 SLG PCT

Notable Achievements

- Batted over .300 five times.
- Four-time AL champion.
- Two-time world champion.

61—C. C. SABATHIA (P, 2009–2011)

Yankee Numbers

Record: 59–23, .720 WIN PCT, 3.18 ERA

Notable Achievements

- 21-game winner in 2010.
- Won 19 games two other times.
- Threw more than 230 innings three times.
- Struck out more than 200 batters once (230 in 2011).
- Led AL in wins twice.
- WIN PCT of .720 is second best in franchise history (Johnny Allen—.725).
- 2009 ALCS MVP.
- Two-time AL All-Star.
- 2009 AL champion.
- 2009 world champion.

62—ROGER CLEMENS (P, 1999–2003, 2007)

Yankee Numbers

Record: 83–42, .664 WIN PCT, 4.01 ERA

Notable Achievements

- 20-game winner in 2001.
- Threw more than 200 innings twice.
- Struck out more than 200 batters once (213 in 2001).
- Led AL with .870 WIN PCT in 2001.
- 2001 AL Cy Young Award winner.
- Two-time AL All-Star.

- Four-time AL champion.
- Two-time world champion.

63—WADE BOGGS (3B, 1993–1997)

Yankee Numbers

24 HR, 246 RBIs, 355 runs scored, 702 hits, .313 AVG, .396 OBP, .407 SLG PCT

Notable Achievements

- Batted over .300 four times.
- Compiled on-base percentage in excess of .400 twice.
- Led all AL third basemen in fielding percentage twice and assists once.
- Won 2 Gold Gloves and 2 Silver Sluggers.
- 1994 *Sporting News* All-Star selection.
- Four-time AL All-Star.
- 1996 AL champion.
- 1996 world champion.

64—JASON GIAMBI (1B, DH, 2002–2008)

Yankee Numbers

209 HR, 604 RBIs, 515 runs scored, 764 hits, .260 AVG, .404 OBP, .521 SLG PCT

Notable Achievements

- Surpassed 40 home runs twice.
- Topped 30 homers three other times.
- Knocked in more than 100 runs three times.
- Scored more than 100 runs once.
- Batted over .300 once.
- Drew more than 100 bases on balls four times.
- Compiled on-base percentage in excess of .400 four times.
- Posted slugging percentage in excess of .500 five times.
- Led AL in walks twice and on-base percentage once.

- 2002 Silver Slugger winner.
- 2002 *Sporting News* All-Star selection.
- Three-time AL All-Star.
- 2003 AL champion.

65—CATFISH HUNTER (P, 1975–1979)

Yankee Numbers

Record: 63–53, .543 WIN PCT, 3.58 ERA, 65 CG, 11 shutouts

Notable Achievements

- 23-game winner in 1975.
- Compiled ERA below 3.00 once (2.58 in 1975).
- Completed more than 20 games twice.
- Threw more than 275 innings twice, surpassing 300 once.
- Led AL with 23 wins, 30 CG, and 328 IP in 1975.
- Two-time AL All-Star.
- Three-time AL champion.
- Two-time world champion.

66—MARK TEIXEIRA (1B, 2009–2011)

Yankee Numbers

111 HR, 341 RBIs, 306 runs scored, 478 hits, .266 AVG, .363 OBP, .514 SLG PCT

Notable Achievements

- Surpassed 30 home runs three times.
- Knocked in more than 100 runs three times.
- Scored more than 100 runs twice.
- Posted slugging percentage in excess of .550 once.
- Led AL in HR, RBIs, runs scored, and total bases once each.
- Second in AL MVP voting in 2009.
- Won 2 Gold Gloves and 1 Silver Slugger.
- 2009 AL All-Star.

- 2009 AL champion.
- 2009 world champion.

67—TOM TRESH (OF, SS, 1961–1969)

Yankee Numbers

140 HR, 493 RBIs, 549 runs scored, 967 hits, .247 AVG, .337 OBP, .413 SLG PCT

Notable Achievements

- Hit more than 20 home runs four times.
- Hit 3 home runs in one game in 1965.
- 1962 AL Rookie of the Year.
- 1965 Gold Glove winner.
- 1962 *Sporting News* All-Star selection.
- Two-time AL All-Star.
- Three-time AL champion.
- 1962 world champion.

68—FRITZ PETERSON (P, 1966–1974)

Yankee Numbers

Record: 109–106, .507 WIN PCT, 3.10 ERA, 81 CG, 18 shutouts

Notable Achievements

- Won 20 games in 1970.
- Surpassed 15 victories three other times.
- Compiled ERA below 3.00 three times.
- Threw 20 complete games once.
- Threw more than 250 innings four times.
- Led AL in fewest walks allowed per nine innings five straight times (1968–1972).
- Led AL in WHIP (walks + hits per innings pitched) twice.
- Compiled lowest career ERA (2.52) of any pitcher at Yankee Stadium.
- 1970 AL All-Star.

69—GEORGE SELKIRK (OF, 1934–1942)

Yankee Numbers

108 HR, 576 RBIs, 503 runs scored, 810 hits, .290 AVG, .400 OBP, .483 SLG PCT

Notable Achievements

- Batted over .300 five times.
- Hit more than 20 home runs once.
- Knocked in more than 100 runs twice.
- Scored more than 100 runs once.
- Walked more than 100 times once.
- Compiled on-base percentage in excess of .400 four times.
- Posted slugging percentage in excess of .500 three times, topping .600-mark once.
- Two-time AL All-Star.
- Six-time AL champion.
- Five-time world champion.

70—BOBBY RICHARDSON (2B, 1955–1966)

Yankee Numbers

34 HR, 390 RBIs, 643 runs scored, 1,432 hits, .266 AVG, .299 OBP, .335 SLG PCT

Notable Achievements

- Batted over .300 twice.
- Collected more than 200 hits once.
- Posted best at-bat-per-strikeout ratio in AL three times.
- Led AL second basemen in putouts twice.
- Led AL with 209 hits in 1962.
- 1960 World Series MVP.
- Holds World Series records for most RBIs in a World Series (12 in 1960) and most RBIs in a single game (6 in 1960 game 3).
- Second in AL MVP voting in 1962.
- Won five straight Gold Gloves (1961–1965).
- Six-time *Sporting News* All-Star selection.
- Seven-time AL All-Star.
- Seven-time AL champion.
- Three-time world champion.

71—CHRIS CHAMBLISS (1B, 1974–1979)

Yankee Numbers

79 HR, 454 RBIs, 415 runs scored, 954 hits, .282 AVG, .323 OBP, .417 SLG PCT

Notable Achievements

- Batted over .300 once (.304 in 1975).
- Led all AL first basemen with .997 fielding percentage in 1978.
- Hit pennant-winning home run vs. Kansas City in 1976 ALCS.
- 1978 Gold Glove winner.
- 1976 *Sporting News* All-Star selection.
- 1976 AL All-Star.
- Three-time AL champion.
- Two-time world champion.

72—JOE PEPITONE (1B, 1962–1969)

Yankee Numbers

166 HR, 541 RBIs, 435 runs scored, 967 hits, .252 AVG, .294 OBP, .423 SLG PCT

Notable Achievements

- Hit more than 20 home runs four times, topping 30 HR once.
- Knocked in 100 runs in 1964.
- Led AL first basemen in fielding percentage three times, putouts twice, and assists once.
- Three-time Gold Glove winner.
- 1963 *Sporting News* All-Star selection.
- Three-time AL All-Star.
- Three-time AL champion.
- 1962 world champion.

73—DAVID WELLS (P, 1997–1998, 2002–2003)

Yankee Numbers

Record: 68–28, .708 WIN PCT, 3.90 ERA, 19 CG, 9 shutouts

Notable Achievements

- Surpassed 15 victories four times.
- Threw more than 200 innings four times.
- Led all AL pitchers with .818 winning pct., 5 shutouts, and WHIP of 1.045 in 1998.
- Pitched perfect game against Minnesota on May 17, 1998.
- 1998 *Sporting News* All-Star selection.
- 1998 AL All-Star.
- Two-time AL champion.
- 1998 world champion.

74—CARL MAYS (P, 1919–1923)

Yankee Numbers

Record: 80–39, .672 WIN PCT, 3.25 ERA, 91 CG, 9 shutouts

Notable Achievements

- Two-time 20-game winner.
- Compiled 1.65 ERA after joining team at midseason in 1919.
- Threw more than 20 complete games three times.
- Threw more than 300 innings twice.
- Led all AL pitchers in wins, WIN PCT, innings pitched, shutouts, and saves once each.
- Second-highest single-season win total in club history, 27 in 1921 (Jack Chesbro, 41 in 1904).
- Three-time AL champion.
- 1923 world champion.

75—TONY KUBEK (SS, 1957–1965)

Yankee Numbers

57 HR, 373 RBIs, 522 runs scored, 1,109 hits, .266 AVG, .303 OBP, .364 SLG PCT

Notable Achievements

- Batted over .300 once.
- 1957 AL Rookie of the Year.

- 1961 *Sporting News* All-Star selection.
- Three-time AL All-Star.
- Seven-time AL champion.
- Three-time world champion.

76—TOMMY JOHN (P, 1979–1982, 1986–1989)

Yankee Numbers

Record: 91–60, .603 WIN PCT, 3.59 ERA, 53 CG, 12 shutouts

Notable Achievements

- Two-time 20-game winner.
- Compiled ERA below 3.00 three times.
- Threw more than 250 innings twice.
- Led all AL pitchers with 6 shutouts in 1980.
- Second in AL Cy Young balloting in 1979.
- 1980 *Sporting News* All-Star selection.
- Two-time AL All-Star.
- 1981 AL champion.

77—TINY BONHAM (P, 1940–1946)

Yankee Numbers

Record: 79–50, .612 WIN PCT, 2.73 ERA, 91 CG, 17 shutouts

Notable Achievements

- Won 21 games in 1942.
- Compiled ERA below 3.00 five times.
- Threw more than 20 complete games once.
- Threw more than 200 innings three times.
- Led all AL pitchers with .808 winning pct., 22 complete games, 6 shutouts, and WHIP of 0.987 in 1942.
- 1942 *Sporting News* All-Star selection.
- Two-time AL All-Star.
- Three-time AL champion.
- Two-time world champion.

78—HANK BOROWY (P, 1942–1945)

Yankee Numbers

Record: 56–30, .651 WIN PCT, 2.74 ERA, 53 CG, 11 shutouts

Notable Achievements

- Compiled ERA below 3.00 three times.
- Threw more than 250 innings once.
- 1944 AL All-Star.
- Two-time AL champion.
- 1943 world champion.

79—BOB TURLEY (P, 1955–1962)

Yankee Numbers

Record: 82–52, .612 WIN PCT, 3.62 ERA, 58 CG, 21 shutouts

Notable Achievements

- Won 21 games in 1958.
- Compiled ERA below 3.00 twice.
- Threw more than 240 innings twice.
- Struck out more than 200 batters once (210 in 1955).
- Led all AL pitchers with 21 wins, .750 winning pct. and 19 complete games in 1958.
- 1958 Cy Young Award winner.
- Second in 1958 AL MVP voting.
- 1958 World Series MVP.
- 1958 *Sporting News* All-Star selection.
- Two-time AL All-Star.
- Seven-time AL champion.
- Four-time world champion.

80—RALPH TERRY (P, 1956–1957, 1959–1964)

Yankee Numbers

Record: 78–59, .569 WIN PCT, 3.44 ERA, 56 CG, 14 shutouts

Notable Achievements

- Won 23 games in 1962.
- Surpassed 16 victories two other times.
- Threw more than 250 innings twice.
- Led all AL pitchers in wins, complete games, innings pitched, and WHIP once each.
- 1962 *Sporting News* All-Star selection.
- 1962 AL All-Star.
- Five-time AL champion.
- Two-time world champion.

81—ALFONSO SORIANO (2B, 1999–2003)

Yankee Numbers

98 HR, 270 RBIs, 326 runs scored, 571 hits, 121 stolen bases, .284 AVG, .322 OBP, .502 SLG PCT

Notable Achievements

- Hit more than 30 home runs twice.
- Knocked in more than 100 runs once.
- Scored more than 100 runs twice.
- Batted over .300 once.
- Stole more than 40 bases twice.
- Surpassed 200 hits and 50 doubles once each.
- Compiled slugging percentage in excess of .500 twice.
- Led AL with 128 runs scored, 209 hits and 41 steals in 2002.
- 51 doubles in 2002 are third-highest total in franchise history.
- Third in 2002 AL MVP voting.
- 2002 Silver Slugger winner.
- 2002 *Sporting News* All-Star selection.
- Two-time AL All-Star.
- Two-time AL champion.

82—JOE PAGE (P, 1944–1950)

Yankee Numbers

Record: 57–49, .538 WIN PCT, 3.44 ERA, 76 saves

Notable Achievements

- Won more than 10 games twice.
- Saved more than 20 games once.
- Compiled ERA below 3.00 three times.
- Led AL in saves twice.
- Two top-5 finishes in AL MVP voting.
- 1949 *Sporting News* All-Star selection.
- Three-time AL All-Star.
- Three-time AL champion.
- Three-time world champion.

83—JOHNNY MURPHY (P, 1932, 1934–1943, 1946)

Yankee Numbers

Record: 93–53, .637 WIN PCT, 3.54 ERA, 104 saves

Notable Achievements

- Won at least 10 games four times.
- Posted double-digit saves five times.
- Compiled ERA below 3.00 twice.
- Led AL in saves four times.
- Three-time AL All-Star.
- Seven-time AL champion.
- Six-time world champion.

84—AL DOWNING (P, 1961–1969)

Yankee Numbers

Record: 72–57, .558 WIN PCT, 3.23 ERA, 46 CG, 12 shutouts

Notable Achievements

- Compiled ERA below 3.00 twice.
- Struck out more than 200 batters once (217 in 1964).
- Threw more than 200 innings four times.
- Led all AL pitchers with 217 strikeouts in 1964.
- 1967 AL All-Star.
- Two-time AL champion.

85—ED FIGUEROA (P, 1976–1980)

Yankee Numbers

Record: 62–39, .614 WIN PCT, 3.53 ERA, 42 CG, 9 shutouts

Notable Achievements

- 20-game winner in 1978.
- Won at least 16 games two other times.
- Compiled ERA below 3.00 once.
- Threw more than 230 innings three times.
- Three-time AL champion.
- Two-time world champion.

86—MONTE PEARSON (P, 1936–1940)

Yankee Numbers

Record: 63–27, .700 WIN PCT, 3.82 ERA, 54 CG, 4 shutouts

Notable Achievements

- Surpassed 16 victories twice.
- Threw more than 200 innings twice.
- Threw no-hitter vs. Cleveland on August 27, 1938.
- Won all four World Series starts, going 4–0 with a 1.01 ERA and 3 complete games.
- Two-time AL All-Star.
- Four-time AL champion.
- Four-time world champion.

87—GENE WOODLING (OF, 1949–1954)

Yankee Numbers

51 HR, 336 RBIs, 361 runs scored, 648 hits, .285 AVG, .388 OBP, .434 SLG PCT

Notable Achievements

- Batted over .300 twice.
- Led AL with .429 on-base percentage in 1953.
- Five-time AL champion.
- Five-time world champion.

88—GEORGE PIPGRAS (P, 1923–1924, 1927–1933)

Yankee Numbers

Record: 93–64, .592 WIN PCT, 4.04 ERA, 84 CG, 14 shutouts

Notable Achievements

- Won 24 games in 1928.
- Surpassed 15 victories three other times.
- Threw more than 20 complete games and 300 innings once each.
- Threw more than 200 innings three other times.
- Led AL in wins, innings pitched, and shutouts once each.
- Won all three World Series starts, going 3–0 with a 2.77 ERA and working 26 out of a possible 27 innings.
- Three-time AL champion.
- Three-time world champion.

89—MICKEY RIVERS (OF, 1976–1979)

Yankee Numbers

34 HR, 209 RBIs, 289 runs scored, 598 hits, 93 stolen bases, .299 AVG, .324 OBP, .422 SLG PCT

Notable Achievements

- Batted over .300 twice.
- Stole more than 20 bases three times, topping 40 mark once.
- Third in 1976 AL MVP voting.
- 1976 *Sporting News* All-Star selection.
- 1976 AL All-Star.

- Three-time AL champion.
- Two-time world champion.

90—FRANK "HOME RUN" BAKER (3B, 1916–1919, 1921–1922)

Yankee Numbers

48 HR, 375 RBIs, 314 runs scored, 735 hits, .288 AVG, .347 OBP, .404 SLG PCT

Notable Achievements

- Batted over .300 once (.306 in 1918).
- Second in AL with 10 home runs in 1916 and 1919.
- Led AL third basemen in putouts three times and in assists and fielding percentage once each.
- Two-time AL champion.

91—WILLIE KEELER (OF, 1903–1909)

Yankee Numbers

10 HR, 206 RBIs, 482 runs scored, 974 hits, 118 stolen bases, .294 AVG, .347 OBP, .341 SLG PCT

Notable Achievements

- Batted over .300 four times.
- Stole more than 20 bases three times.
- Second in AL in batting average twice and in runs scored, hits, and on-base percentage once each.

92—DAVID CONE (P, 1995–2000)

Yankee Numbers

Record: 64–40, .615 WIN PCT, 3.91 ERA

Notable Achievements

- Won 20 games in 1998.
- Compiled ERA below 3.00 twice.

- Struck out more than 200 batters twice.
- Threw more than 200 innings once (208 in 1998).
- Led AL in wins in 1998.
- Second in AL with 3.44 ERA in 1999.
- Threw perfect game against Montreal on July 18, 1999.
- Compiled 6–1 record for Yankees in postseason play.
- Four-time AL champion.
- Four-time world champion.

93—CLETE BOYER (3B, 1959–1966)

Yankee Numbers

95 HR, 393 RBIs, 434 runs scored, 882 hits, .241 AVG, .298 OBP, .371 SLG PCT

Notable Achievements

- Led AL third basemen in assists three times and putouts once.
- Five-time AL champion.
- Two-time world champion.

94—GEORGE "SNUFFY" STIRNWEISS (INF, 1943–1950)

Yankee Numbers

27 HR, 253 RBIs, 562 runs scored, 899 hits, 130 stolen bases, .274 AVG, .366 OBP, .382 SLG PCT

Notable Achievements

- Batted over .300 twice.
- Scored more than 100 runs three times.
- Surpassed 200 hits once.
- Finished in double digits in triples twice.
- Stole more than 30 bases twice, including 55 in 1944.
- Led AL in runs scored, hits, triples, and stolen bases twice each and in batting average, slugging percentage, and total bases once each.
- Second-highest total of triples in franchise history, 22 in 1945.
- Finished in top five of AL MVP voting twice.
- 1945 *Sporting News* All-Star selection.

- 1946 AL All-Star.
- Three-time AL champion.
- Three-time world champion.

95—JIMMY KEY (P, 1993–1996)

Yankee Numbers

Record: 48–23, .676 WIN PCT, 3.68 ERA

Notable Achievements

- Surpassed 17 victories twice.
- Threw more than 200 innings once (237 in 1993).
- Led AL with 17 wins in 1994.
- Second in AL Cy Young voting in 1994.
- 1994 *Sporting News* Pitcher of the Year.
- Two-time *Sporting News* All-Star selection.
- Two-time AL All-Star.
- 1996 AL champion.
- 1996 world champion.

96—ROBERTO KELLY (OF, 1987–1992)

Yankee Numbers

57 HR, 259 RBIs, 324 runs scored, 640 hits, 151 stolen bases, .278 AVG, .331 OBP, .411 SLG PCT

Notable Achievements

- Hit 20 home runs once.
- Batted over .300 once.
- Stole more than 30 bases three times, topping 40 mark once.
- 1992 AL All-Star.

97—ROGER PECKINPAUGH (SS, 1913–1921)

Yankee Numbers

36 HR, 427 RBIs, 670 runs scored, 1,170 hits, 143 stolen bases, .257 AVG, .334 OBP, .342 SLG PCT

Notable Achievements

- Batted over .300 once (.305 in 1919).
- Scored more than 100 runs twice.
- Stole more than 30 bases once (38 in 1914).
- Third in AL with 128 runs scored in 1921.
- Led AL shortstops in assists three times.
- 1921 AL champion.

98—RUSS FORD (P, 1909–1913)

Yankee Numbers

Record: 73–56, .566 WIN PCT, 2.54 ERA, 100 CG, 10 shutouts

Notable Achievements

- Two-time 20-game winner.
- Compiled ERA below 3.00 three times, including a mark of 1.65 in 1910—the second-lowest figure in team history.
- Threw more than 25 complete games and 250 innings three times each.
- Struck out more than 200 batters once (209 in 1910).
- Eight shutouts in 1910 are second most in team history.
- Career ERA of 2.54 is fourth best in franchise history.

99—SCOTT BROSIUS (3B, 1998–2001)

Yankee Numbers

65 HR, 282 RBIs, 264 runs scored, 507 hits, .267 AVG, .331 OBP, .428 SLG PCT

Notable Achievements

- Batted .300 and knocked in 98 runs in 1998.
- 1998 World Series MVP.
- 1999 Gold Glove winner.
- 1998 *Sporting News* All-Star selection.
- 1998 AL All-Star.
- Four-time AL champion.
- Three-time world champion.

100—GARY SHEFFIELD (OF, 2004–2006)

Yankee Numbers

76 HR, 269 RBIs, 243 runs scored, 381 hits, .291 AVG, .383 OBP, .515 SLG PCT

Notable Achievements

- Hit more than 30 home runs twice.
- Knocked in more than 120 runs twice.
- Scored more than 100 runs twice.
- Compiled slugging percentage in excess of .500 twice.
- Second in AL MVP voting in 2004.
- Two-time AL All-Star

Glossary: Abbreviations and Statistical Terms

AVG. Batting average. The number of hits divided by the number of at bats.

CG. Complete games pitched.

CL. Closer.

ERA. Earned run average. The number of earned runs a pitcher gives up per nine innings. This does not include runs that scored as a result of errors made in the field, and it is calculated by dividing the number of runs given up by the number of innings pitched and multiplying the result by 9.

HITS. Base hits. Awarded when a runner safely reaches at least first base upon a batted ball, if no error is recorded.

HR. Home runs. Fair ball hit over the fence or one hit to a spot that allows the batter to circle the bases before the ball is returned to home plate.

IP. Innings pitched.

OBP. On-base percentage. Hits plus walks plus hit-by-pitches, divided by plate appearances.

RBI. Runs batted in. Awarded to the batter when a runner scores upon a safely batted ball, a sacrifice, or a walk.

RUNS. Runs scored by a player.

SB. Stolen bases.

SLG PCT. Slugging percentage. The number of total bases earned by all singles, doubles, triples, and home runs, divided by the total number of at bats.

SO. Strikeouts.

SP. Starting pitcher.

SU. Setup reliever.

WIN PCT. Winning percentage. A pitcher's number of wins divided by his number of total decisions (i.e., wins plus losses).

Bibliography

All quotes were retrieved from the following sources:

BOOKS

Halberstam, David. *October 1964*. New York: Villard Books, 1994.

Shalin, Mike, and Neil Shalin. *Out by a Step: The 100 Best Players Not in the Baseball Hall of Fame*. Lakeville, IN: Diamond Communications, 2002.

Thorn, John, and Pete Palmer, eds. (with Michael Gershman). *Total Baseball*. New York: HarperCollins, 1993.

VIDEOS

New York Yankees: The Movie. Magic Video, 1987.

Pinstripe Power: The Story of the 1961 New York Yankees. Major League Baseball Productions, 1987.

INTERNET WEBSITES

"The Ballplayers," BaseballLibrary.com, http://www.baseballlibrary.com/baseballlibrary/ballplayers.

"Historical Stats," MLB.com, http://www.mlb.com/stats.historical/individual stats player.

"MLB Awards," MLB.com, http://www.mlb.com/awards/mlb_awards/mvp_history.

"The Players," Baseballink.com, http://www.baseballink.com/baseballink/players.

"The Players," Baseball-Reference.com, http://www.baseball-reference.com/
    players.
"The Teams," Baseball-Reference.com, http://www.baseball-reference.com/
    teams.
"TSN-All-Stars," BaseballChronology.com, http://www.baseballchronology
    .com/Baseball/Awards/TSN-AllStars.asp.

Index

About the Author

Robert W. Cohen was born in the Bronx, New York, in 1956. He grew up just a few miles from Yankee Stadium, a huge fan of the New York Yankees. After spending many years working in a large corporate environment, he began writing professionally in 2004. His first published work, *A Team for the Ages: Baseball's All-Time All-Star Team*, clearly reflects his great love of the game of baseball and his vast knowledge of the sport. A sports historian, Cohen has appeared on numerous sports-talk radio programs around the nation to discuss his previously published works. His first nonsports book was released in December 2008. A labor of love, *My Life with Rusty* describes the unique 14-year relationship he shared with his first cat, Rusty, whom he lost to cancer in February 2003. Robert returned to his primary area of expertise in his June 2009 release entitled *Baseball's Hall of Fame—Or Hall of Shame?*—the most comprehensive book ever written on the Baseball Hall of Fame. His latest work, *MVP*, was released in August 2010. Robert is also a contributing writer at the Internet website TheBaseballPage, where he has written player bios and various historical articles on the national pastime and shared with readers his various player rankings. Robert currently lives in northern New Jersey.